THE DARK CLOUD

THE
DARK
CLOUD

how the digital world is costing the earth

GUILLAUME PITRON

translated by Bianca Jacobsohn

SCRIBE
Melbourne • London

Scribe Publications
18-20 Edward St, Brunswick, Victoria 3056, Australia
2 John St, Clerkenwell, London, WC1N 2ES, United Kingdom
3754 Pleasant Ave, Suite 100, Minneapolis, Minnesota 55409, USA

First published in France by Les Liens qui Libèrent as *L'Enfer numérique* in 2021

Published in English by Scribe in 2023

Typeset in Portrait by the publishers

Printed and bound in the UK by CPI Group (UK) Ltd, Croydon CR0 4YY

Scribe is committed to the sustainable use of natural resources and the use of paper products made responsibly from those resources.

978 1 922585 52 3 (Australian edition)
978 1 914484 44 5 (UK hardback edition)
978 1 915590 23 7 (UK paperback edition)
978 1 957363 01 1 (US edition)
978 1 761385 10 0 (ebook)

This book is supported by the Institut français (Royaume-Uni) as part of the Burgess programme and by the Institut français (Paris) Acquisition of Rights Grant.

Catalogue records for this book are available from the National Library of Australia and the British Library.

scribepublications.com.au
scribepublications.co.uk
scribepublications.com

To Camille, Victor, Anaïs.
To Roland Boman and his lost river...

'Our future is a race between the growing
power of our technology
and the wisdom with which we use it.'
Stephen Hawking

CONTENTS

Introduction

LET'S TURN BACK THE CLOCKS. TAME THE FURIOUS CHARGE of time. And reflect on the daily life of our pre-nineteenth-century contemporaries. Their endeavours, both big and small, from growing crops, raising armies, or building pyramids, depended very much on the muscle power of the enslaved, the flow rate of rivers, and the unpredictability of ocean winds. Today the vestiges of certain ancient communication networks remain, such as Roman roads, colonial trading posts, and the old Pony Express stables built in the American West by postal workers.

The sixth of October 1829 marked a turning point for these ancient routines, some spanning thousands of years. On this day, British engineer George Stephenson's 'Rocket' — the first modern steam locomotive — clocked up a speed of forty kilometres per hour on the Liverpool and Manchester Railway, relegating stagecoaches and caravels to the annals of ancient history. With the telegraph and then aircraft, our connection to time was changed, as people, goods, and ideas could now criss-cross the globe at unprecedented speeds, thanks to a worldwide transport network of ports, air terminals, and transmission towers.

The second of October 1971 marked a new step when American engineer Ray Tomlinson sent the first email on Arpanet—the computer network prized by US scientists and military personnel.[1] This technology would project humanity into the era of immediacy. Today, everything shifts and moves at the speed of light, or just about. After the gently paved streets of antiquity and the railroads of the industrial era, have you ever wondered what makes our daily digital life possible? What happens when you send an email or a 'like' on social media by hitting that ubiquitous thumbs-up icon? What is the geography of those billions of clicks, and what is their material impact? And what environmental and geopolitical challenges are we not seeing?

That is what this book is about.

Today, Arpanet is ancient digital history, and its designers—pioneers of information and communication technology (ICT)—are like a distant breed of early man. Designed in 1969, the network was originally meant to connect a handful of computers installed in California and Utah, before that network grew over the next decade to include the rest of the United States, and then Europe. In 1983, the TCP/IP protocol was deployed, making it possible for computers all over the world to communicate with one another, ushering in the birth of the internet—a network of networks, which we are all cohabitants of today.[2]

Since then, the internet has given digital technologies the means to colonise the furthermost reaches of our planet. The transformation of every possible tangible activity into a computerised process has given everything we do an invisible digital shadow. An application on your smartphone to monitor your sleep cycles makes sleeping a digital action; the same applies to praying once you download a meditation from any of the online spiritual communities out there; an ISIS solider waging war in Syria also exists in the digital world, as the US stores the geolocation of his mobile phone as part of its 'Gallant Phoenix' project aimed at turning data into justice; and even playing with your cat becomes a digital action once you post clips of its adorable antics on social media.[3]

In short, our every move in the real world is now duplicated in the virtual realm—a process of digitalisation that Covid-19 has accelerated. The global pandemic irrefutably made us more reliant on digital tools for working from home, buying books online, or having a virtual get-together with friends. In fact, the online world is expanding so fast that its players sometimes struggle to keep up: in 2020, several operators were forced to downgrade the quality of their online video services to keep the networks from saturating; PlayStation and personal computer sales skyrocketed; and connected-car manufacturers are still contending with a computer chip shortage.[4]

This virtualisation of the perceptible world is only in its infancy. By 2030, the giants of the internet will have connected all of humanity to the World Wide Web.[5] The concepts 'internet of senses', 'merged reality', and 'green artificial intelligence' will become part of everyday language, energising an astounding cross-pollination of ideas and cultures.[6] Having taken control of cyberspace, the US and China will dominate the world. Yet, despite all this, the vast majority of us cannot explain the infrastructure behind our connected computers, tablets, and smartphones.

This is firstly because of the common misconceptions about the digital realm, which is touted as being no more concrete than the much-vaunted cloud where we store our documents and photos. But it is in fact more like a blob—a unicellular organism fed by a network of slimy, amorphous veins.[7] In this digital world synonymous with 'nothingness' or a 'void', we are invited to make online purchases, play virtual games, and spill our guts on Twitter, seemingly without involving a single gram of matter, the tiniest electron, or a drop of water. In short, the digital world has the reputation of having no material impact at all. 'We don't even know how much power a single room with the lights left on consumes', comments Inès Leonarduzzi, director of an organisation for more eco-responsible digital.[8] Let alone the power consumption of the digital networks ...

A supposed lack of physical barriers gives digital capitalism the freedom to grow and thrive. The digital industry can even boast its positive role in preserving the planet by optimising our farming, industrial, and service methods, as we shall discover. According to such accounts, only by using digital technologies wholesale will we 'save' the planet. Besides, it is very difficult to explain what exactly this 'blob' is. Like a growing forest of sequoias, or ocean acidification, the expansion of the digital industry is real, but invisible to the naked eye. And what cannot be seen is seldom understood.

But crucial questions need to be addressed. How much physical space is taken up by the digital world? Are these new communication networks compatible with the 'ecological transition'? Will we need to guard them with infantry regiments and aircraft carriers to enable us to continue to amuse ourselves on the Web? What entity will govern the world of tomorrow on the basis of its control of the physical architecture of our supposedly dematerialised lives?

For two years, across four continents, I followed the trail of our emails and the 'likes' of our holiday photos: from the steppes of northern China, to find a metal that makes our smartphones work; to the vast expanses of the Arctic Circle; where our Facebook accounts cool off; to one of the most arid states in the US, where I investigated the water consumption of one of one of the world's biggest data centres, that of the National Security Agency (NSA). I wanted to understand why the tiny Baltic country of Estonia had become the most digitised nation on the planet, to investigate the secretive and coal-hungry world of algorithmic finance, and to track down the connection of a transoceanic cable to Western Europe's Atlantic seaboard.

I discovered that the internet has a colour (green), a smell (rancid butter), and even a taste (salty, like seawater). It also emits the strident din of an enormous beehive. All senses were engaged as I sized up the sheer excess of the digital world. To send a 'like', we use what is set to become the largest infrastructure ever created by humankind. We have built a realm of concrete, fibre, and steel that is hyper-available and at our command within a microsecond; our very own 'infra-world' of data centres, hydroelectric dams, coal-fired plants, and strategic-metals mines, all aligned in the triple quest for power, speed, and cold.

It is also an amphibious realm, traversed by cableships and supertankers, and populated by businessmen, sailors, miners, computer scientists, builders, electricians, streetsweepers, and tanker escorts—men and women pitted against fascinating ecological, economic, and geostrategic challenges. They are the machinists of the digital exodus, and are braving the laws of physics so that billions of internet users are fooled into thinking that these very laws do not apply to them.

A dozen countries visited later, this is the reality I found:

digital pollution is colossal, and it is the fastest-growing type of pollution. 'When I put numbers on the pollution, I couldn't believe my eyes', recalls IT research engineer Françoise Berthoud.[9] Making the biggest contribution to this pollution are the billions of interfaces (tablets, PCs, smartphones)—our point of entry into the internet. Also weighing in is the data we produce at every moment. It is transported, stored, and processed in massive, energy-hungry infrastructures, and used to create new digital content requiring even more interfaces. These two families of pollution complement and feed one another.

There are numbers to back up this reality. The global digital industry consumes enough water, material, and energy to give it a footprint triple that of a country such as the UK. Digital technologies currently use 10 per cent of the world's electricity, and account for close to 4 per cent of global carbon dioxide emissions—almost double that of the global civil aviation sector.[10] 'While digital companies prove to be more powerful than the regulators that govern them, there is a real risk that we can no longer control their environmental impact', warns Jaan Tallinn, the founder of Skype and the Future of Life Institute, which specialises in the ethics of technology.[11] That digital pollution undermines the ecological transition is a compelling argument and will be one of the greatest challenges we face over the next thirty years.

Meanwhile, the race has begun. On the one side, we have digital companies exerting their formidable financial and innovative power to optimise and 'green' the internet and smartphones—like they do with their lawns flanking their head offices. The industry is astutely focused on the 'ecological' and 'responsible' digital agenda, which is the only way to keep us 'liking' to our hearts' content. At its head, the five most powerful US companies in the digital economy—Facebook, Amazon, Apple, Netflix, and Google ('FAANG')—even want to keep us in the dark about its material impact.[12] These giants that pervade our screens but are hard to nail down onto terra firma have dissipated their physical assets—as we shall discover in Scandinavia. By being truly 'untouchable', they are unattackable. They are accountable to no one ... because they don't exist. If the French expression is anything to go by, a happy life is a hidden life. If not a dematerialised one.

On the other side, we have 'pioneer' networks and communities advocating for moderate, responsible, and eco-friendly digital habits.[13] Among them is a Dutch entrepreneur who repatriates tens of thousands of mobile telephones from Africa to Europe; an Estonian activist who launched the first international day for cleaning up our digital acts; a Dutch sailor who recovers old cables from the ocean floor; and an army of engineers from all walks of life who have designed the world's most environmentally friendly smartphone. Their values of collaboration, moderation, and sharing are all in aid of achieving truly sustainable digital infrastructures.

Enter the powerful media tsunami that is the 'climate generation'. From Sydney to San Francisco, from Berlin to Manila, 'Friday strikes' have been galvanising young activists to take political leaders and businesses to task for their lack of action on the climate crisis.[14] It is more than a spontaneous, horizontal, mostly female movement led by idealists of justice and solidarity: it is a digital phenomenon, amplified by a flood of hashtags and YouTube videos. It began in 2018 when young Greta Thunberg organised the first climate strike on the day students went back to class. The bold Swedish activist became an icon after a photo of her holding a placard in front of the Swedish parliament went viral in just two hours. That's how the legend goes, at least. Less known is that the photo was taken by a professional photographer sent by a Swedish climate-focused start-up looking to create a buzz.[15] The images then landed in the hands of talented community managers, who calibrated a powerful message for social media. A star is born ... digitally![16]

None of this takes away from the sincerity of Greta Thunberg's fight. But let us not forget that, like this stroke of marketing genius now subscribed to by 16 million followers on Twitter and Instagram, the 'climate generation' is predominantly made up of young consumers hooked on digital tools. In the US, teenagers spend up to seven hours and twenty-two minutes of their free time per day in front of a screen.[17] Three hours of that time is spent watching videos on Netflix or Orange Cinema Series (OCS), and at least one hour is spent on social networks such as TikTok, SnapChat, Twitch, House Party, and Discord. In France, eighteen-year-olds have already owned an average of no fewer than five mobile telephones. And the younger you are, the more often you change your devices, despite these accounting for nearly half of digital pollution.[18]

For the first time in history, an entire generation has taken a stand to 'save' the planet, to bring governments to justice for climate inaction, and to plant trees.[19] Parents lament having 'three Greta Thunbergs at home' up in arms against eating meat, using plastic, and air travel.[20] This is also the generation that makes the most use of e-commerce, virtual reality, and gaming websites. Young people also get their television fix from online videos, which, as we shall discover, makes very little ecological sense. A study in the UK confirms that 'digital natives'—the generation born with the internet—will be the first to adopt the future services and interfaces on offer from the digital industry giants.[21] The climate generation will be one of the main culprits of the expected twofold increase by 2025 of the digital sector's electricity consumption (20 per cent of global generation), and in its greenhouse-gas emissions (7.5 per cent of global emissions). In 2020, I attended a panel discussion where a young subject-matter expert dismissed this paradox with the offhand reply: 'We use digital products because they're there for us to use.'

The reality is that the climate generation is inheriting an infrastructure that can be used for good or for evil. My questions to them are: how will you use the formidable powers of this infrastructure? Will you know how to tame the hubris triggered by these technologies, or will you, like Icarus, be sent crashing to earth by the all-consuming rays of this artificial sun? Whose side are you on in the race between the growing power of technologies and the claimed wisdom of their use? You are on the verge of 'saturation', says the European statistics agency Eurostat, as the FAANG continue to bombard you with avalanches of content.[22] You don't realise that by making digital the instrument of your emancipation, you are rushing into the arms of your new masters. The benefits of your new vegan and locavore habits risk being wiped out by the explosion of your digital footprint and the aftershocks this electronic tsunami will produce.

'This situation of a young generation taking to the streets takes me back to the anti-capitalist riots of 1968 in France', said a digital expert. The movement took inspiration from Karl Marx, who called on the proletariat of the world to come together. This never happened, whereas capitalists managed to unite to shape globalisation. And for good reason: '[S]ome activists were socialists who went on to become executives in big oil companies', effectively betraying the very ideals they fought for, paving stones in hand, explained the expert, who concluded by saying that, fifty years later, 'I feel like history is repeating itself.'

Can you prove him wrong?

History has shown that we should distrust the fears sparked by new inventions. From newspapers, cinema, and paperbacks, to the telephone, 'New forms of media have always caused moral panics', Canadian psychologist Steven Pinker points out.[23] In the fifteenth century, the printing press was seen as a 'danger to the soul', and in the twentieth century, the radio was disparaged as a threat to good morals and democracy. In the 1960s, it was argued that television would destroy our mental and physical wellbeing.[24] Information and communication technologies attract similar criticism, along with the novel addition of causing harm to the environment. It seems that digital technologies mirror our contemporary concerns and our new environmental angst.

Yet these technologies also offer the prospect of astonishing progress for humanity: longer lifespans, exploration of the origins of the cosmos, broader access to education, and modelling pandemic scenarios. They will lay the groundwork for incredible ecological initiatives. But let us not be so naïve in our commitment to this early century's mother of battles. The digital world unfolding before our eyes is, by and large, for the good of neither planet nor climate. The paradox is how something so intangible can so starkly confront us with our planet's physical and biological limits.

That is the driving force of this investigation whose substance eludes us. I want to make sense of the dark side of this industry as it shies away from the light; to explore the geography of a supposedly abstract notion; to reveal the anatomy of a technology that, in the name of a dematerialistic ideal bordering on the mystic, is building a modern world that is completely materialistic; and to expose the plain fact that every email and 'like' we send produces enormous challenges that have so far escaped our senses.

CHAPTER ONE

The digital world's environmental benefits: fiction vs. fact

FROM THE ROARING CITY OF ABU DHABI IN THE UNITED ARAB Emirates it is a half-hour drive to Masdar City. Built over 640 hectares of burning desert sand, running alongside the Persian Gulf highway to Saudi Arabia, Masdar City is an inward-facing fortress of aluminium, glass, and red-tinted concrete. Silhouettes wearing *dishdasha*, traditional long white garments, glide through the inner city's narrow streets shaded by palm trees. Mashrabiya lattices adorning the facades of the buildings further soften the intrusive rays of the sun. And placed in the middle of a small square is a windcatcher that, like its predecessors in ancient Persian cities, redirects air currents to cool the city's core.

What makes this dune-locked city out of the space age so fascinating are the technologically ambitious plans in store for its development.[1] The Emirati government plans to make Masdar—the Arabic word for 'source'—the world's most sustainable eco-city, using the most modern digital technologies ever designed.[2] By 2030, and with 17 billion euros in investments, Masdar promises to be the regional if not global model of smart urban design.[3] One promotional video boasts that the city's 50,000 future inhabitants will enjoy 'the highest quality of life with the lowest possible environmental impact'.[4] Masdar City is already a dream coming true, and that is to be one of the most enjoyable cities to live in on Earth.

Smart cities in aid of the planet

Masdar City is the embodiment of the hopes that have been pinned on smart cities and digital technology to improve our lives. And there's good reason to believe that they can. Over half of the world's population is now concentrated to urban areas, and while they only cover 2 per cent of the Earth's surface, they are responsible for generating 75 per cent of the world's power, and producing 80 per cent of the world's carbon dioxide emissions. This puts immense pressure on water and food resources, and on electricity grids. The challenge therefore is to manage the flow of people, goods, and electricity as efficiently as possible to make the cities of the future more pleasant and sustainable places to live. So no more brigades of whistle-blowing pointsmen to direct traffic at intersections, nor relying on word-of-mouth to find buyers for perishable goods. In smart cities, the data collected and processed by information and communication technologies — sensors, geopositioning systems, and even artificial intelligence — will exponentially increase our interaction and collaboration as citizens in the interest of our planet. And the starting point of a greener world is a more organised one.

Masdar is the full-scale test of just this. The city must rely solely on renewable energy without producing any carbon dioxide emissions or waste. To achieve this, it is equipped with movement sensors and smart meters that can more than halve the city's electricity and water consumption; 1,800 self-driving vehicles making up the Personal Rapid Transit (PRT) transport network (according to current plans); and smart homes that adjust the air conditioning depending on whether their occupants are in or out, bringing household energy consumption down by 72 per cent. 'The Emirati authorities see technology as the solution to all urban challenges!' says Federico Cugurullo, an Italian scholar who has long been researching Masdar City.[5]

In 2007, the British architectural practice Foster + Partners was commissioned to raise Masdar from the sand, which it did using good common sense.[6] The city is north-east facing, limiting its exposure to the sun; its streets run in the direction of the wind to allow a flow of air; and staircases are placed in front of lifts to encourage more physical exercise. But the Emirati authorities preferred to bank on technological innovations, with the result that nothing went according to plan. As the technical hurdles piled up, officials conceded that the city could only run on 50 per cent renewable energy rather than almost double that as anticipated. The PRT also came up short for technical reasons, and was ultimately replaced by a fleet of more modest autonomous shuttle buses.[7] As for smart homes, the implementation of the ambitious Building Management System for optimising Masdar residents' electricity consumption has been held up, as users try to figure out how to get it to work.[8]

The real environmental price to pay for smart cities

Today, only 10 per cent of the initial plans for the eco-city have been built, and the city barely has 2,000 inhabitants. Is Masdar condemned to become the first 'green ghost town', as suggested by some news sources?[9] And it is really the eco-friendly city its developers repeatedly claim it to be? The question seems scandalous when we know that making everything 'smarter' is supposed to be the new frontier of sustainability. Was it not the European Parliament that said smart cities will generate 'economic prosperity and social wellbeing' in 'an efficient and sustainable way'?[10] This is why 286 cities around the world have already launched some 443 smart-city projects.[11]

But 'a city is like a person: it needs food, water, and space in order to thrive', explains Federico Cugurullo. Urban planners study what is termed 'urban metabolism'—the movement of matter, energy, and waste moving in and out of built-up areas—as way of assessing cities' environmental performance. So what kind of metabolism does a smart city such as Masdar have? 'It's a legitimate question; smart technology requires material, and we need to factor in that material', insists Cugurullo who, in vain, requested detailed reports from developers. In any case, 'you'll never be able to get that kind of information in Abu Dhabi', says Gökçe Günel, a Turkish academic and author of a book on Masdar City, in a thinly veiled comment on the authoritarian Emirati regime.[12]

Most astonishing of all is that, up until recently, not a single global impact study had been conducted on a smart city anywhere in the world.[13] It was only in 2016, in an article published by a group of Danish researchers, headed by Kikki Lambrecht Ipsen, in a scientific journal that a theoretical analysis framework was finally set out.[14] Over six months, Ipsen reviewed the costs and benefits of seven categories of smart technologies, including smart windows, water meters, and energy grids—making up millions of pieces of hardware.[15] He and his team found that, while they reduce the electricity consumption of urban areas, this benefit has a high material and energy cost, as large quantities of parts and equipment need to be industrialised and transported. Indeed, Lambrecht Ipsen's cost-benefit analysis, published in 2019, reaches the astonishing conclusion that: '... the implementation of Smart City Solutions generally has a negative influence on the environmental sustainability performance of an urban system'.[16]

Don't get me wrong. Smart cities can be clean and enjoyable places to live in for their billions of inhabitants, especially since technological progress is making them even more efficient, and will no doubt reduce their environmental impact even more. Local councillors wouldn't be out of their minds to make such smart solutions the cornerstone of their political campaigns. But if we take into account the true borders of these cities, which extend thousands of kilometres beyond the outer city limits to where smart technologies are manufactured, we are in fact making their overall impact worse. 'The conclusions of the study cannot be generalised to the entire planet', warns Ipsen. 'But when it comes to smart cities, we should remain circumspect.'[17] For his part, Federico Cugurullo has the intuition—but not the proof—that 'the environmental costs of Masdar City [also] exceed the desired benefits'. He assures me that 'advanced solutions are the very cause of the problem: talk to geographers and urban planners, and you'll find that 95 per cent of them remain sceptical about smart cities'.

How could we have overlooked this?

Mathematics at the service of nature

We can begin to answer this question by looking back into the long history of mathematics. For thousands of years, humans have used numbers and calculations to understand the world around them. As a starting point, in Mesopotamia on the shores of the Euphrates 5,000 years ago, the shepherds in the prosperous agrarian society used clay tokens to count each head of cattle at the end of each day.[18] The various branches of mathematics thereafter (such as algebra, statistics, geometry, and arithmetic) continued this numerical conceptualisation of the world, extending humanity's grip on its surroundings.

In Ancient Rome, for instance, the aqueducts were built using a dioptra—a levelling tool used to measure the angles of structures. In the Middle Ages, Arab land surveyors used trigonometry to translate their steps into geographic distances, giving birth to the first land registries. At the dawn of the Renaissance, exploration of the seas would not have been possible without using geometric calculation instruments, including the compass, the protractor, and astrolabes. In eighteenth-century France, statistics and probability were used to better administer the state by measuring tax revenues in relation to demographic changes. Over the course of history, mathematics has proved to be a powerful discipline for humankind to understand and organise the world, and therefore conquer it.

But over the last three centuries, mathematicians have been working towards a different objective. Since the early eighteenth century, foresters in Germany have been rotating logging operations as a way to accelerate forest regeneration and increase profits. In the fishing industry, from the post-World War

II period, the concept of maximum sustainable yield—measuring the maximum quantity of fish that can be fished—was applied to ensure the survival of the species.[19] 'Mathematics has long been used to control resource and energy consumption, improve research into the evolution of flora and fauna, and optimise travel', confirms an expert.[20] In other words, human societies measure nature to both dominate and protect it.

Enter digital technologies—the most advanced representation in figures, numbers, characters, and other signals of the world around us. Coupled with the formidable processing power of contemporary information tools, digital technology has simultaneously intensified our thirst for knowledge and conquest into the furthermost reaches of the distant galaxy, and helped to protect forests in Germany.

- We can use digital technologies to gain unprecedented insight into the state of the planet. The extraordinary mass of images and data it provides deepens our understanding of pollution and the threat it poses. Up until recently, scientists had for years observed the persistent presence in the atmosphere of CFC-11—a gas responsible for the hole in the ozone layer, prohibited by the Montreal Protocol in 1987—but without being able to pinpoint which countries the emissions were coming from.[21] In 2019, using satellite images, and by modelling the winds spreading these gases, a team of international experts was able to identify the source of emissions—factories in the east of China—thus putting an end to CFC-11 trafficking.[22] What other technology could make such ecological advances in such a short amount of time?

We have only scratched the surface of the powerful effect of digital on the environment. In George Orwell's *1984*, Winston Smith's only scant refuge in Oceania from Big Brother is in a copse of ash trees, a lambent clearing of hyacinths, a pasture, and a stream—places in nature.[23] Today, reality has gone beyond fiction. 'Megaconstellations' of thousands of satellites catapulted into space make it possible to observe plastic pollution in the oceans, measure the soil acidity of agricultural areas, the erosion of the Great Barrier Reef, and snowmelt on top of Kilimanjaro—all in real time. We have gone from gazing at the sky to get a reading of the world below, to the very opposite. Thousands of electronic celestial bodies are observing us around the clock, as they are tuna in the Mediterranean, penguins in Cape Town, and Paraná pines in Brazil. Never has nature been subject to this degree of surveillance!

• Digital technologies are gradually optimising how we organise our everyday lives. '[T]hey provide the means of adapting street lighting to real population requirements, locating leaks in water distribution networks [...], providing real-time information about mobility solutions available to users. They contribute to better energy network functioning [...]. They can help to optimise waste collection, and the use of inputs in agriculture', according to a report published by a leading French research institute.[24] For example, the Chinese government has put its money on road traffic data to curb air pollution. This is the 'city brain' concept developed by the Chinese company Alibaba in the city of Hangzhou, using hundreds of thousands of cameras.[25] Alibaba claims that the information collected is used to adjust traffic lights to the flow of traffic, reducing traffic jams by 15 per cent and therefore carbon dioxide emissions.[26] In connected homes, sensors anticipate our exact energy requirements, turning down the air conditioning when no one is home, or automatically lowering the electric shutters during heat waves, generating as much as 30 per cent in energy savings.[27] Extend these technologies to the rest of the planet, and the benefits would be unprecedented.

- Lastly, digital technologies encourage us to be more eco-responsible consumers. In the US, platforms such as CropSwap and FarmMatch have multiplied the number of short food-supply chains by putting consumers in direct contact with local farmers.[28] The Danish startup Too Good to Go now covers fourteen countries, connecting producers of perishable foods to buyers who are happy to take them off their hands at a reduced price.[29] The company claims that since 2016 almost 50 million meals have been 'saved' around the world. The ecological gain is massive, considering that a third of the food produced on Earth is thrown away, representing a sizeable 8 per cent of carbon emissions. And that's not all, since digital technologies 'help to integrate goods into sharing systems [such as loans and cash gifts between individuals]', 'facilitate crowdfunding for renewables or agroecology [...]', and are 'helping to combat planned obsolescence, such as Spareka, a platform selling spare parts connected to a community of repairers', states the same leading report.[30]

In a time of fake news and alternative facts, never have we had such accurate information with which to improve our understanding of the world. This is attributable to the engineering behind digital technologies, for one smartphone alone is more powerful than all the information systems used to send a man to the Moon.[31] Now multiply these tools by the number of humans on Earth, picture the legions of super calculators capable of executing billions of operations per second, and you have a new gospel: 'Green IT'. According to a working group of the think tank The Shift Project, 'It is increasingly considered that it would not be possible to control climate change without massive recourse to digital technology.'[32] And why not 'green artificial intelligence', as we will discover further on, that can plan environmental policies for the next 200 years? In this future already envisaged by certain techno-prophets, humans would give algorithms the mandate to both master and own nature for the good of the planet.

When the digital industry rewrites the future

The battle to become an opinion leader required irrefutable figures, the first of which appeared from 2003 in confidentially distributed reports.[33] From 2015, the message gained currency among intergovernmental bodies, such as the United Nations Educational, Scientific and Cultural Organization (UNESCO): 'Whereas the carbon footprint of ICTs should reach 1.27 GtCO2e from now to 2020, the total potential for reduction [of this footprint thanks to] ICTs is seven times higher.'[34]

If there is one organisation with more clout than any other on this terrain, it is the Global e-Sustainability Initiative (GeSI)—a group of private players from the digital sector and international organisations, based in Brussels.[35] The GeSI describes itself as a 'a leading source of impartial information ... for achieving integrated social and environmental sustainability through ICT-enabled transformation'. Put plainly, it is a lobby group defending the interests of its members, making it a powerful communication machine. Its first report in 2012, *SMARTer2020*, predicted a 16.5 per cent decrease in greenhouse-gas emissions by 2020, thanks to ICTs.[36] Its second report, three years later, *SMARTer2030*, made bolder estimations still: 'The emissions avoided through the use of ICT are nearly ten times greater than the emissions generated by deploying it.'[37]

The digital industry is not saying it has a limited environmental impact; it is outright promising a net positive effect on the environment, with knock-on benefits for economic players transitioning to digital: small-scale farmers using satellite images to more accurately manage their inputs; car manufacturers developing eco-navigation tools capable of optimising fuel efficiency; and major mining houses that, using sensors, can switch off the ventilation to unused galleries, lowering their electricity consumption. The examples are compelling. Perhaps this is why the foreword was written by none other than Christiana Figueres, secretary-general of the United Nations Framework Convention on Climate Change from 2010 to 2016.[38] The UNFCCC's supreme body is none other than the Conference of Parties—better known as COP—where, every year, the future of the planet is discussed. Figueres even goes as far to say how 'the report underlines the pivotal role of Information and Communication Technology' for achieving the goals of the fight against climate change.

International organisations, including the UN and the International Telecommunication Union (ITU), have used their communication channels to relay the GeSI's key conclusions, while the World Bank included them in a public note.[39] The same goes for powerful firms such as McKinsey, the Boston Consulting Group, Deloitte, and Orange. The result is that the GeSI reports are being taken as gospel, with the Brussels-based lobby boasting that it is one of today's leading sources of global information on 'green IT'.

Very quickly, however, a number of experts raised their doubts about the reliability of the research. One of them was Françoise Berthoud, a researcher at the French National Centre for Scientific Research (CNRS): 'the criteria used for judging the robustness of the data used are at times insubstantial', and 'the assumptions are based on sources that are unclear'.[40] Moreover, 'the two reports only look at carbon dioxide emissions. E-waste is not fully accounted for, excluding the likes of connected vehicles, and the reports have not been sanctioned by an independent body.'[41]

Could the story of the report's production tell us more about its credibility? For weeks, I tackled the question by meeting with several of the report's co-authors in exchange for their anonymity. First revelation: thirteen of the seventeen organisations providing their expertise are from the private sector.[42] Such an overwhelming majority should have been counterbalanced by specialist input from the non-commercial sector, as the international non-profit Collaborating Centre on Sustainable Development (CSCP) appears to have done. I also learned that while a number of NGOs, including the World Wildlife Fund (WWF), were approached to participate, they would have had to pay to do so, which they refused to do.[43]

'The first thing I thought when I saw the panel was that it was inexperienced', one participant told me. 'I didn't know any of the experts. There was no academic credibility.' Despite that, they began to work on the report, and at several points my source worried about the lack of impartiality of the research. Too many of the assertions 'were unverifiable'. 'The experts could not support their claims, especially about the amount of electricity savings by going digital. I think the data they suggested gave little credibility to the GeSI.'

Tensions flared as work on the report progressed. Some researchers challenged their colleagues to prove their overly optimistic base assumptions in five years' time. At one point, two representatives of the Swedish telecommunications group Ericsson unceremoniously left the project due to the apparent lack of scientific rigour. But what did they expect? 'Everyone knew from the outset that the report's findings would be positive', one of my sources stated baldly. 'Business is business! It was pure "green marketing", which would only ever come up with glowing statistics.' Another dissident admitted being 'very sceptical about all the assertions' contained in the report: 'I'm not very comfortable with the idea that my name is associated with the report. Today, I would do things differently.'

One of our renegades went as far to say that, 'It would be very dangerous to use GeSI reports for public policy purposes.' Only, that is precisely what happened. And why wouldn't they be? 'It was so very appealing to believe that digital could generate economic growth and be good for the environment', said one sustainable IT specialist.[44] There was very little push-back from independent studies. Too little time, and too little money. 'It's David against Goliath. The industry confiscated the message on the internet's environmental benefits, and has been pushing it by all means since then.'[45]

Thousands of years of wars have taught us how the victors seek to rewrite history to their advantage. In the twenty-first century, digital companies are taking this further by trying to go as far as rewrite the future. That is because digital is dirty. Very dirty. As pointed out earlier, the sector's water and energy consumption, and its contribution to the drying-up of mineral resources, gives it a carbon footprint two to three times that of a country such as the UK or France.[46] And this is unsurprising: there are some 34 billion pieces of digital equipment in circulation on the planet, representing a total of 223 million tonnes, or 179 million cars.[47] In terms of energy consumption, ICTs account for around 10 per cent of the world's electricity, equivalent to the power generation of 100 nuclear reactors.[48] If the digital world were a country, it would be the third-biggest consumer of energy after China and the United States, bearing in mind that 35 per cent of today's energy is coal-based.[49] All told, digital represents just under 4 per cent of global greenhouse-gas emissions.[50]

This is the current situation. But it is just a snapshot of a very long process—one that led me to the final chapter of this book, uncovering the internet's ballooning and seemingly unstoppable impact on the environment along the way. Digital technologies consume 5 to 7 per cent more electricity every year, and could increase to as much as 20 per cent of global electricity by 2025.[51] ICT's share of global carbon dioxide emissions could double just as quickly.[52] 'We don't realise just how huge an impact digital has. It's monstrous, and we need to take it very seriously', GreenIT. fr founder Frédéric Bordage told me.[53] It is a fact that we tend to overlook, for 'this kind of pollution is colourless and odourless, and doesn't have any black smoke coming out of a factory', argues Inès Leonarduzzi, founder of the consultancy Digital For The Planet.[54] But it could also be because we barely understand how this nascent technology actually works. Now seems a good time to take a deep dive into the belly of the internet.

The geography of a 'like'

We're in Montreal, in autumn 2020, where a snowstorm has just hit Quebec's capital. An icy white blanket covers the pavements, softening the steps of pedestrians, hunched over under the frozen weight of gravity, and absorbing the sound of their breath. At the same time, in a luxury hotel in old Montreal, one of the foremost conferences of the digital industry is taking place: Digital Infra Network Montreal. The event is abuzz with topics such as 'hyperscale data centres', 'digital infrastructure energy efficiency', 'long-haul fibre optic networks', 'peripherals', and 'cloud computing'. Let's face it: these are opaque concepts to most of us. And yet, without them, the everyday lives of billions of people would be thrown into disorder. For one thing, we would no longer be able to send billions of 'likes' every day on Facebook, YouTube, and LinkedIn.

You're dying to do it, and you click that ubiquitous, irresistible thumbs-up icon to woo that cute colleague at work—you 'like' a photo on their Facebook profile. But for that 'like' to reach the object of your affection, it has to travel through the seven layers of the internet, the seventh layer being your smartphone, laptop computer, or other connected device. (See appendix 1.)

Your gallant notification then sinks into the intermediary levels of the net (data link, network, transport, etc) until it reaches the first physical layer of the internet—the application—comprising undersea cables. From sender to receiver, the notification uses the 4G antenna of a mobile operator or a cable modem, and runs the length of the building's shared telecoms infrastructure to reach the copper cables buried eighty centimetres under the pavement. It then travels along the cables running the length of major communication routes (such as highways, rivers, canals, and railroads) to join other 'likes' in the operator's technical rooms. From there, it crosses the oceans via a data centre. From the inmost depths of the net, your 'like' finally takes the reverse journey back to the seventh layer: the mobile phone of your crush. And even though your colleague is just ten metres away, your signal has travelled thousands of kilometres.[35] There truly is a geography of a 'like'.

As a result of our intangible activities—sending an email via Gmail, a message on WhatsApp, and an emoticon on Facebook, or posting a video on TikTok or photos of amusing felines on Snapchat—we have built an infrastructure that, according to Greenpeace, 'will likely be the largest single thing we build as a species'.[36] Yet, as we have seen so far, the available literature tends to prove that the benefits of digital outweigh the drawbacks. That is, until the think tank The Shift Project really put its foot in it with its thoroughly researched report published in 2018: 'The digital transition as it is currently implemented participates in global warming more than it helps to prevent it.'[37] Furthermore, the risk that digital results in 'a net increase in the environmental footprint of digital sectors is therefore very real'.[38]

So who do we believe? On the one hand, academics and

NGOs point to the biased nature of research by industrial groups who, in turn, denounce the overly theoretical approaches of the academic world. 'We have neither the time nor the money to verify the research carried out [by industrial groups] on digital technologies', admits a researcher specialising in digital matters.[59] 'Lots of people give their opinion; very little research has been done. And, ultimately, no one knows anything', summarises Mark Acton, a data centre specialist.[60] One thing is certain: 'The decades of digitalisation in our societies have also seen the highest increase in our ecological footprint', as stated in the White Paper on Digital Technology and Environment, published by a number of research bodies and non-profits, including the WWF.[61]

The reality of digital pollution sinks in

Sweden was the first country to address digital pollution when, in the early 1990s, the non-profit TCO Development introduced the first global certification label for responsible digital equipment.[62] Before then, IT was more for secretaries ... only they were ruining their eyes in front of screens and were on the receiving end of electromagnetic fields. 'To protect their health, we required that computers comply with certain manufacturing criteria', TCO CEO Sören Enhold explained to me when we met in Stockholm. He told me how 'the ICT industry first saw the certification as an obstacle to their interests', but that 'hundreds of thousands of employees responded by putting pressure on employers to provide equipment that met the certification criteria'.

From there, the grievances with ICTs turned to the pollution generated by their manufacture. The results included limits on the use of heavy metals, a ban on 'conflict metals', and proper working conditions on production lines.

In the rest of the world, the wake-up call came later with the help of sharp-shooters such as Eric Williams who, at the turn of the millennium, was one of the first American researchers to write a book entirely on ICT pollution.[63] 'Intel [the American semiconductor chip manufacturer] complained a lot about what I had to say, but in the end, they gave up on contradicting me', Williams told me.[64] In Europe, the American consultant, editor, and researcher Michael Oghia may have been the first to organise an international conference to address this topic. With the emergence of reports on digital pollution, seminars on sustainable electronics, and NGO-led protests in front of the FAANG head offices, an opposing view began to form, particularly from the likes of Greenpeace. On the academic front, Swedish researcher Asta Vonderau confirmed that 'a growing number of researchers are weighing in on the debate, with more and more articles being published in the press'.[65]

Yet the message is barely being relayed at an institutional level. 'Digital pollution is a blind spot in European political thinking', says a parliamentary attaché at the European Parliament in Strasbourg.[66] The European Commission, for its part, is a staunch supporter of digital for the ecological transition. 'The Green Pact [a road map for a sustainable Europe presented in 2019 by the president of the European Commission, Ursula von der Leyen] is based on the idea that digital is the answer to everything', says a parliamentary adviser. 'Digital pollution is very much back-of-mind for the Brussels institutions.'

Perhaps the private sector should be the first to grasp the nettle. 'The digital ecology is an emerging concept in the business world', explains the corporate and social responsibility manager of a European bank, adding that large corporations 'are still in the very early stages of tackling these issues'. Yet the director of the IT department of a European insurance company admitted to me that ICTs account for 30 per cent of his company's carbon footprint.[67] Figures such as these are bound to poke holes in the shining green reputation so very dear to the key players of the economy. Some companies have already given into pressure to act, Google being one of them: in 2019, 2,000 employees signed a letter demanding that the internet giant cut all its carbon dioxide emissions by 2030.[68] Companies are also realising that a tarnished image can have a damaging effect on recruitment. As one digital entrepreneur explained to me, 'Students today no longer want to work for companies with questionable ethics.'[69] Another compelling argument is cost, as every employee in the service sector represents an IT equipment and management budget of up to 20,000 euros.

We are left with the impression that everything we read, hear, and are told about 'green', 'sustainable', and 'eco-friendly' digital technologies is helping to entertain a dangerous illusion. More and more activists, entrepreneurs, and politicians are now asking what until recently was a preposterous question: can IT truly be a force for the good of the environment if it is not in itself eco-friendly? This is a question that will become increasingly pertinent as we uncover the conditions in which the IT equipment used for connected objects are manufactured.

CHAPTER TWO

Smartphones and the art of Zen

'THE POLICE JUST CALLED ME ON MY PHONE! THEY WANT TO know what we're doing here!' Xian gasps as she tears across the slope.¹ Her heavy breathing covers the distant hum of the drone we have been using to film an illegal dump from the nearby graphite mines and plants. For the past hour we have watched truck after truck climb to the top of this section of hill to discharge their dark loads. Over the years, these open-air torrents of waste have created a tortuous, chaotic, and artificial landscape.

Our fixer gives me a worried look; everything about her body language says that it's time to move. 'We have half an hour at best before they find us', Xian insists. 'They' have effortlessly found the contact details she used to book our Airbnb in the nearby city of Jixi where neighbours alerted local police to the presence of a *laowai* (foreigner). It won't be long before police officers reach Mashan, our current location. My investigation will be compromised: if they're the overzealous kind, they won't let us out of their sight. There is also the real possibility of being expelled from China.

And yet two days ago it was all going well. It was spring 2019, and I had come to do a story in Heilongjiang, China's northernmost province.[2] Just 200 kilometres away was the border with Primorsky Krai in the far-eastern side of Russia. It is a harsh territory, petrified by the severe climate, and banished from economic development. Huge clusters of pine and silver birch trees, corn, wheat, and flax grow out of the chernozem.[3] But Heilongjiang is better known for what is underneath its crops and vegetation: an abundance of coal, but graphite, too—a mineral that is indispensable to our connected lives, and without which the vast majority of smartphones and computers would not work.

We land the drone, I pack up the cameras, and run to our vehicle. Before I do anything else, I save the video recordings onto a hard drive that has been encrypted in case of a search. And now we wait for a car decked in flashing lights to arrive ... Unless we change our mode of transport to be more discreet. A taxi parked on the main square of a nearby village is our salvation. It takes us to Jixi airport, where we will take the first flight far away from here. A few hours later, a propeller plane lands on the tarmac in the city of Harbin, 400 kilometres further west, where no homeland security agents await us upon arrival.

Journey to the heart of graphite mines

Had the Chinese authorities confiscated our footage, they would most certainly have erased evidence of the pollution from the graphite mines. China produces close to 70 per cent of this mineral whose particles, under the microscope, are the shape of snowflakes. Except that these dark, twinkling snowflakes don't drift down from the sky, but are lifted out from the Earth's core—an operation that takes place in Liumao. This small town in Heilongjiang, teeming with surveillance cameras, is one of the epicentres of the country's graphite production.

Standing at the bottom of the valley, it is hard to make out the mines tucked away in the folds of the surrounding mountains. To get closer, I navigate a sinuous maze of dirt roads in the pine forests. After weaving through the undergrowth, I scramble up to the top of a steep scree slope that offers a view of one of the mines.

Ringed in by an impressive mineral arena and steeped in clouds of dust are excavators tearing down Nanling mountain. From there, the whitish rocks are transported to dilapidated factories at the bottom of the valley where they are crushed, immersed in an acid bath, and then loaded into very high-temperature furnaces.[4] The end product—a grey powder that smells of rancid butter—is packed up in 25-kilogram sacks that are stored in run-down hangars. Some of the workers have wrapped a scarf around their grimy features as protection. In their blue coveralls, they move furtively in near silence, their eyes cast down. All I can get from them is permission to examine their hands, which are covered in a greasy substance resembling anthracite soot. Despite the harsh working conditions, there are no complaints. Do they know that this graphite powder contains hydrofluoric acid, a highly corrosive, extremely toxic, and potentially lethal solution?

After a one-hour drive from Liumao, we have arrived in Mashan—another Chinese graphite-manufacturing landmark. The narrow road on the way brushes alongside agricultural plains filtered by cold, white light. As the vehicle comes to a stop, our eyes are drawn below the embankment to a procession of skips: this is the illegal dump described above. In an hour from now, Xian will raise the alert. This is enough for Wei, a farmer whose house stands defiantly next to the scrap heap, to pass comment from the middle of his field: 'Graphite is our salvation! The entire region depends on it. So it's just one hole after another!', he says, leaning on his spade.[5] 'They use it to make very good batteries, right?' We nod. The batteries of billions of telephones around the world each contain little more than two grams of graphite in order to have electric conductivity. But its manufacture comes at great human and environmental expense because of the residue emitted from the nearby mines and factories that, says Wei, 'can spread into the atmosphere for dozens of kilometres in all directions. Mashan has lost its greenery, its clear water, and, unfortunately, the manufacturers do very little to prevent that.'

In principle, there are strict environmental regulations in place governing industrial operations in China. But they fail to take into account just how strategic graphite is to Heilongjiang. Every year, the 'black snowflake' brings 1.2 billion euros into the province—an amount that the authorities hope to increase tenfold by 2030, thanks to the global craze for electronic goods.[6] How can this forced-march growth accommodate President Xi Jinping's recurring promise of a 'blue and green', or more ecological, China?

By keeping up appearances: bring a few 'model' factories up to standards in time for an official visit, and allow the reality of operations to slide back into place once the apparatchik returns to Beijing. The central government apparently has little control over how local businesses are run. 'It's what we say around here: the mountains are high and the emperor is far', Wei tells us. 'The bosses make huge profits. The money is all they think about; they don't care about the pollution we have to live with. We're just the little guys; we can't reach them. All we can do is cry about it.'

The China I explored in Heilongjiang province is the invisible, voiceless China, far from the opulence of the big cities. It is also where I unearthed the primary cause of digital pollution: the raw materials needed to manufacture the 34 billion mobile phones, tablets, and other devices in circulation in the world. These 'interfaces' and 'terminals' are, for 4.5 billion users, the gateway to the global information-technology network and its infinite services. Whether it's to order a pizza with anchovies, book a flight, stream a miniseries, or find a soulmate on a dating app, internet and digital technologies have turned every single one of us into modern lords who, with the tip of our fingers, can command a multiplicity of virtual assistants to do the work of serfs and the enslaved of centuries ago.

And it's early days still: by 2025, every one of us (or almost) will be responsible for some 5,000 digital interactions a day.[7] To keep up with such inflation in the use of digital devices, equipment manufacturers are being challenged to multiply interfaces that are even easier to use, with better performance, versatility, and sophistication. Look no further than the standard smartphone, whose features now include two cameras, three microphones, an infrared sensor, a proximity sensor, a magnetometer, multiple GPS antennas, WiFi, 4G, and Bluetooth.[8]

What is the physical cost of these marvellous objects? A visit to a car-boot sale might give you an idea. There you might find an old 1960s telephone, complete with a rotary dial, whose manufacture at most would have required around ten different raw materials, such as aluminium and zinc. You might also dig up a mobile phone from the 1990s, affectionately known as a 'brick'.

A few steps up from its spin-dial predecessor, it contains another nineteen raw materials, including copper, cobalt, and lead.

Now take a look at your smartphone. It is much smaller, but don't let this fool you: it contains more than *fifty* raw materials, including gold, lithium, magnesium, silicon, and bromine (see appendix 2 for the full list), all found in the smartphone's battery, casing, screen, and electronics, making it a more enjoyable product to use. The obscure metal neodymium, for example, is what makes your phone vibrate. The touchscreen is thanks to traces of ITO—indium tin oxide. Every day, we are walking around with an array of raw materials in our pockets without even knowing they are there or what they do. There is less than a gram of each, yet this is more than enough to have completely changed our lives.

Then there's the internet and its litany of telecommunication networks (cables, routers, and WiFi) and data centres, where connected objects can talk to one another. This gigantic infrastructure is drawing on a growing share of the Earth's resources, with ICT accounting for 12.5 per cent of global copper production, and 7 per cent of global aluminium production (both abundant metals).[9] ICT also uses minute metals with exceptional chemical properties. We also find them in flatscreen televisions, condensers, hard drives, integrated circuits, fibre optics, and semiconductors. These digital technologies guzzle a large share of annual global output: 15 per cent of palladium, 23 per cent of silver, 40 per cent of tantalum, 41 per cent of antimony, 42 per cent of beryllium, 66 per cent of ruthenium, 70 per cent of gallium, 80 per cent of germanium, and as much as 88 per cent of terbium. (See the complete list in appendix 3.)

Assembling these resources into a smartphone that fits into

the palm of your hand has become a feat of insanely complex and notoriously energy-intensive engineering. Its manufacture alone makes up half the carbon footprint and 80 per cent of the energy consumption of its entire life cycle.[10] We therefore cannot talk about the digital revolution without turning our attention to the bowels of the Earth—in Chile, Bolivia, the Democratic Republic of Congo, Kazakhstan, Russia, and Australia—from where the resources of a more connected world are extracted. 'Digital is very physical!', an engineer tells me, almost embarrassed by how obvious this is.[11] It is becoming increasingly clear how absurd it is to talk about the 'dematerialisation' of our economies when the virtual has such a tremendous physical impact in the real world.

More from less

But for the billions who subscribe wholesale to the discourse of the digital gurus, admitting that our economies and way of life cannot be dematerialised without material is nothing short of heresy. Wasn't the eruption of the digital realm, which is obviously 'virtual', supposed to curb our consumption of resources, if not stave it off entirely in some cases? It is extremely tempting to believe so, given how much pressure the globalisation of trade has put on raw materials. In a *New York Times* op-ed published in 2008, the American anthropologist Jared Diamond wrote that, 'If India as well as China were to catch up, world consumption rates would triple'—a scenario he believed would be untenable.[12] His prediction was confirmed in 2019 in a fascinating report by the Organisation for Economic Co-operation and Development (OECD): by 2060, the global use of materials may be two and a half times higher than that of 2011, increasing from seventy-nine gigatons to 167 gigatons per year.[13]

Such scenarios have been distorted by enticing terms such as 'the circular economy', 'process efficiency', and 'resource productivity gains', with the aim of disassociating the consumption of materials from the generation of wealth—in a nutshell, 'more from less'.[14] It's a concept also lauded by 'ecomodernists' who state in their techno-optimistic manifesto published in 2015 that 'Thanks to technological improvements in agriculture, during the half-century starting in the mid-1960s, the amount of land required for growing crops and animal feed for the average person declined by one-half.'[15]

The internet is changing the rules of the game: other than enhancing manufacturing processes and reducing the flow of materials, the internet offers to eradicate the overconsumption of resources. The utopia of a world without the spectre of a shortage of resources has become reality, with both the private and public sectors waxing lyrical about 'paperless' tax declarations, payslips, letters, and invoices, and favouring 'virtual human interaction' over face-to-face team meetings.

In a tiny northern European country on the Baltic Sea, I experienced the full extent of this powerful shift.

Estonia: the country that went fully digital

Nothing about the fortified old city of Tallinn, the capital of Estonia, gives any indication that I am in the kingdom of geeks. The city's gothic buildings, red-shingled roofs, and cobblestone streets certainly don't look like they were modelled using 3D software.

Likewise, I'd sooner expect arrows to rain from the medieval fortification girding the city than face the threat of a cyberattack. Yet this tiny republic with a population of 1.3 million—the next stop in my investigation, in the summer of 2020—holds the prize of the most digitalised and 'dematerialised' country in the world.

Ninety-nine per cent of Estonia's public services are online. Other than getting married, divorced, or carrying out major banking transactions, everything is handled remotely. Its 'digital citizens' have an electronic identity card with which to pay their taxes, create a start-up, join the municipal library, take public transport, and even cast their vote. Public services are managed centrally via a data-exchange platform called 'X-Road'. For citizens, it is simplicity incarnate, from birth ... right until death, as the e-administration considers developing an 'e-death' service to automatically settle any outstanding debts the deceased may have left. The reputation of 'e-Estonia' is so persuasive that its engineers consult for other countries looking to successfully engage in their own digital transformation.

A thirst for democracy after decades under Soviet rule would explain the decision of this state, known worldwide for its transparency, to go digital. Estonia also trains engineers (the electronic systems of the 1957 Sputnik were designed in Tallinn), making it culturally more open to digital technologies. Or could this all-digital promised land be the result of Estonians' determination to free themselves of the agricultural enslavement endured by the generations of farmers before them? 'Our philosophy, including with regards to e-administration, has always been to design easy-to-use systems and infrastructures precisely because the lives of Estonian farmers never had it easy', a Tallinner senior official tells me.[16] It's a compelling explanation: the black band on the national flag represents both the land and Estonia's painful past.

The result is a country that prides itself as 'the most digitalised society in the world.'[17] 'We are working towards automating everything we can', says Ott Vatter, the managing director of e-Residency.[18] 'We envisage a data-driven state able to pre-empt the needs of citizens and anticipate certain political strategies.'[19] The gains generated by this digital orientation are indisputable: Estonia's gross domestic product (GDP) is higher than that of its Baltic neighbours; the government is more efficient, and its operating costs are lower than anywhere else. And what a boon for the environment! Every month, the digital state saves piles of paper as high as a stack of Eiffel Towers and many kilometres of transport, as well as energy. 'As a consequence, our government saved 2 per cent of GDP every year', says Estonia's former president Toomas Hendrik Ilves.[20]

Everything in Estonia bears the seal of simplicity. Life in digital is smooth sailing. What we don't see or hear about, however, is the physical, energy, and software infrastructure that keeps the state machine running. I queried this, but was met with vague replies, as if my questions were completely off-topic: the means to achieve the desired result are irrelevant. It's a bit like admiring the great masterpieces for their balance of depth, play of light, hyperrealist, or figurative style while ignoring the role of the materials and the colour merchants in enabling artists to apply paint to canvas.[21] Likewise, we inherently discount the basic, fundamental question of 'How?' Yet no question could be more noble; possibly not even 'Why'. Before we become drunk on our ideas and concepts, there is the mundane but inescapably real matter of materials and their production. How many of us smartphone and tablet users ask, let alone seek, the answers to such questions?

In their defence, three types of professionals have, over the last few decades, played a role in detaching users from this reality: theorists, advertisers, and designers.

- First, the theorists. These pioneers designed the internet as a forum for total freedom of speech, where libertarians and radical libertarians advocated the removal of the state. One of these radicals was political activist John Perry Barlow. In 1966, opposed to state control of the internet, he put forth his famous Declaration of the Independence of Cyberspace: 'Your legal concepts of property, expression, identity, movement, and context do not apply to us. They are all based on matter, and there is no matter here.' According to Barlow, only in an electronic world, free of the shackles of the physical world, is political emancipation possible: 'Our identities have no bodies, so, unlike you, we cannot obtain order by physical coercion.'[22]

  This utopia of liberation from matter is echoed in the business world. The knowledge economy (or 'economy of the immaterial') is based on knowledge, creativity, and imagination, rather than on resources.[23] It is arguably synonymous with infinite and sustainable growth, and follows the natural course of history.[24] Indeed, in the early 1980s, the 100 richest companies in the United States 'either dug something out of the ground or turned a natural resource (iron ore or oil) into something tangible that you could hold', writes the American star business expert Seth Godin.[25]

  Today, according to the American physicist-turned-journalist Chris Anderson, 'Only thirty-two of the Top

100 companies today make things you can hold, from aerospace and motor vehicles to chemicals and food, metal, bending, and heavy industry. The other sixty-eight traffic mostly in *ideas*, not resource processing. Some offer services rather than goods, such as health care and telecommunications. Others create goods that are mostly intellectual property, such as drugs and semiconductors, where the cost to produce the physical product is tiny compared to the cost of inventing it.[26]

Corollaries to this cognitive capitalism are new economic models, including that of services, where selling a service or access to an experience replaces the sale of a physical object. This is the genius behind streaming platforms such as Spotify and Apple Music, which sell music rather than CDs. Take this reasoning further, and you could have hordes of salespeople selling you anything from light instead of lightbulbs, mobility instead of cars, and printing services instead of printers. Thus the object drifts further and further away from its intrinsic value. The Greek philosopher Plato spoke about this very dualism: in his dialogue *Phaedo*, the body—made of matter, and therefore worthless—is an impediment to the search for truth. Which is why Plato prefers spirit over body—the nobler of the two. Fast-forward to the twenty-first century: by ascribing more intellectual than material value to objects, depriving patents, trademarks, algorithms, designs, or organisation models of their underlying physicality, armies of engineers and traders are transposing the teachings of Plato to the market economy via Excel spreadsheets and PowerPoint presentations.

- Next are advertisers. They have institutionalised a marketing vocabulary to sex up the digital world with the attributes of virtuality. Without giving much thought to the words we use, we talk about 'dematerialised payments', and 'holographic', 'virtual', and 'augmented reality' headsets for entertainment. But the most ambiguous of all these is 'the cloud'—a supposedly dematerialised place where we can store our documents.[27] 'The cloud is ethereal, woolly', says a specialist in responsible digital activities.[28] How do we find the right words? 'When you see the market cap of a company such as Apple, you realise the kind of marketing pressure that can represent', says Frédéric Bordage.[29]

- Then there are the brains behind the design of electronic goods who have rolled out their treasures of creativity to remove the physical from the digital. The consumer's first—and sometimes only—contact with the digital world is such a treasure, the smartphone: a superb object that conveys the idea of purity. And how could something so sleek be so impure? The aesthetic perfection of these products is intuitively incompatible with the notion of pollution.

  The clean design of Apple's devices has contributed a lot to this ambiguity. For its co-founder Steve Jobs, this quest draws on the precepts of Zen Buddhism—a philosophy that advocates simplicity and asceticism.[30] The aesthetic results are polished temples with minimalist decoration. 'Steve Jobs was not Buddhist, but he was very much inspired by the simplicity of Zen, and how he thought about Apple's design', says Erick Rinner, an investment professional who practises meditation.[31] Jobs described how he had always found Zen Buddhism 'aesthetically sublime'.[32] After all, Apple's first marketing brochure in 1977 declared that 'Simplicity is the ultimate sophistication.' Under Jobs' influence, 'The trend became about simplifying what was turning into an increasingly complex technological world', Rinner continues. 'In the digital world, everything is clean and perfectly in place. There are no bad vibes, and that's dangerous because that's not real life!'[33] That is, the sophistication of Steve Jobs and his search for aesthetic harmony has contributed to feeding billions of consumers with the illusion that the digital world is harmless for the planet.[34]

Yet all dematerialised enterprises over the last 5,000 years tell another story. While it may not seem obvious how writing fits in, its invention by the Mesopotamians would become the very first tool for dematerialising people themselves. 'The written word has the characteristic of being accessible on demand and able to be consulted at any point. It is thanks to writing that a precise order can be issued by a person without their being physically present', writes a technology expert.[35] Moreover, as ancient societies become more complex, currency would come to symbolise the value of a marketable product. 'Thus, goods, objects, and foodstuffs existed not in relation to themselves, but in relation to their monetary value, to the point that "commercial trade" would be able to take place without the physical presence of the object being traded.'[36] Then came the bill of exchange, 'at which point money itself was dematerialised to promote trade, and, from the fifteenth century, would become the elemental tool of international trade and the first major step towards the dematerialisation of the world of the economy.[37] Now, with modern technologies, 'man will task the machine with the ability to think for him, dematerialising in a way his thoughts' (with the calculator), but also his words (the telephone) and his image (visual media).[38]

Dematerialisation therefore began well before the advent of computer technology, by replacing animal with metal, metal with paper, and paper with digital media. The resource did not disappear with each shift; rather, another resource, with more beneficial properties, was added. And given our colossal need for materials to design modern electronic equipment, computerisation just confirms this mechanism. In fact, says a specialist in sustainable IT, 'Dematerialising means materialising in another way.'[39]

An era of electronic purges

The design of digital interfaces is one thing; their fate at our hands and the compounded material cost/burden is another, as demonstrated by the spectacular announcement made by China at the end of 2019. In the midst of its trade war with the United States, and consumed with the security of its data, Beijing ordered all government bodies and businesses in China to replace within three years their Dell, HP, and Microsoft computer hardware and software with Chinese products.[40] The decision is a stark illustration of the 'digital separation' at play between the two superpowers, with China pursuing its goal of self-sufficiency by ending its reliance on foreign technologies. But no one seems to have dared ask the most basic questions: what will become of the

20 to 30 million electronic products in perfect working order, yet unusable because a high-ranking official decreed them so? Will they be repurposed? Will the servers, stripped of all sensitive information, be carted off to the shredders? Or will they end up in illegal landfills, such as the one in Guiyu in Guangdong province in southern China?

It's extremely difficult to know the answers; what we can be sure of is that this move essentially eliminates an entire generation of IT equipment in a way that is both radical and abrupt. There have been myriad political purges throughout history of opponents whose ideas do not align with those of the dominant party or ruler. Now we are entering an era of electrotonic purges, with millions of computers, deemed undesirable on account of their origin, all of a sudden stopping working. And this is not the exclusive domain of China: fearing espionage operations, the US mobilised nearly $2 billion at the end of 2020 in order to 'rip and replace' all communication and video-surveillance equipment installed on American soil by Chinese companies.[41] Several European countries followed suit for the same reason, and announced that they, too, would rid their territory of thousands of Huawei 5G antennas.[42]

This junking of equipment, while the result of political decisions, remind us of manufacturing strategies of planned obsolescence, aimed at speeding up a product's demise. Such obsolescence can be 'material', whereby a component of a smartphone—more often than not, its battery—stops working or is impossible to replace because it is glued fast to the rest of the device, condemning the entire smartphone to the scrap heap. We can also talk about cultural obsolescence, when an earlier technology becomes less desirable, and therefore useless, with the release of a new technology. By 2025, 80 per cent of companies will have shut down their own data centres to move their contents to external providers that offer cloud services. This migration will lead to the liquidation of millions of servers around the world.[43] Then we have software obsolescence, whereby an electronic product no longer works following a software update that renders it incompatible. For example, in 2020, Sonos announced that the connected speakers it sold between 2011 and 2015 would no longer work properly, because there would be no further software updates.[44] 'They are taking a speaker that is in perfect working order, and throwing it into the bin. It's completely scandalous!', fumes a campaigner for the HOP (Stop Planned Obsolescence) association.[45]

Software developers are largely to blame, as new applications and programs take up more and more memory and processing power, earning them the name 'bloatware': complex software that includes countless battery-guzzling features. GreenIT highlights this trend: 'The average weight of web pages increased by 115 times between 1995 and 2015.'[46] Similarly, the power needed to compose a text message doubles every two or three years.[47] Devices slow down under the processing burden of such increasingly complex code, prompting users to replace them with better-performing products.

This explains why, over the last three decades, the lifespan of a computer has dropped from eleven to just four years.[48] *Homo sapiens* becomes 'homo detritus', producing the equivalent of 5,000 Eiffel Towers of electronic waste, or e-waste, every year.[49] In fact, the impact of the Anthropocene epoch does not stop at climate change and ocean acidification. In 2017, researchers made the staggering discovery that humankind is a geological force, for its activities have engendered 208 new minerals due mostly to the alteration of mining and e-waste, such as semiconductors and batteries that have been buried in the ground.[50] Simply put, our consumer behaviour—especially with regard to digital—is changing the composition of the Earth's crust. By exhuming exotic minerals such as nealite, devellina, and hydromagnesite from archaeological sites, geologists in the thirtieth century will be able to piece together our lifestyles, just as we do by digging up the vestiges of ancient Rome and Egypt.

We are only scratching the surface of what is a profound and historical mutation of the very nature of waste. In a world where the 'internet of everything' will thrive (more on this in chapter seven), every object and every organism—from homes, wild animals, and pine forests to cars—will be 'smart' and 'connected'. And at the end of their lifespans, these hundreds of billions of objects and living creatures, packed with sensors, will transmute into e-waste: a chipped dalmatian, after eating a spoiled can of dog food; a connected oak tree sent to the sawmill; or a cow with a microchip, on its way to the abattoir. May the reader forgive me for this next grim conjecture: even the departed, endowed with brain implants and artificial organs, will become e-waste. There will need to be approved collection services, a competitive recycling industry, and a well-oiled circular economy. The four cardinal Rs —recover, repair, reuse, and recycle—will be the solution to the accumulation of all this hybrid scrap of animal, vegetable, and mineral matter, and future generations will use more of their creativity to come up with ways to extend the lifespan of what already exists, rather than bring to life new, revolutionary products.

But will our children have the right to do more than just patch up these objects? It's an absurd yet relevant question, unfortunately. For many years now, manufacturers have been increasingly denying users the basic freedom of repairing their electronic products. When a manufacturer sells a smartphone, for instance, it relinquishes the effective ownership of the device, and grants the user a licence to use the operating system (Android, for example) that makes the device work. But while the user owns the smartphone, they only hold the licence to use the software, and don't have the right to touch it. This is how the American company John Deere stops its customers from repairing their tractors, despite owning them, because doing so would require altering the software, which is owned by John Deere![51] In 2020, Apple applied this strategy by only allowing authorised service-providers to repair the camera on the iPhone 12.[52] The built-in software in any product 'allows the vendor to control who can carry out repairs, when and at what price ... and because the product can't even be repaired a lot of the time, you have to buy a new one', says Kyle Wiens, founder of the Californian company iFixit, which helps users fix their electronic devices.[53]

This user-unfriendly approach is one long perfected by Monsanto. The US agrochemical company grants Indian farmers the licence to plant Monsanto's Roundup-resistant seeds (a powerful herbicide), but does not sell the seeds to them. And so, every year, because the farmers do not own the seeds, they have to buy new seeds from Monsanto instead of replanting the seeds they save.[54] We may all become like those Indian farmers if our right to own any object is systematically restricted by all sorts of patents that, in practice, prevent us from using our electronic products as we see fit.

Another kind of digital world is possible

This is how the contents concealed inside the cover of a smartphone, under the bonnet of a connected car, and beneath the keyboard of a laptop will be, over the next few decades, at the frontline of a major confrontation. On one side: manufacturers, using all forms of cunning to make us ever more dependent on their products. On the other: increasingly well-organised consumer networks, working to take back control of the objects around them. This movement began twenty-five years ago in Germany and the US with the concept of 'makers', from which thousands of 'FabLabs' around the world have sprung. Their philosophy? 'If you want to know how something works, make it yourself!'[35] Other community groups have emerged, including thousands of Repair Cafés where anyone can walk in with their broken electronic item and fix it with the help of volunteers. This global phenomenon began in 2009 at the instigation of Martine Postma, whom we met in 2020. The former journalist, whose global Repair Cafés boasts 350 tonnes in e-waste avoided annually, estimates that the approach 'is at a tipping point; consumers are realising that reparable products are desirable products. More and more of them no longer want to be enslaved to their coffee machines or mobile phones.'[36]

There are myriad solutions for limiting the physical footprint of devices, all well referenced in online guides.[37] Sell your items second-hand on platforms such as Swappa and Back Market; connect to Spareka for spare parts for electrical appliances and repair tutorials; lease a smartphone from Commown instead of buying one new; have just one smartphone for both work and personal use, etc. Such concrete actions show that consumers recognise that they, like tech companies, are responsible for digital pollution, and can do something about it. Governments could stimulate a 'repair and reuse' economy, extend legal guarantee periods, prescribe a ten-year compatibility period of devices with new software, and demand that manufacturers provide spare parts for the products they sell.[58] In France, significant progress has been made with the introduction of a compulsory repairability index in 2021 to give intending consumers an indication of the durability of electronic tools and appliances before buying them.[59]

Collecting e-waste promises to be a herculean task, since less than 20 per cent of it is recovered and recycled.[60] A story I was covering in Amsterdam in 2020 led me to Joost de Kluijver—the director of Closing the Loop since 2012.[61] The forty-something-year-old is running an insane project to import back into Europe the same quantity of old phones that Europe has offloaded to e-waste dumps in Africa, and to recycle them. The company essentially wants to reverse the journey of our used phones, and trigger a backwards migration of electronic goods. There is enormous potential. De Kluijver believes they can reimport as many as two million mobile phones every year. All that's left then is to find a way to collect them in Rwanda, Zambia, and Nigeria, right from under the noses of highly organised Indian and Chinese recycling networks, brave the nightmare of African administrations, avoid being ripped off by intermediaries who 'strip the mobile phones of their metals and replace them with cement or soap'... and set up a sustainable economic model.

Joost de Kluijver believes he has found such a model in the form of a compensation scheme: 'For every smartphone a company such as Samsung sells, it commits to financing the repatriation of a phone from Africa.' The scheme has already been taken up by several corporations (KPMG, ING Bank, and Accenture) and administrations in the Netherlands (the municipalities of Amsterdam, Utrecht, and Groningen), which have bought thousands of phones for employees. The scheme is a way for them to improve their reputation as responsible players, while making de Kluijver's repatriation activities cost-effective.[62]

Finally, phones should overwhelmingly be bought from Fairphone, the first company to bring 'ethical' smartphones to the market. Hailing from the Netherlands, Fairphone operates out of the IJhaven port in Amsterdam, which I was invited to visit in winter 2020. In an immense workspace, dozens of engineers and salespeople speaking a variety of languages bustle about in a relaxed atmosphere. What makes the phones manufactured here the most sustainable in the world are, first and foremost, the company's efforts to ensure that the metals used to make them are mined ethically. It also designs its phones to last as long as possible. 'We want our users to keep their phones for seven to eight years', a member of the team tells me.[63] The trick is modularity, meaning the Fairphone's parts can be assembled and disassembled separately, and therefore replaced separately. 'This is especially important for the battery and the screen', says a technician. 'We also need to be able to change the speaker, the front camera, the selfie camera ... I won't lie, it's a real nightmare', she sighs.

And it doesn't stop there. The company needs to open new phone-repair centres and fight to keep the new versions of Android compatible with the SIM cards in older phone models.[64] 'Every day, I have moments of discouragement', says the technician. Another limit is that the hundreds of thousands of third-generation Fairphones the company plans to sell is a mere fraction of the 1.5 billion mobile phones sold worldwide every year. Be that as it may, more and more entrepreneurs, campaigners, and activists are mobilising every day so that we can truly comprehend our devices—and our future. Such initiatives are all the more vital, as an unfamiliar indicator is about to tell us: the physical impact of the digital world is far greater that what we, up until now, could have imagined.

CHAPTER THREE

The dark matter of a digital world

WE HAVE LOOKED AT WHERE OUR DEVICES COME FROM, BUT we have only scratched the surface of the Earth's crust. The internet has a far greater reach both in time and in space, and to get a sense of its proportions, we need to immerse ourselves in a multidimensional universe about which most of us haven't the first clue.

Astrophysicists will tell you that the naked eye can make out only an infinitesimal part of the cosmos—around 3,000 stars—when, in fact, the Milky Way comprises at least 100 billion stars. There are also 100 billion galaxies in the universe. Yet all this, combined, is only 20 per cent of the universe's mass. The remainder is likely to be composed of a mysterious substance—dark matter—about which we know very little. And so, to broaden our scope of observation, technologies measuring gamma rays, ultraviolet light, infrared light, and gravitational waves are used. I suggest we, too, should use little-known tools to explore the extent of the largely invisible pollution generated by digital: the dark matter of the nonmaterial.

MIPS and the inner workings of matter

Jans Teubler, a German science researcher at the Wuppertal Institute in Germany, remembers the moment like it was yesterday.[1] It was at a conference at the institute in its namesake city in the region of Westphalia: 'I stopped dead in my tracks when I saw this drawing of a man wearing a wedding band ... and an enormous rucksack on his shoulders, representing the true physical weight of the ring. It made a huge impression on me.'[2] The image Teubler saw is an illustration of the ground-breaking 'MIPS' method developed by the institute in the 1990s for calculating the material impact of our consumer habits. It stands for Material Input Per Service unit, and quantifies the resources needed to manufacture a product or provide a service.[3]

To measure their environmental impact, industries start by looking at their carbon dioxide emissions. And it makes sense to do so. The fight against global warming is at the forefront of today's environmental priorities: the European Green Deal of 2019 aims for greenhouse-gas emissions neutrality by 2050; and China recently pledged to become carbon neutral by 2060—a commitment forming the backbone of its environmental transformation plan. But by measuring emissions alone, other forms of pollution, such as the impact of chemical waste on water quality, tend to be overlooked. Moreover, only considering the carbon dioxide emissions of consumer products is 'a very reductionist approach', says Karine Samuel, professor of business sciences and an expert in the internet of things (IoT).[4] Since the 1990s, the MIPS method offers an entirely new approach: instead of taking into consideration the environmental damage as a result of what an object produces (such as carbon dioxide emissions), the MIPS approach factors in what goes into producing an object. Looking at what goes *into* an object as opposed to what comes *out of* it delivers a radical change of perspective.

The method assesses all the resources mobilised and displaced for the manufacture, use, and recycling of a given object — whether it's a garment, a bottle of orange juice, a carpet, or a smartphone. Everything is covered: renewable and non-renewable resources (plants and minerals), agricultural land shifts, and the use of water and chemicals.[5] For example, a T-shirt made in a factory in India requires electricity that is generated by coal, which requires cutting down a pine forest ... The T-shirt's MIPS factors in the cotton that is used, but also the bricks used to build the factory, the tungsten filament lighting the premises, the coal used to generate electricity, and the trees that were felled to plant the cotton, etc. Teubler likens the method to 'shifting a car's gear stick, which sets a series of wheels in motion right under your seat'.

We could also see it as a 'butterfly effect of materials'. Just as a butterfly flapping its wings can cause a storm at the other end of the world, making a simple item of clothing can have an impact on all stages of its production, scattered across the globe. The MIPS method exposes a causal chain on a planetary scale. It is translated into a number — an 'ecological rucksack' — which is the multiplying factor of every one of our acts of consumption. The method is not perfect: 'Most of the data used for calculating MIPS is based on experts' opinions and estimates', and are often inaccurate, Teubler points out. This does not lessen the impact of what I'm about to learn: making a T-shirt requires 226 kilograms of resources; a litre of orange juice, 100 kilograms of raw materials; and a newspaper, 10 kilograms.[6] But what really blew Teubler away at the conference was the wedding band in the drawing, whose few grams of gold had a MIPS of three tonnes! Clearly, the weight of the objects that surround us is far greater than we think—an average of thirty times more.[7]

The MIPS of a service or an act of consumption can also be calculated. A one-kilometre car ride and an hour spent watching television use one and two kilograms of resources respectively. One minute on the telephone 'costs' 200 grams. A text message 'weighs' 0.632 kilograms.[8] You can even measure the material impact of your own lifestyle by using one of the countless MIPS calculators online—a quick fifteen-minute test with questions including your country of residence, the surface area of your home, the type of power you use, and where you go on holiday.[9] I'll admit, it was not a pleasant experience, as I learned that my ecological rucksack is around thirty-eight tonnes per year.[10] The Wuppertal Institute test even proposes a punishing 'diet' to reduce this number to seventeen tonnes per year by 2030.

The dizzying MIPS of digital technologies

Many products have quite a low MIPS ratio. Manufacturing a steel bar 'only' requires ten times more resources than its final weight. But, as Jens Teubler points out, 'The MIPS is higher as soon as technology is involved.' Digital technologies are proof of this on account of the vast number of metals they contain, and especially 'rare metals that are hard to extract from the ground'. A two-kilogram laptop involves twenty-two kilograms of chemicals, 244 kilograms of fuel, and 1.5 tonnes of clean water, to list but a few resources.[11] The MIPS ratio of a television is 200:1 and to 1,000:1. (A fifteen-kilogram television would require between three and fifteen tonnes of raw materials.)[12] That of a smartphone is 1,200:1 (183 kilograms of raw materials for an end product weighing 150 grams).[13] But the prize for the highest MIPS goes to the microchip: 32 kilograms of materials for an integrated circuit weighing two grams—a hair-raising ratio of 16,000:1.[4]

'People are often surprised by the difference between the perceived effect and the actual impact of their decision to buy a consumer product', says Teubler. And for good reason: the geographic region that is located furthest upstream of the production chain, and therefore furthest away from the final point of sale, pays the highest material cost. Thus well-intentioned urbanites continue to praise the environmental and nutritional benefits of chickpea-flour pasta, rave about using public-access bicycles to get to their Bikram yoga class, and happily trade in their mobile phone for a new model every eighteen months. It's a feel-good but dangerous lifestyle, because of how dramatically and imperceptibly the digital world has increased our material impacts. Multiply this volume by the MIPS of billions of servers, antennas, routers, and other WiFi terminals currently in service by 100, 1,000, or even 10,000, and you will reach the conclusion that these 'dematerialised' technologies not only consume materials, but are quite simply becoming one of the most massive enterprises in materialisation in history.

Companies in sectors as diverse as glass, textiles, automotive, and software have their MIPS calculated, but if the results are unflattering, they go undisclosed ... and the consumer remains uninformed. And while 'MIPS is now an established indicator in Germany, we have failed to popularise it in the rest of Europe and the US', says Teubler, as 'the demand for pollution measurement continues to focus on carbon emissions'.[14] Considering how little we know about the 'ecological reality of technologies' every day, we are leaving future generations with the responsibility of having to deal with a colossal physical challenge.[15]

MIPS should be seen as a fantastic tool for action. It is also the basis of the Wuppertal Institute's 'Factor 4' theory: by decreasing fourfold our material and energy consumption, we can halve the production of goods *and* halve its overall material impact—producing twice as much material wellbeing for half as many resources consumed. It's within our reach.[16] 'The Wuppertal Institute's goal is eight tonnes [of resources per person per year] by 2050', says Teubler. This is why smartphone manufacturers should be made to display the MIPS on their products. Otherwise, everything happening below our feet will continue to go completely over our heads.

It is not enough to be 'low carbon' to be eco-friendly; it takes being 'low resource' as well. The uncomfortable truth is that the more wearable, discreet, and light the technology, the greater the material legacy of our existence. But it's not enough to explore the physical impact of our miniaturised world: we need to scrutinise a much smaller world, indistinguishable to the naked eye. 'We're constantly talking about Apple, but we never mention microchip manufacturers', laments Agnès Crepet, an engineer at Fairphone.[17] 'Yet they're at the heart of a huge environmental and social mess.'

The environmental toll of nanotechnologies

'Step through the airlock and put on this anti-static suit', instructs engineer François Martin.[18] 'Leave your notebook behind, otherwise there will be fuzz.' He sees the surprise on my face and explains: 'Paper spreads fibres, and you're entering a zero-particle environment where fine particles are the arch enemies of semiconductors.' It's morning in September 2019, and I am at LETI, the Laboratory of Electronics and Information Technologies at the CEA French government agency.[19] Located in the city of Grenoble between the Vercors and Chartreuse massifs, LETI-CEA is a unique industrial site in Europe for its new-generation chips—also known as integrated circuits—that it develops for the electronics sector. Since their invention in 1958 by the American engineer Jack Kilby, these minuscule silicon chips have completely changed our lives.[20] They are the brains of electronics, receiving and processing the information needed to operate all sorts of objects. A handful of companies, such as Samsung in South Korea, Intel and Qualcomm in the US, and the Taiwan Semiconductor Manufacturing Company (TSMC)[21] now produce some 100 billion chips every year for everything from laptop computers, washing machines, and rockets to, of course, mobile phones.[22]

It was no easy feat getting access to LETI's clean room. Given the amount of intellectual property between its walls, my credentials as a journalist were thoroughly scrutinised. Another airlock, and I had arrived. My very first thought was that I had just entered the international space station: there were hundreds of engineers in white coveralls, masks, and hairnets, working around the clock, seven days a week, in an obstacle course of ultra-modern facilities interconnected by a maze of pipes. The end products of this strange laboratory are in what look like small incubators, and are round 'wafers' the size of a vinyl disk and composed of small rectangular chips. The clean room lives up to its name in every respect, with the requirements for cleanliness infinitely more stringent than in an operating theatre. It's as big as a football field, with no running, shaking hands, or any other sudden movements allowed. 'Make-up is tolerated, but not perfume', explains a laboratory worker.

This extreme level of precaution signals that I have entered the world of nano manufacturing. For a mobile phone to be able to take photos, film, record, use geopositioning, capture data, and—why not—even make calls, its chips had to be made exponentially more powerful without increasing its size. To print even more transistors on a square wafer, the industry abandoned the micrometre (one-thousandth of a millimetre, or the thickness of a strand of hair) in favour of the nanometre—a thousand times smaller still. Now I understand better why the smallest speck of dust can have a disastrous effect on the quality of the products in this environment. 'If we want a chip to work, there needs to be military organisation and constant attention', Marin adds. 'Even the air in the clean room is renewed every six seconds.'[23]

The result of such engineering is astounding: 'Every smartphone today has a computer that is 100 times more powerful than the best computers designed thirty years ago', says Jean-Pierre Colinge, a former engineer at TSMC, who couldn't help but add: 'And when you know that they're mainly used for taking selfies, it's a bit galling.'[24] Especially since chips are among the most complex electronic components out there. Making them requires some sixty raw materials, including silicium, boron, arsenic, tungsten, and copper, all of which are 99.9999999 per cent purified. Printing transistors is no easy feat. 'Microchips can contain up to 20 billion transistors. Imagine 20 billion little ball bearings in a watch—it's astounding!' says the former engineer. So, fifty microchips on a wafer equals as many as 1,000 billion transistors, or 'four times the number of stars in the Milky Way, all studded on the surface of a vinyl record'.[25]

The 500 steps it takes to manufacture an integrated circuit involves thousands of subcontractors across dozens of countries. If there is one object that represents globalisation, it would without a doubt be the microchip. As Jean Colinge says:

> The quartz mine is probably in South Africa; the silicon wafers are manufactured in Japan; the photolithography equipment comes from the Netherlands; Austria is home to one of the world's biggest manufacturers of vacuum pumps, the ball bearings of which are made in Germany; the integrated circuits are probably packaged in Vietnam to keep costs down;[26] from there they are sent to Foxconn in China to be put into iPhones; and to optimise all these processes, TSMC would use software developed by Italian and Scottish universities.[27]

The logistics alone 'consume an absolutely monstrous amount of energy', says the researcher Karine Samuel.[28]

The scramble for energy

Extracting and refining silicon, casting wafers at 1,400 degrees Celsius, producing extreme ultraviolet light using machines drawing on light energy, and the dozens of cleaning operations of the wafers all require exorbitant amounts of energy.[29] Would it not make more sense to minimise the amount of energy these industrial processes need, if not just to lower costs? 'The less energy microchip manufacturers use, the lower their profits', Jean-Pierre Colinge explains. It's a highly competitive sector, and signing just one contract with the likes of Apple or Huawei might keep a business going for an entire year. And what do smartphone manufacturers want? Faster, more functional phones. 'The advertising boasting the increasingly high performance of their electronic products speaks for itself', says Colinge.

Enslaved to the technical specifications of its clients, companies such as TSMC are doomed to multiply its technological prowess in record time. Soon, patterning transistors of five to seven nanometres will not be enough to stay in the game, with TSMC having already committed to lowering the count to three nanometres, or even one nanometre. In these conditions, 'Never has the company's energy consumption been this concerning', says the former TSMC engineer.[30] So it comes as no surprise that the total amount of fuel burned is hundreds of times higher than the final weight of the integrated circuit. According to Agnès Crepet, the vast majority of integrated-circuit manufacturers 'couldn't care less about improving their carbon footprint'.[31] In their defence, consumers are no more environmentally conscious than manufacturers. 'Do people worry about the energy it took to make that?' asks Colinge. 'No, they don't. They're more concerned about getting the latest iPhone and getting rid of the one they got two years ago. It's painful to see all that science and expertise go into the bin.'[32]

The impact of this industrial logic on health and the environment are laid bare in Taiwan—the country that holds the record of producing more electronics per capita than anywhere else in the world.[33] The island nation located 180 kilometres from the coast of China is home to TSMC, which alone represents over half of the global manufacture of semiconductors. In recent years, it has also had to contend with myriad accusations of pollution, because 'the microprocessor industry releases liquid, solid, and gaseous waste' into the environment, says a Taiwanese chemist.[34] The exact figures are hard to come by, but producing one kilogram of silicon purportedly generates some 280 kilograms of chemicals.[35] Not all the waste is treated, and since 2013 several of TSMC's subcontractors, including the electronics groups ASE Korea and Nerca, have had to suspend their operations after spilling toxic substances into nearby rivers.[36]

Colinge further explains that 'because integrated circuits need to be rinsed with deionised water [purer than distilled water] at every step of the manufacturing process, it takes a lot of water to develop chips'. This puts TSMC's water consumption at some 156,000 tonnes per day. Although 86 per cent of it is recycled, Colinge recalls a recent episode involving his former employer.[37] 'Taiwan was hit with a drought in 2017, but TSMC needed so much water that it had to transport it by the truckload from a river close to the factories. 'There were so many heavy-duty trucks that you couldn't drive into the Hsinchu Science Park [an industrial park of 1,400 hectares in the north of Taiwan].'[38]

More staggering still is TSMC's energy consumption: 'The smaller the object you produce, the larger energy-guzzling machines you need', adds Colinge. TSMC's factories in Taiwan supposedly require the equivalent of three nuclear reactors to operate, or 3 per cent of Taiwan's national peak energy consumption—a number that is expected to double over the next ten years.[39] With 43 per cent of the country's electricity coming from coal- and oil-fired plants, 'the carbon footprint of Taiwan's electronics industry makes up 10 per cent of the country's total emissions', explains Colinge.[40] Its air pollution, together with that of the petrochemical industry, has already driven thousands of protesters onto the streets of the industrial cities of Kaohsiung and Taichung.[41] According to Taiwanese activist Han-Lin Li, 'The rate of lung cancer is fifteen times higher here than in Taipei.'[42] As a result, the sector's management boards (with TSMC in the lead) recently issued the order to shift to renewable energies.

But why did it take so long to react? 'The microelectronics industry has the reputation of being at the cutting edge of progress. And perhaps we failed to understand that it could also be the source of environmental and health impacts', says Li.[43] Does the economic clout of this strategic industrial sector bypass all checks and balances? 'TSMC is so important to Taiwan that the authorities would give them anything they ask for', he says. The reality is that the demands for change in Taiwan's industry are being made by foreign clients. Like TSMC, 'companies are under immense pressure by groups such as Apple, which want their suppliers to transition to green energy', says Li. But it's too early to celebrate. The energy consumption of Taiwanese chip manufacturers has become so high that they are not prepared to wean themselves off coal. And with total indifference, they continue to emit another, imperceptible type of pollution: fluorinated gas.

Digital's hazardous haze

Spring 2019. The view from the seventeenth floor of a hotel in Datong, a city with a population of 3.4 million, 300 kilometres west of Beijing, could be a scene straight from the film *Blade Runner*: high-rise buildings, like modern-day haunted castles, reach up into an ominous sky. For three days, this megacity will remain trapped in a fog where night and day become indistinguishable. The number-one enemy of conurbations in China is carbon dioxide, and when the wind sweeps the smoke from coal-fired plants into the city centres, you're better off staying at home. Yet carbon dioxide is not the only gas threatening humanity. Colourless, odourless, and non-flammable, other products used by the digital and microelectronics industry are contributing to global warming.[44] Among them are the fifty or so fluorinated gases (F-gases), which we know little about.

HFCs, SF_6, PFCs, NF_3, and CF_4 are just some of the chemical formulas of these gases comprising one or several fluorine atoms. The gases are used in air-conditioning systems for cooling down cars, buildings ... and data centres (the case for HFC).[45] As for microelectronics, 'They're full of gas!', says academic Karine Samuel. Fluorinated gases are used for their chemical properties in the manufacturing of semiconductors, integrated circuits, and flat-panel displays.[46] They are produced in very small proportions, totalling only 2 per cent of total greenhouse-gas emissions. The main F-gas, the HFC family, has the immense advantage of not destroying the ozone layer, unlike the CFC gases they replace. This takes HFCs a step forward in the right direction for the environment. But it's not that simple.

The office of Bas Eickhout is a choice vantage point for contemplating nightfall in Brussels. It is from this glass perch that this Dutch member of the European Parliament has for many long years been leading a fierce battle to limit—if not ban outright—the use of fluorinated gases in Europe. The MEP explains: '[A] single molecule of this type of gas is far more potent than carbon dioxide.' Their warming ability is a confounding 2,000 times higher on average. NF_3 is 17,000 times more effective than carbon dioxide at trapping heat in the atmosphere. SF_6 is an even more impressive 23,500 times more effective than carbon dioxide, making it the most potent greenhouse gas ever produced on Earth. 'A single kilogram of SF_6 heats the planet as much as twenty-four people taking a flight from London to New York', British journalist Matt McGrath tells me.[47] Logically, we should be limiting their use to fight climate change. Except the exact opposite is taking place, driven by our desire for air-conditioned buildings and cars, 5G, algorithms, and data storage. Despite all the regulations being drawn up around the world to limit the use of these F-gases, Guus Velders, a researcher at the National Institute for Public Health and the Environment in the Netherlands, warns, 'If nothing wakes up to this reality, by 2050 these chemicals will represent 10 per cent of greenhouse gases.'[48]

Because fluorinated gases are synthetic, nature cannot break them down. Consequently, they remain in the atmosphere for a very long time: 740 years for NF_3, up to 3,200 years for SF_6, and 50,000 years for CF_4—the greenhouse gas with the longest lifespan that we know of so far.[49] In summary, our digital lifestyles, celebrated as the quintessence of eliminating our carbon footprint, require substances that have the highest heat-trapping potential and the most unalterable properties in existence.[50] Moreover, the solutions for recovering and eliminating fluorinated gases only exist in developed countries. Such substances are effectively an ecological time bomb; it's no wonder Greenpeace calls them 'the worst greenhouse gases you've never heard of'.[51]

Yet their effects were identified very early. In 1975, an Indian climatologist named Veerabhadran Ramanathan sounded the alarm on the potential impact of HFCs on global warming.[52] Why did no one listen? Because their effects remain far less harmful than the CFCs they substitute, which are responsible for the hole in the ozone layer. But, as pointed out by Durwood Zaelke, president of the Institute for Governance & Sustainable Development, in Washington, the main reason is that, 'In 1975, nobody paid attention to climate change!' Fluorinated gas was massively used until 2016, when the international community met in Kigali, the capital of Rwanda, to try to get rid of it. 'For anyone who has a sense of the urgency to fight climate change, since 2009, if anything had to be done, it would be on those gases', says Zaelke, who is also an environmental activist, and who played an important role during the talks in Kigali.[53] Put simply, the unintended impacts of decisions made decades earlier needed to be rectified with full knowledge of the facts, and with the planet at stake. It was not easy to build a consensus, the industries that make fluorinated gases having no interest in amending international regulations. The 197 signatory countries finally agreed on a progressive ban on HFCs. The Kigali Amendment should have been a major breakthrough. But to reach this agreement, certain countries needed to be given a grace period. Thus China, the world's biggest producer of HFCs, will only start phasing them out in 2029, and India will do so in 2032.

Honeywell: the oil and the spanner in the works

In theory, there is no need to take so long to ban HFCs, for their substitutes have already been found: HFO (hydrofluoro-olefin) gases, better known under the Solstice range, developed by the US chemical company Honeywell.[54] HFOs, which can be used for refrigerating data centres, have a much lower warming potential than HFCs.[55] But before these miracle gases can be used, we have to abide by the laws of business. Honeywell invested hundreds of millions of dollars into the Solstice range.[56] To get a return on its investment, the chemistry company has patented the range until 2030, and sells the gases at a cost that is twenty times higher than that of HFCs.[57] While the prices are arguably justified, they are completely out of reach for developing countries. 'India is too poor to stop using HFCs', confirms Durwood Zaelke, who has pointed this out to Honeywell representatives on many occasions. 'Yes, I raised this point many times at Honeywell: if the prices could go down, we could go faster. Honeywell's answer is: "I spent a lot of time and money for this gas, and I need to be paid back. I want to be rewarded." Every investor would tell you that. People just want to make money.'[58]

Zaelke makes a direct causal link between the grace period granted to India and China, whose populations make up a third of humanity, and Honeywell's prohibitively priced HFOs. In effect, while the company holds an invaluable solution, it also blocks action. 'Honeywell is keeping a lock from moving faster away from climate change' says Zaelke, while Paula Tejon, a campaign strategist at Greenpeace, laments how 'developing countries are stuck [with HFCs] for decades'.[59] The situation will continue to drag on in this fashion so long as Honeywell can continue to count on Washington's support. 'These corporations are so powerful that they can dictate the US government's action', says Tejon. Like banning the use of 'natural' refrigerants, which are far less harmful to the climate and to which no intellectual property rights apply.[60] 'Such substitutes would mean less profit for American chemical companies, and therefore they are banned in the United States', says Tejon. 'The government says they're too dangerous to use, when in fact it is protecting the country's industry.'

To date, the US has not banned the use of HFCs.[61] Europe, however, is more proactive. Since 2006, the use of fluorinated gases has steadily been decreased. But the Old Continent only represents one-fifteenth of humanity.[62] The MEP Bas Eickhout is optimistic, all the same, and believes that the regulations established in Brussels will force Chinese fluorinated gas producers to align with the requirements of the European market, thereby accelerating their conversion to a new generation of substances that are less harmful to the climate. A major obstacle remains: how do we know if the Kigali Amendments will be properly applied? 'There are no clear recommendations on how to best calculate fluorinated gas emissions', says Guus Velders.[63]

Europe might be making itself review its emissions every year, but we can't say the same for the rest of the world. Numerous companies in the digital sector stand to become less cooperative. From the perspective of Kristen Taddonio, a colleague of Durwood Zaelke, Amazon's greenhouse-gas emissions report is so vague that she couldn't work out what portion of its refrigerant emissions comes from its vehicles and what portion comes from its data centres.[64] Such discrepancies put the onus on scientists to do the assessments themselves by taking atmospheric measurements.

But when it comes to climate change, there is little time. Zaelke thinks we have a decade to do something about greenhouse gases, including fluorinated gases. 'If we don't take aggressive action this decade on short- and long-term pollutants, we'll break the 1.5-degree barrier and we'll make climate change harder to change in the future', he warns.

So, phones, tablets, and computers most certainly have a hidden cost. It is the submerged part of the iceberg: unaccounted for, invisible to our senses, and therefore largely ignored. And the billions of connected objects we use every day generate and exchange a stream of data for which the digital industry has, over the last few years, rolled out phenomenal infrastructure: data centres.

CHAPTER FOUR
Investigating a cloud

'THAT PLACE IS A MYSTERY', SAYS A PASSER-BY BUNDLED UP IN a thick scarf, pointing to the twelve-storey building nearby, surrounded by moats and railings. 'You can see shafts of purple, sometimes red light through the bay windows, day and night. I'd love to see what's in there!' she adds. I am at Science Park 610 in a suburb west of Amsterdam. Under the pale sky of this winter day in 2020, gusts of wind whistle against the black and grey ridges of what the Syrian refugees living in the nearby prefabs call the 'red building'. This may be its only distinguishing feature, for neither window nor logo gives an indication of what goes on inside. A shadow behind the central security station is all that moves. 'It's not very welcoming. It's a bit scary, even!' says Ugnius Rimsa, a local shopkeeper. 'I wonder which companies store their data there.' Since going into operation in 2017, the Equinix AM4 data centre exchanges data with 80 per cent of the European continent in under 50 milliseconds. The metal building is as intimidating as it is splendid. More importantly, it is part of what is commonly called 'the cloud'. One that, under the low skies of this winter morning, blends into other clouds that are far more imposing.

Factories of the digital age

Regardless of how we use our smartphones, they are connected to a data centre. When we book a flight, order a pizza, or call a friend, our interfaces do not communicate directly with those of EasyJet, Pizza Hut, or Mike. Rather, there is a point of interconnection or transit between the two where information is stored and processed, or which it uses to leave just as quickly (for a telephone call), or where it comes to be conserved and analysed (for ordering a pepperoni pizza). Our photos on Instagram, our videos on Facebook, and our WhatsApp messages are not only on our phones; they are held at these interconnection points—servers (computers), to be precise—with which we communicate when surfing the web. Likewise, without this infrastructure, platforms for bartering with neighbours, dating sites, smart meters, and connected cars could not exist.

For a long time, companies used to store their data on site in so-called technical rooms exiled to the back of a broom cupboard or the bathroom. Today, the biggest companies in the world (such as Google, Facebook, and Apple) still manage their own servers in privatised spaces. But for cost and security reasons, a growing number of companies prefer entrusting the management of their servers to specialist providers such as Equinix, Interxion, EdgeConneX, CyrusOne, Alibaba Cloud, and Amazon Web Service. As good 'hosts', they accommodate their clients' data in 'colocation' data centres—a bit like 'hotels for servers' linked to the internet. These facilities make up what is known as 'the cloud'—an outsourced service for storing data that is accessible from absolutely any interface, and so popular that it is the transit point for a third of the data produced in the world today. 'Every day of your life, for your most basic needs, you are likely to use 100 data centres in ten different countries', explains Fredrik Kallioniemi, commercial director of the data centre operator Hydro66'.[1] 'Without them, there's nothing!' comments Yves Grandmontagne, editor-in-chief of *Datacenter Magazine*. 'They're at the heart of our computerised life.'[2]

Yet rarely do we give a thought to their existence. 'There aren't a lot of open days in this business!' says Paul Benoit, co-founder and director of Qarnot Computing.[3] It is an emerging, discreet industry that loves filling its trade brochures with incomprehensible acronyms. And there is nothing to distinguish a data centre from any other old building, factory, or warehouse. In fact, you've probably walked past dozens of them without noticing. The hip neighbourhood of Sentier in central Paris is a veritable constellation of data centres built inside old industrial buildings. A few cable lengths away, at number 138 Boulevard Voltaire, a red-brick building houses a 7,000-square-metre data-processing centre belonging to the operator Telehouse. You can find these clusters of servers in the very heart of major cities—an old hotel, a fallout shelter, an air bunker, a post office sorting centre, or a disused car factory.[4] In New York, the old twenty-three-storey Western Union Telegraph building at 60 Hudson Street now serves as a data warehouse. In London, the campus of the University of East London in the Docklands district accounts for as many as around twenty of these digital factories. Because of their size, they are increasingly relegated to soulless, prefabricated warehouses outside city limits. But that doesn't rule out efforts towards architectural integration, as Facebook has done with its elegant data centre in Prineville (Oregon), or its futuristic annexe built by CoreSite in Santa Clara (California).[5] There is even a beauty contest for the world's most beautiful data centre, recently won by MareNostrum in Barcelona—a 44.5 tonne beast encased in a glass box built in the nave of a deconsecrated chapel.[6]

Over ten or so years, the cloud has grown roots in all major communication hubs, from Washington, Hong Kong, Johannesburg, to Sao Paulo, and notably in the world's most prominent financial centres, including London, Frankfurt, New York, Paris, and Amsterdam. Consequently, there are nearly three million data centres with a minimum surface area of 500 square metres, 85,000 intermediate-sized data centres, and 10,000 or so data centres more or less the same size as Equinix AM4.[7] In the midst of this web of steel and concrete thrive over 500 'hyperscale' data centres with surface areas sometimes as big as a football pitch. (See appendix 4.) Paul Benoit describes this concentration of cables, security equipment, IT and electric facilities as 'ocean liners, the monsters of technology'.[8] It's an interesting paradox: the more we celebrate the shift of our economies towards the service sector, the more we talk about data 'farms', the 'factories' of the digital era, information 'hubs', 'routes', and 'highways'—remnants of agriculture and industry that the service sector was supposed to supplant ...

But why put so many cement mixers to work—at a considerable ecological cost, as we shall discover further on in the book—if it's only to accumulate impalpable cat videos, emails, and geopositioning data? Because humanity is already producing an absolute deluge of data: '[T]here was five exabytes of information created between the dawn of civilisation through 2003.'[9] That is enough data to burn onto ten million Blu-Ray disks, which, if stacked, would be four times the height of the Eiffel Tower. And with hundreds of billions of objects connected to 5G, soon to be rolled out worldwide, 'the quantity of data is exponential, and we cannot stop this trend', warns Fredrik Kallioniemi of Hydro66.[10] Meanwhile, the global market for this infrastructure, currently worth in the region of 124 billion euros, is growing at an annual rate of 7 per cent.

Let's try to visualise what this data tsunami looks like. The Web is often associated with liquid: we 'surf' the internet; we talk about data 'flows', and we 'stream' online videos. Take this metaphor at face value and go to a washbasin. Collect in a glass all the drops of water dripping from the tap. (I did this experiment, and have reproduced it in appendix 5.) If one drop is worth one byte—a unit for measuring digital information. One thousand drips (or one kilobyte, the equivalent of a quick email) later, you will have collected 100 millilitres of water, or half a glass. Repeat the operation a thousand times to get a megabyte, the equivalent of a one-minute MP3 audio file, and also 100 litres of water. A gigabyte (one thousand times more) is the equivalent of a two-hour film, which is as much as a rainwater tank. A terabyte can store almost half of the catalogue of the national library of France, but is also as much as twenty-seven Olympic-size swimming pools. It follows that the five exabytes of data produced globally every year is enough to fill Lake Geneva five times. We'll end our experiment with the forty-seven zettabytes of data produced every year, or the volume of the Mediterranean and the Black Sea combined. Humanity is quite literally drowning in a sea of data.

The fundamental question is *why* are we creating so much data? We are all more or less aware that our geopositioning information, internet search history, and interaction on social media generate data.[11] But how and in what quantity is our data being processed, and by whom? I spent many weeks trying to find the answer to this question. I turned my investigation to the incredible binge of data by a seemingly innocent everyday object: those shared electronic scooters parked on the pavements of major cities.

The little-known powers of e-scooter sharing

Since hitting the streets of Santa Monica, California, in 2017, free-floating e-scooters have become increasingly popular around the world. Cheap, practical, and fun, they help decongest cities saturated with traffic. Pioneering this growing trend are operators including Lime, Bird, Jump, and Lyft, with market capitalisation at record levels. Indeed, investors have hit the sweet spot: according to one consulting firm, 'A dozen e-scooter startups have already attracted more than $1.5 billion in funding, and we estimate that the global market will reach about $40 billion to $50 billion by 2025.'[12] But the e-scooters themselves are not all that sturdy, and last little more than a few months—hardly enough to make a dent into their production and maintenance cost. So renting out e-scooters today is not a profitable business; yet, despite this, the sharing service is the darling of investment funds.

Maybe it's because we can rely on the e-scooters of tomorrow to be more robust and therefore more profitable. Or maybe it's mostly because the companies renting them out 'are collecting huge quantities of data generated by users' mobility habits', explains

Mohammad Tasjar, an American civil liberties defender and staff attorney at the American Civil Liberties Union (ACLU).[13] When creating an account on a dedicated app, you enter your name, email address, postal address, telephone number, banking details, and payments history, among other information.[14] The operator can then collect information about your journeys from the sensors built into the e-scooters and from the data sent by your mobile phone.[15] Bird even takes the liberty of enhancing your profile by ingesting information gleaned from other companies that already have your data, and even queries your solvency with credit-check companies! That's a lot more than just taking a Sunday cruise ... Of course, all this intelligence can prove indispensable for satisfying the client, who is king: 'The data is used to refine the company's pricing policy, identify the most frequently used routes, and therefore optimise the placement of the e-scooters, all in the interest of better service quality', a professional from the mobility company Bolt tells me anonymously.

However, operators have a far greater horizon than the e-scooters themselves ... In collecting a maximum amount of information, they are taking a very keen interest in how we move around, especially since there are more and more ways of travelling in cities. Getting from A to B can involve a shared taxi, followed by an e-scooter, then a bus. The Holy Grail of operators has a name: 'Mobility as a Service', or a single gateway that aggregates all these modes of transport. 'Operators want to offer a multi-mode transport system, covering bicycles, cars, and e-scooters', confirms a member of La Quadrature du Net.[16] Renting out e-scooters is just one means of penetrating the gigantic mobility market, contingent on having the most extensive and precise information on traveller habits as possible. 'What will a company such as Bird do with all this accumulated data on our movements? Make loads of money!' says a geo-marketing specialist.[17] 'At least, that's what investors are betting on by putting the company's market value at $2 billion after just one year in operation.' This makes data a strategic asset—the black gold of mobility companies dedicated to finding us ways of getting around that are best adapted to our needs.

But there's a catch ...

When stepping on that e-scooter platform, you are also giving consent for the operator to share some of your data 'with third parties for research, business, or other purposes', says Lime, for example, but without elaborating.[18] Such provisions 'are written using unclear and vague terms, because they are intended to be unintelligible', says the ACLU attorney Mohammad Tasjar.[19] In fact, you are agreeing to the operator using a tracker—a piece of software that collects additional information about you, often unrelated to your use of an e-scooter. It's not about keeping the information, but sharing it with other companies as part of their own commercial activities. Generally speaking, 'Facebook and Google's trackers are the most prevalent in apps', a 'hacktivist' from Exodus Privacy, a non-profit that lists trackers, tells me.[20] When connecting to BabyPlus, for example, a 'prenatal education system', and despite using a telephone that has never connected to Facebook, the hacktivist 'discovered that the information on the child's name, sex, and nursing routine went to Facebook all the same'.[21] The child already existed for the social network, because a tracker had apparently made sure of it.

Back to e-scooters: the tracker AppsFlyer (Bolt, Bird) looks into your search history on the web or on other applications installed on your smartphone, while Tune (Bold) collects some of your geopositioning data. The tracker Adjust (Bird, Dott, Hive), remembers every one of your purchases. Branch (Lime) collects your digital fingerprints. Such trackers make it possible to then deploy targeted marketing strategies, such as tailored advertising.[22] They can also facilitate geofencing (a special offer on a jacket that pops up walking past a clothing shop) or segmentation (a precise message sent to a population group).

No one knows if e-scooter operators have already shared or sold the information collected in this way. A geomarketing specialist even believes that that immediate challenge for service providers 'is not to leverage their data, but first acquire a critical mass. They can't do anything with their data so long as they haven't won the loyalty of hundreds of millions of users.'[23] But we have reason to be circumspect, as 'our mobility data says far more about our lives than any other data', explains Mohammad Tasjar. 'It's among the most sensitive data there is.'[24] An analysis of our raw data can easily produce our home address (where we leave from every morning at the same time), our faith (the church we go to every Sunday at 11.00 am), or political views (a protest we attended), and why not our ailments while we're at it (an appointment made at a specialist clinic).

The end of anonymity

In 2014, the Australian researcher Anthony Tockar, using freely available data, tracked the comings and goings of New York taxis in front of a strip club, and identified with uncanny accuracy the home address of regular clients.[25] Around the same time, a Belgian researcher confirmed, with evidence, that 'four spatio-temporal points [were] enough to uniquely characterise 95 per cent of the traces amongst 1.5 M users'.[26] One might argue that the data is anonymised, whereas the path to uncovering an identity is very short. In fact, concludes the Californian engineer and subject-matter expert Liam Newcombe, 'It is virtually impossible to anonymise the data, and essentially the best way not to misuse it would be not to collect it in the first place.'[27] German academic Thorsten Strufe flatly states that 'anonymous data is one big hoax'.[28]

The data accumulated by e-scooters could then aggregate with information that other companies already have about you. Enter data brokers: discreet individuals or companies that buy information and complete profiles, and sell them to the highest bidder. A consumer's profile can encompass 1,500 parameters sold piecemeal (around 30 euro cents for a name and surname), or wholesale (600 euros on average). The global market represents around 300 billion euros. By agreeing to the service, you are giving away control over your own data. Parts of your identity could be spread across an incalculable number of data centres around the world, without you having the faintest idea of what it is used for. You are putting a finger into a vast machine with no understanding of its parts, let alone its purpose.

In 2018, the mighty American Civil Liberties Union (ACLU) warned against the true intentions of e-scooter rental companies: 'When you scan a QR code, you are unwittingly hopping onto a two-wheeled data-hoarding device that is collecting far more of your personal information than the product really needs.'[29] The issue is so serious, in fact, that non-profits have recently worried that all sorts of positioning data could be used by governments for surveillance purposes.

Didn't the Trump administration use this kind of data from the phones of illegal immigrants and activists for the purposes of prosecuting them?[30] Companies such as Lime and Bird admitted that they send user information to governments if they feel they are obliged to do so.[31] This is an assault on a freedom as fundamental as our privacy. 'China's social-credit system is just a slightly more obvious transcription of what we are already seeing in countries in the West', observes Liam Newcombe. 'We are going to have contend with particularly dangerous challenges in the future, and I don't think people are really aware of this.'[32] A year after ACLU, the Hamburg (Germany) commissioner for data protection and freedom of information also warned its citizens, 'A centre [sic] component of privacy is being able to move around in public space without being tracked. However, anyone who makes use of the new offers of e-scooters loses this protection.' In conclusion, 'users must consider whether paying with this much data is worth the service they receive' from the operator.[33] Translation: think twice before trading something that has a price for something else that doesn't ...

Responding to these warnings, a number of e-scooter rental companies stated that 'protecting the data of [their] users is an absolute priority'.[34] Do they mean it? It's hard to say. What is certain is that by installing a tracker in their app, operators have legally given themselves the freedom so that, one day or another, a company you've never even heard of can learn everything about you. Yet we can refuse, thanks to the General Data Protection Regulation (GDPR) voted in by the European Parliament in 2016, to share our data by practising digital hygiene at all times.[35] 'I'm no longer on Facebook nor Instagram, I've installed ad blockers,

I've stopped working on Windows, I don't use GPS, and use Tor as my search engine to keep my IP address anonymous', says the academic Thorsten Strufe.[36] But how many of us are prepared to make the same effort?

The harm is imperceptible when compared to the instant benefits ... If you had to pay the real price for your trip on an e-scooter, it would cost much more. Would you still be willing to pay for the service? The operator knows that the digital industry no longer thrives from selling computers or software, but from commercialising information.[37] The more a company is embedded in the cloud, the greater its potential to become rich and powerful. And so consumers are drawn in with supposedly 'free' services in order to keep siphoning more and more of their data.[38] Facebook, the true champion of this economic model, 'has become the most effective advertising authority in the world', and sells a lot of intelligence on who you are, explains a specialised journalist in his book on the social network's founder, Mark Zuckerberg.[39] It is so successful that in the US more than half of the $240 billion of its annual advertising revenue is generated online. Why not apply this logic to selling vegetables, cinema tickets, and when billing medical procedures? After all, says Dutch privacy activist Douwe Schmidt, 'everything can be free as long as we are willing to give our data away'.[40] Do we really want every aspect of our behaviour to be entirely transformed into data by these platforms?

Extending the reach of data

Since data became the new philosophers' stone that can transform a loss-making business into a money-making machine, companies have been storing anything and everything. Data that is not useful right away might be crucial tomorrow for a goal yet to be determined. Or, if a company already knows how the data can be used, but doesn't yet have the technical means (such as algorithms or supercomputers) to turn it into bank notes, it's still worth storing. This makes the 'tech world' buzz with wildly exciting expressions such as 'machine learning', 'quantum computing', 'deductive reasoning', and, of course, 'big data'—gigantic volumes of data that, once analysed, can be used to identify complex systems, recommend targeted content that is increasingly adapted to consumers' taste, and, while we're at it, predict their behaviours, thereby making even more profit.[41]

Let's be objective: whether produced by individuals, machines, or organisations, data has the potential to make the world infinitely better. Using data, we can better diagnose cancers, model with greater granularity the evolution of epidemics, and develop predictive medicine more quickly and more cheaply, therefore making it more accessible for more people. Big data will also make governments more efficient, enable non-profits to better provide for the neediest, accelerate the reconstruction of cities affected by earthquakes, and better shape school curricula to the needs of pupils. Given the mass of data that is currently being compiled on the universe, it is even possible, says Swedish academic Karl Andersson, that we already have, tucked away on a server, proof of life on other planets, but which, at this stage, we lack tools that are powerful enough to translate into understanding. 'Maybe we don't know what we do know', he adds.[42]

The corollary of free, resulting from the generation of data, is more consumption of the internet. 'As soon as it's "open bar", I won't stop at the tenth cat video; I'll watch the eleventh video!', says Hugues Ferreboeuf of The Shift Project ideas laboratory.[43] With 'free' comes 'data inflation', which helps to explain why, unbeknownst to us, each of us generate nearly 150 gigabytes of data per day—enough to fill the memory of nine iPhones with sixteen gigabytes every twenty-four hours.[44] And after twelve zettabytes of data stored in 2015, humanity will generate 2,142 more in 2035—that is, almost 180 times more. (See appendix 6.)[45] 'The numbers are insane', exclaims Fredrik Kallioniemi. 'If we converted into paper the rate at which the production of data is increasing, you'd have a pile shooting up in the sky faster than a rocket at take-off!'[46]

The data gleaned by e-scooter operators is just a tiny drop in what is a sea of data, yet enough to saturate a few hundred servers at the most.[47] This needs to be put in its context: the systematic collection worldwide of all sorts of data that is 'multiplying the need for data centres', says a specialist at Bolt. The result is a proliferation of business parks across all five continents so that users can store the world's memory on the cloud. In the north of Paris, the Plaine Commune Conurbation Community, which already has forty-seven data centres, is preparing to host a digital factory of 40,000 square metres—five times the size of the Stade de France pitch.[48] In China, 'cloud cities' for data storage are springing up across the country. In fact, the biggest data centre on the planet is a one-hour car ride south of Beijing in the city of Langfang, and has a surface area of 600,000 square metres, the equivalent of 110 football pitches.[49] To support this spectacular growth, the industry has turned to real estate agents, or 'site selectors', who scour the globe for the most appropriate location for stowing the next fragment of the cloud: preferably as far as possible from any flood, farming, or residential areas, air routes, and railway lines in order to limit the risk of accidents, but less than an hour's drive from an international airport so as to attract top talent. That's not all: electricity transmission grids must be robust, the tax environment favourable, the cost of land attractive, and the construction workers competent so that the future data centre can be up and running in less than eighteen months.

When the 'East Coast Silicon Valley' wants to protect its forests

It's a tall order! And it is not uncommon to find data-centre hubs encroaching on densely populated urban areas. Nowhere else in the world does the growth of data exert more pressure on land than in Ashburn, which I visited in spring 2021. Located some fifty kilometres north-west of Washington in the state of Virginia, Ashburn is more than just a small, quiet town whose 50,000 inhabitants brighten up its dull business district and clutch of shopping malls; it is the 'East Coast Silicon Valley', and handles no less than 70 per cent of the world's internet traffic. The creation of one of the first internet exchange points in the world in 1992 triggered an influx of the big players of the digital economy, such as the US firms America Online, Verizon, and Telos.[50] In their wake, fifty-seven data centres have converged on Ashburn, which was soon dubbed by the trade press as the 'data centre capital of the world'.[51]

The economic effects are obvious: Loudoun County, which includes Ashburn, has the highest median household income in the United States.[52] And the hub is growing. Gentrified, yet surrounded by massive buildings, Ashburn's residents are having to contend with this urban manifestation of the immaterial. The infrastructures are noisy and ugly. 'You know the number-one complaint I've got in the last four months?' one county supervisor is quoted as asking. 'It wasn't traffic. It wasn't tolls. It was data centre design.'[53] Ecological concerns have also emerged: 'There are so few green areas around here', laments Brian Carr, a resident. 'You reach a point where enough is enough! We don't need to destroy the nature we have left.'[54] As recently as 2018, Loudoun County authorised the company Compass to build its True North data centre at the expense of forty-three hectares of wooded areas.[55]

In 2019, another plan to extend buildable areas in Loudoun County revived tensions with the local population, fearing that farmland would be next to be sacrificed on the altar of data.[56] But how could the local representatives 'focus on the ecological impacts [of data centres] when they've got $22 million in tax benefits being waved under their noses?' stated one observer.[57] And indeed, Loudoun County planned to approve the new land development plan post-haste ... 'We have seen massive reductions in open and green spaces in just seven years', continues Carr. 'At this rate, Loudoun is going to become a county of data centres.'[58] Ashburn is the site of one of a growing number of disputes that are emerging as the cloud grows. In the US alone, there are reports of tensions in the metropolitan areas of New York, Newark (New Jersey), Haymarket (Virginia), Chandler (Arizona), and Quincy (Washington).[59] But one Homeric battle surpasses all others: that between activities and a politician in Utah over the biggest data centre that belongs to the National Security Agency.

The man who tried to dry up the National Security Agency

In addition to collecting our data for commercial purposes, Google hands over our search history to the NSA. The American intelligence agency also collects the content of our emails, phone calls, parking tickets, travel itineraries, book purchases, etc.[60] How much of the world's electronic memory is targeted by this surveillance? No one knows, but here's a clue: in 2013, when the NSA commissioned its flagship data centre on a training site of the National Guard on the outskirts of the city of Bluffdale, northern Utah, it was then the third-biggest data warehouse in the world. A machine known for storing, every minute, as much information as that held in the US National Library of Congress.

Why Bluffdale? For its qualified and patriotic workforce (therefore less inclined to contest the agency's activities), but also for its incredibly low cost of water, which is indispensable for cooling data centres.[61] Cooling an average-sized data centre can take as much as 60,000 cubic metres of water per year — enough to fill 160 Olympic-size swimming pools, or meet the needs of three hospitals.[62] But Utah is the second-most arid state in the US. Nate Carlisle, a journalist at the local daily paper *The Salt Lake Tribune*, takes a dim view of this anomaly. From where is the water sourced? Would there be enough? Could it lead to conflict over its use? Carlisle filed a public records request for information on the NSA's use of water in Bluffdale. At first, it was rejected by the agency, who responded: 'Armed with this information, one could then deduce how much intelligence NSA is collecting and maintaining.'[63] Pressured into transparency, the agency caved in two months later, and it was revealed that its facility was consuming between 100,000 and 200,000 cubic metres of water every month.[64] This was not enough to dry up Utah's Jordan River, which the municipality uses to meet its own needs, but let it be said: there can be no generalised surveillance without water. Yet the public disclosure of this information sparked an unexpected battle ...

Alerted to the matter, the Tenth Amendment Center (TAC)—a non-profit dedicated to the protection of the American Constitution—took up the case. The recent revelations of the whistleblower Edward Snowden had shaken the defenders of civil liberties. They wanted to thwart the activities of the NSA. TAC's executive director, Michael Boldin, discovered through his investigations that a few years prior, another one of the agency's data centres, operating in the city of Baltimore, had 'maxed out' the local power grid.[65] 'We understood that the NSA needed natural resources, so we thought "Why not cut off supply?"' recalls Michael Maharrey, who campaigned alongside Boldin.[66] As demiurgic as it is, the architecture of global surveillance is always governed and constrained by a physical underpinning. Like electricity in Baltimore, water is the crucial element of the Bluffdale data centre. Without blue gold, 'the NSA can't operate its infrastructure', says Maharrey, concluding that '[w]ater is clearly the Achilles heel of the NSA'.

Michael Boldin wanted to challenge the NSA on legal grounds. To do so, he drew on the tenth amendment of the American Constitution, in virtue of which a state is not required to provide material assistance to the federal state. He also invoked a precedent that took place in Nevada in 2007, when the state opposed the opening of a nuclear-waste storage site under Yucca Mountain by denying the federal authorities access to its water resources, indispensable to the site's construction, thus forcing the Obama administration to back down.[67] Boldin also had the support of a large citizen movement across the US. 'A lot of people were shocked by the degree of surveillance. The public were happy that activists were tackling the issue', recalls Maharrey.[68] Boldin drew up a draft registration, from which sixteen states would subsequently take their cue. They saw fit to deny all assistance to Washington in order to discourage the NSA—with its facilities already multiplying in Georgia, Texas, and Colorado—from spreading out even further. California and Michigan voted in favour of the bill. Could Utah literally turn off the taps on the NSA?

This is where a surprising politician entered the scene. Marc Roberts, a member of the Republican Party and the Utah House of Representatives, and a defender of the tenth amendment, was protective of the prerogatives of his circumscription against Washington.[69] He didn't pull his punches: 'When the federal government gets too big and gets out of control, the states have to step up', he argued.[70] The Buffdale case was his opportunity to put his opinions into practice, and in 2014 he put forward a bill authorising Utah 'to refuse material support or assistance to any federal data collection and surveillance agency'.[71] In short, 'If you want to spy on the whole world and American citizens, great, but we're not going to help you', Roberts told the press.[72] Marc Roberts had in mind a disarmingly simple equation: no water equalled no NSA.

Roberts failed to get his bill passed, but reoffended the following year with a new bill.[73] His extraordinary crusade garnered a groundswell of support. 'If they didn't think I was crazy before, they think I'm crazy now!' Roberts said on a local radio station.[74] The NSA kept a low profile while Roberts endured another disappointment. Gradually, the opposition to his voluntarism grew. Seeing that the momentum, including on his side, was waning, he threw in the towel. 'Party leadership has a lot of influence; if you don't agree with them, they can make your life miserable', admits Maharrey, who was in touch with Roberts at the time. 'Marc felt that it would be politically detrimental for him to push further. For him to be willing to take that step, it took a lot of guts to do it.'[75] The citizen movement eventually petered out and disappeared. Resigned, Maharrey explains: 'I think people accepted that the NSA was doing what it had to do.'[76] And all the while, Bluffdale continues to assert itself as a hub for data collection. As recently as 2021, Facebook built an immense data centre in Eagle Mountain, some twenty kilometres away from the NSA data centre.[77]

Dirty surveillance

But all is not lost! Scrutinising the NSA's water consumption means exposing its environmental impact. The Bluffdale data centre affair created a surprising—and quite brilliant—correlation between mass surveillance and ecology.[78] If this reasoning wins over citizens, a powerful opposition to state surveillance could emerge, not only in the interest of civil liberties, but for the preservation of the planet. Defenders of individual liberties could declare themselves as *de facto* environmental activists. Slogans such as 'End mass surveillance, save 2°C', or 'Surveillance is pollution' might be brandished at processions and on walls.[79] Scholars might profess that Article 12 of the Universal Declarations of Human Rights, the fourth amendment of the United States Constitution, and article 8 of the European Convention on Human Rights, which decree the protection of privacy, are intrinsically environmental texts, and that our governments must draw on these sources to lay the foundations of a new social contract.[80]

Such a phenomenon would never come to be, however, as democracies and dictatorships alike would oppose it with the search for the same ideal, but using completely the opposite means. This is the concept of 'surveillance for green'—monitoring our polluting actions in order to save the climate. To protect nature, humans in nature must be managed ... In the shorter term, another concept, this time called 'green surveillance', has already taken shape—a space that the biggest intelligence agencies in the world have been occupying for the last twenty-five years.[81] These agencies include the NSA—a master at glorifying its low-carbon solar panel installations, its green roofs, its fleet of electric vehicles, and even its dry toilets, which save nearly 200,000 litres of water a year.[82] For their part, the British secret service, the famous MI6, patted itself on the back in 2014 for reducing the carbon emissions of its offices.[83]

We see here the potential danger of these justifications for storing more data—unless the growth of the digital industry is held back, as we shall discover, by its colossal needs for an indispensable fluid to our connected lives: electricity.

CHAPTER FIVE

An appalling waste of electricity

EVERYTHING IS GETTING FASTER. EVERY MINUTE, 1.3 MILLION people connect to Facebook, 4.1 million internet searches are made on Google, 4.7 million videos are viewed on YouTube, and $1.1 million are spent on e-commerce websites. (See appendix 7.)[1] But every now and then, these flows grind to a halt when 'blackouts' occur—a data centre shutting down due to a power outage, a leak in the cooling system, or an IT bug. At the mere mention of such an occurrence, users' blood runs cold; words like 'disaster', 'hell', and 'catastrophe' come thick and fast. And for good reason, for such events can have huge consequences. In 2012, Amazon Web Services' data centre was hit by extreme weather, which severed access to Instagram and Pinterest for six hours.[2] In 2016, the world's internet traffic fell by 40 per cent for two minutes after Google went offline.[3] And in 2019, Gmail went down for half a day.[4] According to a survey, one-third of companies admitted to having suffered an outage over the previous year.[5]

Such an event can turn into a nightmare: in 2017, British Airways'
data centre crashed, resulting in 400 flights being cancelled and
75,000 passengers left stranded at London's Heathrow Airport.
'It took two days to fix the problem. Planes were grounded on
the wrong side of the planet. It cost the company hundreds of
millions of dollars ... The fallout was huge,' recalls data-centre
specialist Mark Acton.[6]

Storm in the cloud

If there's one data-centre failure that companies won't forget
it's the one that happened in 2017 at OVH—one of the biggest
cloud-computing companies in the world.[7] The episode was so
severe that it is believed to haunt the company's directors to this
day. A former OVH engineer who was on the bridge the day of
the storm told me more, in confidence. 'I had been at OVH for
two months when it happened. Talk about a baptism of fire!'
he recalls. On the morning of 9 November 2017, the engineer,
responsible for improving the company's industrial processes and
performing maintenance operations, was in Roubaix in the north
of France when two data centres at OVH's Strasbourg site, east
of France, lost power. The cause: 'a piece of worksite equipment
hit the powerline'. The incident could have ended there, thanks
to the centres' two back-up generators. But, for reasons then
unknown, they did not start up. With the servers left without a
single power source, the dreaded words began to ripple over the
phonelines: 'Warning! Strasbourg is down!'

'When you hear that', says the engineer, 'you know it's bad.'

It was battle stations at head office, where the company opted for transparency: 'The set of 4 elec arrivals no longer feed the routing room. We are all on the problem,' tweeted CEO Octave Klaba. A crisis team was quickly mobilised: 'We analysed the problem, the condition of the equipment around the world, and when maintenance last took place,' the engineer told me.

Then the unthinkable happened: another data centre, this time at OVH's Roubaix site, stopped responding. 'The origin of the problem is a software bug on the optical equipment,' the company stated, adding that these were 'two separate incidents that have nothing to do with each other'. The probability of one data centre failing is very low; two failures, occurring almost simultaneously, is exceptionally rare. My source and his colleagues were dumbfounded: 'Two successive outages, two hours apart, and on two critical systems ... We should play the lottery tonight ...' The situation was all the more serious, given that OVH had twenty-seven more data centres in nineteen countries, making it Europe's most important cloud company, with 1.3 million clients, including fourteen of France's biggest companies, and twenty of the world's 500 largest companies, their websites all hosted by OVH.[8] The colossal failure affected tens of thousands of websites. 'A lot of companies were cut off from email servers and websites. You couldn't book train tickets on the French national railway company website, the homepages of numerous French news channels stopped responding, as was the case of several municipalities' websites,' my source explained. How would the cloud provider survive a crisis of this magnitude?

Before going any further, we need to understand that the internet thrives thanks to the intangible and holy commandment of 'service continuity'. The web must work without interruption;

it must be 'hyper-available'.[9] When human lives and state security are at stake, continuous access to medical or military data is a foregone conclusion. But the stakes are no less critical when you need to satisfy billions of users surfing the web non-stop. Not only does the sun never set on the internet, but we can no longer stand having to wait to use it. 'At the end of the 1990s, the home page of a website had to load in less than eight seconds', relates Philippe Luce, director of Institut Datacenter. 'Today, if the homepage hasn't finished loading in less than an eighth of a second, people move on to their third screen'.[10] We have essentially moved from a 'now' to a 'right now' mentality.[11] It is a tyranny that is only growing as the world is increasingly invaded by connected vehicles that analyse obstacles in real time, automatic trading systems that buy and sell in mere microseconds, and e-commerce websites that generate millions of dollars and pounds in revenue every minute.

That's why it is quite simply impossible to stop a data centre. 'Basically, a data centre promises to be online, all the time', says Philippe Luce. 'It doesn't have a "do not disturb" mode!'[12] With more and more competition, many cloud companies promise that their infrastructure will run 99.995 per cent of the time, with no more than twenty-four minutes of unavailability per year. Luce is trenchant: 'Those who experience blackouts on a regular basis have to quit the business.'[13] This puts tremendous pressure on engineers; in the UK, the joke goes that 'CIO' doesn't stand for 'chief information officer' but 'career is over'.

We can also question the resilience of a system in which companies that are prepared to dismiss hundreds, even thousands, of people over a few lost seconds prosper ... Back to OVH: on the day of 9 November 2017, this is what the engineers working themselves into the ground to fix the twin outages had on their minds. They knew that this series of interruptions could ruin the company's reputation and cause it to be downgraded, or even go bankrupt. The more time passed, the unhappier clients became. Power from the grid had to be restored as fast as possible. All the technicians were called in, and those not on duty were hauled from their beds. The grid was restored after a few hours, but there were still significant power cuts. Over several days, 'Dozens of us were working twelve-hour shifts around the clock to the point of exhaustion', said my source. 'It was a combination of panic and adrenaline. There was brainstorming going on in every corner, with the reality changing from one day to the next.' Material support followed: a truck carrying spare parts was rushed in, while two private jets were chartered to transport the teams between Strasbourg and Roubaix. On the morning of 13 November, after a final night of repairs, OVH's CEO could at last declare victory: 'All servers are UP.' The episode lasted for four days.

For the group, it was a seismic event. For many clients, the damage was great; data had more than likely been lost. The company nevertheless demonstrated its responsiveness, and promised to learn every lesson from the crisis. More importantly, its boss, Octave Klaba, responded by communicating.[14] 'This showed the public that the internet is more than just a webpage—there are big players, people, and work as well ... Klaba managed to give a human face to something that was virtual,' said my source. The company recovered well in the end. The client breach was patched up; its status as a world-class cloud service-provider was left intact.

Yet, despite the endless tweets, the company's leadership did not actually reveal the root causes of the double outage: under pressure to increase profits, management apparently put the satisfaction of a clientele demanding more and more 'service continuity' before the safety of its infrastructure. 'The first time I stood in front of OVH's servers [two months before the double outage], I thought: *Wow, they're really behind!* recalls the former engineer. 'The tools were clearly in need of maintenance, and a number of important tasks had been neglected ... Imagine a hotel that goes from zero to 200 rooms in a few years, all in the joyful atmosphere of a start-up. We all knew we were flirting with disaster.'

In OVH's defence, we, the users, are all responsible for putting the internet's architecture under constant pressure. This is something the former engineer can speak to: 'Users don't care how the web works. They're spoiled little brats who expect the internet to work faster and faster. At the end of the day, we are all prisoners of this mentality.'[15]

Digital continuity at all costs

In their quest for absolute availability, cloud companies are taking more precautions:

- First, they use 'redundant' power systems. 'You have two electrical supplies, two generators, and rooms the size of public libraries filled with lead-acid batteries to ensure continuity between the time the outage occurs and the generators take over', explains Paul Benoit of Qarnot Computing.[16] This configuration implies a huge amount of logistics. As an example, the roofs of many of the data centres in the middle of New York 'are dizzying outgrowths' that comprise 'water cooling towers for air-conditioning [...] water tanks in the event of a cut-off, cranes to mount the diesel generators from the street ... Their basements are loaded with cables, equipped with fuel oil tanks that hold several hundred thousand litres to supply the generators', write two researchers who wrote a global report on data centres.[17] Quite simply, Philippe Luce concludes, 'no other building costs as much per square metre as a high-level data centre'.[18]

- And as if that wasn't enough, cloud companies are also duplicating the data centres themselves, and not without making sure that the mirror site is built on a different tectonic plate! The last thing we want is an earthquake to prevent us from posting the contents of our dinner plate on Instagram, or delay a Tinder date ... Apparently, at a conference around 2010, engineers at Google explained that the Gmail email service was replicated six times, while as a rule a cat video was stored in at least seven data centres around the world.[19] An unverified rumour has it that a major financial institution replicated a data centre fifteen times! As a result, the industry is haunted by 'zombie servers' ... Some go as far as speaking about 30 per cent of company material that 'sits around, not doing anything, but is switched on', Mark Acton tells me.[20]

- Lastly, cloud companies 'oversize' their infrastructure in order to anticipate peaks in internet traffic. Consequently, 'when a router is running at 60 per cent, it's actually running at maximum capacity,' says IT researcher Anne-Cécile Orgerie.[21] The corollary to this intemperance is a staggering waste of electricity. An investigation by the *New York Times* revealed that certain underused data centres can waste as much as 90 per cent of the electricity they consume.[22] And, of course, nothing will change so long as technicians' bonuses remain indexed on the hyper-availability of the machines rather than on the reduction of their employer's energy expenditure. 'We can reverse this phenomenon if you and I decide to start communicating using smoke signals. But the reality is that my daughter can't stop posting nonsense on TikTok', complains Philippe Luce.[23] In any case, says engineer Paul Benoit, 'the cost for the environment is having instant access to everything, all the time'.[24]

Obviously, 'we can't even imagine the number of gigawatts it takes to operate this lunacy,' says researcher Thomas Ernst.[25] In fact, we now know very well that data centres are among the biggest consumers of electricity in a metropolitan area. At a conference at Data Centre World's trade show—one of the biggest gatherings of cloud computing professionals—in Paris at the end of 2019, an executive made this stunning statement: '[We] realised that data centres were going to capture a third of electricity of the greater Paris area.'[26] Amazon Web Services, which has been expanding in the Paris region since 2017, 'is believed to have signed, in France, a contract to supply 155 megawatts of electricity, which is enough for the electricity needs of a city of 100,000 inhabitants,' a specialist told me anonymously. Today, the sector would represent 2 per

cent of global electricity consumption, which, given the rate
at which cloud services are growing, could increase fourfold or
fivefold by 2030.[27] In other words, conclude Cécile Diguet and
Fanny Lopez, 'Data centres will be among the most important
electricity consumption elements of the 21st century.'[28] It should
come as no surprise, therefore, that data storage is becoming a
formidable energy challenge for the cities that have made the
cloud the cornerstone of their economic development.

Sparks fly in Amsterdam

Ensconced in a banquette at the Grand Café-Restaurant in
Amsterdam Central Station, interrupted only by the chatter
of a parrot perched above the bar, Mariëtte Sedee is not just in
charge of space development at the Haarlemmermeer council, a
municipality of 150,000 inhabitants adjoining the Dutch capital;
she is also one of the first councillors in the world to wage war on
data centres. As she explained, 'Ten per cent of Amsterdam and
Haarlemmermeer's electricity is siphoned by data centres. That's
a very high number. Where do we want to live? How do we take
back control of this trend?' Indeed, together with Dublin, London,
and Frankfurt, Amsterdam and her region make up one of the
biggest data hubs in Europe.[29] The metropole is perfectly located
on the fibre-optic cable route connecting the United States and
continental Europe: water, essential for cooling the systems, is
everywhere; electricity has always been abundant; connectivity is
excellent; and the municipality is welcoming. Haarlemmermeer
is a cloud paradise, and for thirty years, industry players have
been converging on this Venice of the North to consistently

request more and more connections.

But from 2015, concerns were raised over the capacity of electricity providers to support the phenomenal growth of these data farms. 'At the time, a 60-megawatt data centre was meant to be built in Haarlemmermeer, which was the equivalent of the energy needs of a city of 120,000 inhabitants,' Paul van Engelen, an engineer at Alliander, told me.[30] There was no shortage of electricity, but technicians lacked both the human and technical means to install a transformer in one year, which is what the cloud company demanded. So they put a stop to the project: 'For the first time, we were seeing the limits of the system, and asked the client to wait a few years before connection.'[31] In the months and years that followed, Alliander's engineers realised that the shortfalls in material and human resources were multiplying. The electricity-distribution systems of the Amsterdam region were destabilised. In the press, data-centre specialists sounded the alarm, and in meeting rooms, technicians such as Marco Hogewoning, who works at Europe's internet registry, could now be heard saying, 'I can't extend my data centre because the municipality can't provide me any more electricity.'[32]

In 2019, the situation began to ring alarm bells with Haarlemmermeer authorities. The municipality was already hosting some twenty data centres, with another half dozen lined up. At the same time, the urban landscape was being transformed, and local residents began to complain about the disfiguration of their city. Recently elected, Mariëtte Sedee took on the case, not wanting Haarlemmermeer's citizens to find themselves surrounded by soulless warehouses. She also worried that the increased electricity needs would conflict with those of surrounding greenhouses for flowers, hospitals, and fire stations.

She also questioned just where the 1,000 hectares of solar farms accompanying this digital spread would go: 'That's 2,000 football pitches! It's huge! And right in the middle of my municipality?'

What do data centres mean for spatial development? What will be their future electricity requirements? How will the grid be adapted accordingly? These are unanswered questions. Sedee saw how the political leadership was increasingly overwhelmed by the double-digit growth of the sector; there was a real risk of power outages increasing. It wasn't long before others outside the municipality began to share her view. In June, she was discreetly contacted by the city of Amsterdam. They met and decided to join forces, drawing up a joint statement that, on 12 July 2019, resounded in the data-centre industry like a thunderclap. Realising that 'we want to be online all day on our phones and PCs', but that space in Amsterdam and Haarlemmermeer 'is scarce', the two municipalities fiercely decreed the world's first moratorium on data-centre construction.[33]

This sudden halt created a shockwave; no one saw it coming. The moratorium lasted until June 2020—the time it took the authorities to ready a strategy for controlled urban development. In Haarlemmermeer, the construction of data centres can resume until 2030, 'after which 'there will no longer be space available [...] for [them]', warns the municipality.[34] But challenges remain. 'We are by no means an isolated case. Frankfurt, the Danish peninsula of Jutland, London, Paris, and Dublin all face the same problems,' admits Dutch lobbyist Stijn Grove.[35] The industry is, in fact, experiencing what is called the 'Amsterdam effect', and other municipalities may make similar decisions to avoid overload.[36]

Could Dublin, where data centres, enticed by an attractive tax regime, thrive, be the next city to overheat? In 2020, the Chinese company ByteDance—the parent company of TikTok—announced its intention to build a data centre in the Irish capital to store its videos of teenagers prancing around to music.[37] Only, the announcement came after internet giants Google, Apple, Microsoft, and Facebook set up operations in Dublin, with the result that 'data centres now consume more energy than the city's population!' said Olivier Labbé, managing director of a data-centre engineering firm.[38] According to research by EirGrid Group, Ireland's electric-power transmission operator, data centres could consume up to 29 per cent of the country's electricity by 2028![39] To accommodate such growth, Irish authorities have announced the roll-out of an ambitious green energy-generation program: by 2030, renewable energies should make up 70 per cent of the national energy mix. But for now, 58 per cent of the country's electricity is generated from fossil fuels, compelling academics Patrick Bresnihan and Patrick Brodie to warn in an op-ed that 'the data centre gamble is far from sustainable'.[40]

We are touching on a sensitive topic: the origin of the electricity that keeps the internet running relentlessly is none other than coal. I would learn more about this dependence in one of the wildest regions of the United States.

No selfies without coal

It's a hot day in May 2021. Driving along the Interstate 70 that runs westward from Baltimore across the US, I could not have imagined that I was about to enter such an inhospitable yet lush mountainous kingdom. Spanning 2,000 kilometres from Newfoundland (Canada) to Alabama, the Appalachian Mountains are interspersed by languid plains and sunken valleys, stippled with red oaks and acacias, magnolias and poplars, pine and beech trees. The compact forest locked the roadway in its embrace, and was at times so oppressive that I found myself looking in the rear-view mirror of my Jeep to check that the vegetation wasn't closing up behind me. Here, every kilometre feels like a temporary permit, a fleeting favour from sovereign nature to humankind.

After 700 kilometres of driving, I arrive in the small town of Hurley at the extreme west of the state of Virginia. Since the second half of the nineteenth century, the mining industry has been extracting from the folds of the surrounding mountains coal that is indispensable to the country's steel production and some of its electricity.[41] For a long time, what people here call the 'black diamond' gives the southern Appalachians its wealth and creates jobs, along with pits, mine dumps, and mining villages. In the mid-twentieth century, there were 700,000 people working in the region's 12,000 mines. Mechanisation and the diversification of energy sources then spelled the decline of the American coal industry, which now only employs 52,000 miners.[42] Many of them have left the once-welcoming region. Those not working are retired, or live, so I'm told, off food stamps and drug-dealing. Opioid abuse is rampant. Even the mobile phone network doesn't work here. By all accounts, the American dream has abandoned the river-carved Appalachians.

Yet the moribund American coal industry has not had its final say. The Appalachian region still accounts for a large portion of the 640 tonnes of coal produced every year in the US, 78 per cent of which is mined underground.[43] The rest comes from open-pit mines, like the No. 2 Surface Mine in Hurley. I charge my way up to the gigantic hole on the crest of a mountain in the front seat of a young mechanic Steve Hunt's truck. 'Coal is the only thing this place has going for it', says Steve, whose house is nestled below the mine, and insists on showing me around. 'What else would we do without this resource?' he continues. Entry is forbidden, but my driver doesn't seem terribly concerned. At the end of a rocky road, we hike across the perilous landscape of a massif as vast as several dozen football pitches. Criss-crossed by the heavy machinery of Wellmore Coal Corporation, the mine's northern slope is still active.

My coming here is no coincidence: up until 2008, Ashburn's county—one of the biggest concentrations of data centres on the planet—in all likelihood used electricity that was sourced from numerous Appalachian coal mines, and in particular No. 2 Surface. For its power needs, the state of Virginia relies on Dominion Energy, among others. The US company is even reputed to be a key supplier of the cloud companies concentrated in Ashburn. However, Dominion also used to obtain coal from the same mine for its electricity plant, Altavista Power Station. Located around 300 kilometres east of Hurley, it redistributes its output to the east coast of the US.[44]

An important point here is that the coal from No. 2 Surface mine was extracted using a method called 'mountaintop removal', as was confirmed to me by Erin Savage, an activist with the non-profit Appalachian Voices, by analysing satellite images of the mine on Google Maps.[45] Essentially, Twin Star Mining (which operated the mine at the time) used explosives to flatten the mountain so that it could extract coal, lowering No. 2 Surface mine 'by 30 metres', reckons Steve Hunt, examining the uneven landscape.[46] The effects of mountaintop removal are not limited to the Hurley region. 'I can assure you that a big part of the coal bought and burned by Dominion between 2008 and 2014 in the state of Virginia was mined this way,' says Savage.

That is because this method turns out to be cheaper than digging pits, and became increasingly popular with mining companies from the 1970s. Junior Walk, an activist with Coal River Mountain Watch, who I met the day before in neighbouring Raleigh county, did the maths: by his account, the cumulative power of the explosives used in West Virginia alone is the equivalent of the thirteen 'Little Boy' atomic bombs dropped on Hiroshima.[47] The practice of moving mountain tops apparently accounts for 3 per cent of the country's electricity.[48] And the results are clearly visible, with several hundred Appalachian mountains having been decapitated over the last few decades to produce the black diamond.[49] According to researchers at Duke University in North Carolina, mountaintop removal has contributed to making some of the most active mining areas in West Virginia '40 per cent flatter than they were before excavation'.[50]

There have also been studies on the environmental consequences of open-pit mining on the Appalachians.[51] They conclude, as summarised by the Environmental Protection Agency (EPA), that the result is a significant loss of biodiversity around the mining areas, the loss of streams due to the removal of ground, as well as high concentrations of selenium in the surrounding streams.[52] 'We have data that the water quality impacts can last at least thirty years,' add the researchers at Duke.[53] Then there are the geomorphology impacts, which 'might last thousands of years'.[54] Mining companies are required to decontaminate and reforest mines once they are no longer in operation. However, says Erin Savage, the decline of the coal-mining industry 'will drive a lot of these companies to bankruptcy. They might not have enough resources to redevelop the older mines, which will be abandoned as a result.[35] In other words, the impact of the cloud will still be felt for a long time on what are some of the most ancient mountainous reliefs that the Earth has created.

What is the situation today? Does Dominion still procure coal that is mined using mountaintop removal? It's very hard to verify this. First, because the share of coal in the utility's power output has dropped considerably over the last few years: 12 per cent today from 50 per cent in 2005.[36] Second, because 'electricity companies are not required to disclose the exact origin of the coal powering their stations, meaning the information you find is unclear', says Erin Savage. But the rest of my investigation further enlightens me. Rising out of the plains of West Virginia, a six-hour drive north-east of Hurley, is the coal plant Mount Storm, also operated by Dominion. The black diamond comes notably from a processing facility a half-hour drive away operated by the company Mettiki Coal. I head there in the company of Brent Walls, an employee of the environmental organisation Upper Potomac Riverkeeper.

Against a forest backdrop, my eyes settle on imposing edifices for washing coal, straddled by conveyers on which the raw material is transported. A ten-minute drive past the procession of trucks flooding into the plant, and we have reached an immense open-pit mine that we are prohibited from entering. The waste material from the preparation process has been piling up for decades at a spoil tip located three kilometres from the Mettiki plant. We make our way there. From the boot of his car, Brent Walls takes out a drone mounted with a camera. The device rises into the air. Seen from above, the topography is riveting: a mountain 200 metres high and several kilometres wide, lacerated by the roads used by heavy equipment.[57] Known as Backbone Mountain, this tremendous hill now stands in the middle of the Appalachians.

'This mountain was once a valley', says a resident who bought a house here in 2017. The octogenarian gives his name as just 'James', in case his account might worsen his relations with Mettiki. For a dispute is brewing: a month ago, James and his wife, Wendy, learned from a neighbour that Mettiki was planning to scrap the top of the hill where their house is. 'They're going to remove all the vegetation, and then remove a fifty-metre layer of soil over around thirty hectares', James says, looking up at the summit. 'The recovered material will be used to reforest Backbone Mountain once Mettiki no longer has any use for it.' When will operations begin? Our man doesn't know. 'You won't have any farming or wildlife on this land ever again. The deer, bears, coyotes, and wild turkeys will go!', he cried. 'They'll leave one hell of a mess behind ... and that's the truth!'

Moving the top of a mountain in order to rehabilitate a tip or an old mine doesn't stop at Backbone Mountain. Residents in Hurley told me about similar practices taking place to redevelop part of No. 2 Surface mine. As for the electricity generated by the Mount Storm power station using coal from Mettiki, it will be added to that generated by numerous other Dominion plants (such as from gas, solar, and biomass). It will then have the benefit of the power utility's seven million customers spread across some twenty states, including Virginia, where Ashburn's county is located.[58] It would seem accurate to declare that our digital lifestyles are having an indelible impact on some of the wildest landscapes our planet offers.

The FAANGs at Dominion Energy's heels?

How can digital companies reduce such an ecological footprint? The answer depends, at least in part, on the Dominion Energy group itself. Not only is it a powerful company, but its net income, close to $1.6 billion in 2020, also makes it an influential player on the local political scene. To the extent, reports Josh Stanfield, an activist advocating for the financial transparency of political life in Virginia, that, 'Dominion makes them do what it wants them to do [...] whether it is Republicans or Democrats'.[59] Officially committed to transitioning to clean energy, behind the scenes the company is fighting to delay it. Strategies include lining up its political allies, supplying them with preferred amendments to, say, delay closing down its coal-fired plants ... and knowing how to be generous to them.[60] Between 1997 and 2018, it paid $11.1 million to Virginia officials of all political stripes.[61] And in 2020, it spent another $1.3 million—three-and-a-half times more than all the payments it made in 2018.[62] It can even claim the title of the 'most generous donor in state history'.[63]

Among its sympathisers is Terry Kilgore, a Republican member of the Virginia House of Delegates, and, more importantly, 'one of Dominion's fiercest defenders', says Josh Stanfield. 'Terry Kilgore will keep pushing coal until the industry is gone.'[64] In 2020, he tried—and failed—to push through an amendment to reject the closure of a coal plant.[65] Coincidence? The politician has since 1997 received $230,897 in donations from Dominion.[66] Yet the lobbying by the utility has not produced its desired outcome; over the last five years, it has had to decrease the share of coal in its electricity generation. To offset this decrease, the group is increasingly placing its bets on natural gas, which now represents over 40 per cent of its energy mix. This fossil fuel does indeed emit half as much carbon dioxide as coal, but it also releases methane—a gas that, over a century, has a heating potential twenty-eight times that of carbon dioxide.[67] In conclusion, 'the impact [of Dominion's energy policy] on climate change could get worse,' says Ivy Main, an American lawyer and advocate with the environmental organisation Sierra Club.[68]

Dominion's force of inertia is such that, in 2019, major corporations such as Apple, Amazon Web Services, Adobe, and Microsoft addressed a joint letter to the utility 'to express concern regarding the re-stated intentions of energy providers to meet our energy demand with expensive fossil fuel projects'. Was this a show of impotence by the most powerful companies in the world against the power of Dominion? An attempt to pass their responsibilities onto someone else? These assumptions seem imminently reasonable. Either way, the situation explains—or, at least, partly—why Greenpeace, in a report published in 2017, called out certain digital corporations that store some of their data in Virginia-based data centres.[69] Coal meets 30 per cent of Amazon Web Services' electricity needs. The same applies to Netflix; it's a startling figure, given that 15 per cent of internet traffic worldwide is generated by the video-streaming platform. And 23 per cent of Adobe's mix, 36 per cent of Oracle's, and 23 per cent of LinkedIn's are allegedly also coal-based. Twitter's number is meant to be around 21 per cent—bear that in mind the next time you tweet.

Until Virginia's energy mix becomes 100 per cent renewable between now and 2045 or 2050, as urged by a recent Act, the behemoths of the digital economy can offset their carbon dioxide emissions using 'carbon credits'.[70] Created in the US in 1998, and then in Europe in 2001, the concept is based on the premise that the electrons produced from solar or wind energy are indistinguishable from those from a coal-fired or nuclear power plant once they have entered the electrical grid. But a producer of green energy can—through a specialised intermediary—sell a document to a company wishing to link, virtually, their electricity consumption to a sustainable source of energy. The cumulative credits make it possible for companies such as Netflix to proclaim that they have achieved carbon neutrality.[71]

The streaming platform is undeniably consuming coal, yet this game of accounting entries makes it possible to erase, at least on paper, its carbon footprint. It is greenwashing in its purest form, and in the world of data centres, one of the rare experts daring enough to tell it like it is, Philippe Luce, calls it 'intellectual and moral fraud'.[72] Nevertheless, the intention behind carbon credits is good; by buying green energy, we are financially supporting their development. But surely the price tag should reflect that intention. In the US, a credit costs around 70 cents per megawatt hour, which is too little to seriously support the shift to green sources of electricity. As it happens, an authority on the matter has already stated that the existence or the absence of these credits have absolutely no bearing on the development of renewables.[73] In the meantime, 'cheap green electricity' stands out as an excellent way for companies such as Netflix to delay their energy transition.

Western companies nevertheless often do better than the rest of the world does, as 35 per cent of the electricity used in the world today is generated from coal. Be that as it may, this general addiction to fossil fuels explains why the entire digital industry, which taps 10 per cent of the electricity generated on the planet, is reported to be responsible for 3.7 per cent of greenhouse-gas emissions—a number that could double between now and 2025.[74]

And so we need to realise that even our most banal digital habits have a carbon impact. An email produces a minimum of 0.5 grams, and as much as 20 grams if there is an attachment—the equivalent of a light bulb switched on for one hour.[75] And to think that 319 billion emails are sent every day around the world![76] But the carbon impact of emails is negligible compared to online videos, which make up 60 per cent of data flows.[77] A data-centre company wanting to illustrate these numbers for consumers used the example of the music video *Gangnam Style*. The global smash hit by South Korean singer Psy was viewed around 1.7 billion times per year, requiring the equivalent of 297 GWh, or the average annual electricity consumption of European cities with a population of well over 60,000.[78]

This dark side of the immaterial world is starting to tarnish the reputation of the tech giants. A response is imminent. In the far north of Europe, in the midst of the vast plains of Lapland, the FAANGs believe they have found the answer to creating a greener internet.

CHAPTER SIX

Battle of
the far north

'THIS IS WHERE THE CLOUD TOUCHES THE GROUND! THERE are billions of calculations taking place all around you. The very thought of it is exhilarating!' As he speaks, Fredrik Kallioniemi, the commercial director of the Swedish data centre Hydro66, seems incandescent with excitement. Entering a huge wooden building of 500 square metres, past the meticulous gaze of a security guard, though an airlock set in two-way glass, I am quite literally in the cloud. My ears are the first to be assaulted, as machines emit the strident buzz of a billion bothered worker bees. Next is my sight: row upon row of metal racks containing servers lined up under green lights. Intercepting the waves of heat given off by the machines is an icy breeze brought in from the outside by large fans built into the walls; surrounding the roaring hall is countryside encased in metres of powder snow. Welcome to Boden in Swedish Lapland.

Technology for cleaner data

If my peregrinations have taken me as far as the extreme north of Sweden this winter in 2020, it is because the internet produces heat. Some data-centre equipment can heat up to 60 degrees, whereas a data centre needs an ambient temperature of between 20 and 27 degrees to work optimally. Cooling systems use vast amounts of electricity—as much as 'half of the electricity of a data centre', a computer science university professor tells me.[1] How do you reduce this energy consumption, and use electricity that doesn't emit greenhouse gases? These are two existential questions on the minds of the big digital firms on a quest for respectability. When it comes to image, there is a lot at stake: any association with appalling wastes of energy—not to mention global warming—is out of the question. The banner 'How clean is your cloud?' that was hung over the facade of Amazon's Seattle headquarters in 2012 by Greenpeace activists left a nasty aftertaste, as did its blimp floated two years later over Silicon Valley, using compelling slogans calling on Apple, Google, and Amazon to green up their sources of electricity.[2] The FAANGs also have to contend with reputational risk coming from the inside.[3] Since 2019, Amazon employees have whipped up a media frenzy by protesting in their thousands to make their employer reduce its carbon dioxide emissions to zero by 2030.[4] Financially, there is also more at stake: 'The first expense item of a data centre is energy,' says a director at the Dutch company Interxion. 'By extension, it represents 30 per cent of the bill we send our clients.'[5]

The ecological benefits of shifting to all-renewable energy are up for debate, but do any of the digital players care?[6] Companies are racing to show just how 'green' they are ... FAANG headquarters have become the poster child of a new battle for a respectable image. In Cupertino, California, Apple Park is steeped in an artificial forest of 9,000 trees, and is covered in so many solar panels that CEO Timothy Cook calls it 'the greenest building on the planet'.[7] To perfect this display of purity, the headquarters of some Californian companies are said to paint their lawns green during dry spells. And to decarbonise all their activities, digital companies have, for the last ten years, been signing energy contracts left, right, and centre with solar and wind companies. Apple and Amazon are even directly involved in the construction of renewable-energy power plants in China, the US, and Japan.[8]

Following their lead, the entire industry is claiming adherence to renewables. 'The big data centres like Equinix, Compass, CyrusOne, and Vantage are all working for big Californian firms, which are demanding they convert to cleaner electricity. They have no other choice but to adapt,' says Christian Déjean, an executive at Hydro-Québec.[9] This transformation regularly opens the way to all forms of 'greenwashing'. One example is reported by a trade journalist after a visit to a data centre in Saint-Denis, north of Paris, in 2015. 'There were solar panels on the roof of the data centre. And when I asked what the electricity it generated was used for, the answer was: "Given how much energy the thing needs, there's just enough to power a coffee machine."'[10]

Between window-dressing and buying carbon credits, it is hard to accurately gauge the sincerity of stakeholders. One thing is certain: this transformation is very real, but it is not nearly as awe-inspiring as the industry would have you believe. 'Google recently stated that it uses 100 per cent renewable energy, but we know for a fact that that is not possible', says the journalist trenchantly.[11] 'There is a lot of ill will, lip service, bad intentions, even', Philippe Luce of Institut Datacenter admitted during our interview. 'There is no such thing as a "green" data centre.'[12]

One promising approach is to use the heat from data centres to warm public swimming pools, office blocks, greenhouses, and households. According to Dutch lobbyist Stijn Grove, 'In the Netherlands, a million homes could potentially be heated with this residual heat.'[13] The idea is popular with the media, but matching an offer to a demand that is not located too far away is no easy feat. Nor is it the vocation of data centres to roll out such infrastructure. 'A data centre isn't there to help grow tomatoes,' complains Philippe Luce. 'Let's not confuse their function.'[14] Doing so could even be risky, as highlighted by Dutch local councillor Mariëtte Sedee: 'What would happen if one day a data centre decides to relocate to India? You would lose your heating infrastructure! It is naïve to think that data centres will generate heat for municipalities!'[15]

Especially since such initiatives do not address the essential question of how to manage the digital sector's astronomical electricity consumption. And so, to tackle the root of the problem, phrases and words such as 'energy performance', 'optimisation', and 'power usage effectiveness' have in recent years become music to cloud companies' ears.[16] So much so, in fact, that 'One of the industries making the most progress in terms of energy efficiency is data centres.'[17] A greater centralisation of data in hyperscale structures that can accommodate thousands of servers is already optimising storage. Engineers in Switzerland and the Netherlands have come up with technology that cools data centres by immersing them in liquid solutions.[18] More radical still is Microsoft: off the coast of the Orkney islands in northern Scotland, the company is experimenting with a new generation of subsea data centres, perhaps with the end goal of reflooring the seabed.[19]

Optimistic, if not presumptuous, industry players have the luxury of not having to dwell on the effectiveness of today's technologies, for there are extraordinarily more effective innovations waiting in the wings to replace them. The proof: it is speculated that soon the power of quantum physics will be harnessed to reduce the volume of a data centre to the size of a paperback novel; and DNA storage technology could encode all data to take up no more space than the boot of a car.[20] In a future more optimistic still, humans will desert data centres, which will become entirely automated and populated by autonomous robots capable of scaling columns of servers to replace defective parts. Without having to house humans, the working environment of the machines could reach 35 degrees, reducing the operation of air-conditioning systems and therefore energy consumption.[21] Who knows? Maybe one day we'll launch data centres into space. Equipment will have a longer lifespan suspended in a vacuum, with all the ecological benefits we can imagine. 'Look how efficient telecoms became, thanks to satellites, after all!' says the CEO of an IT consultancy.[22]

Yet, a few years ago, none of this technological speculation could prevent Facebook—now Meta, and one of the world's best-known companies—from having to contend with an unprecedented crisis.

The extra-cool data centre

Back to Earth. In 2010, the world's biggest social network, which outsourced its data storage, announced that it would build its own data centre, measuring 1.3 hectares, in Prineville, Oregon.[23] It was a technological gem, and the internet giant was already making energy gains. But the trade press quickly pointed out that the data centre's power supply came predominantly from a coal-fired plant.[24] These revelations would soon trigger a global campaign by Greenpeace against Facebook's use of fossil fuels. The US non-profit released a series of reports exposing the energy policy of Mark Zuckerberg's company while, on the social network, internet users formed groups to share Greenpeace's petitions. We can imagine the threats this posed to Facebook's reputation. 'Even if they never said it, at the time Facebook's directors were beleaguered by Greenpeace', reported one observer.[25] They had to move quickly by making significant announcements.

This is where Node Pole comes in. Since 2009, the former Swedish professional association had been trying to entice the tech giant to install its data centres in Sweden. Led by Matz Engman, a delegation of businessmen travelled to Silicon Valley to meet with the leaders of the digital industry. Among those approached was Facebook. The group was expanding, and needed to store more and more data, particularly for its users in Europe, Africa, and the Middle East. A new data centre needed to be built on the old continent, providing the shortest possible connection time—or latency—for its 800 million users. Engman recognised that Sweden could be the ideal location because of its exceptional political stability—the last war, with its neighbour Norway, dated back to 1814—and near absence of seismic activity. The businessman was particularly confident about the city of Luleå, located in the far north of the country. It has a reliable power infrastructure: the Luleälv river, one of the longest in Sweden, is known for its reputedly 'green' hydroelectric power generation, and at highly competitive rates. More importantly, temperatures are dreadfully low for a large part of the year, with the thermometer dropping as far as -41 degrees. This environment could cool data centres naturally, thereby reducing cloud companies' electricity consumption and costs. What Matz Engman had on offer was the cold.[26] Sweden's far-north business 'climate' was very suitable to the FAANGs, in all senses of the word.

Listening to Engman's pitch, Facebook's representatives purportedly exclaimed, 'We love this place!' The firm contacted the Swedish government in September 2010. It wasn't looking just to expand its infrastructure; it wanted to sell the story of an eco-responsible company which, to 'save' the climate, would gamble on setting up a '100 per cent green data centre' in one of the most inhospitable regions in the world.

The company proposed some forty locations in Sweden; it selected twenty-two, then eight, then two ... It was at this point that Matz Engman saw a platoon of lawyers and architects travel across the country, led by Thomas Furlong, Jay Parikh, and Darin Daskarolis, three high-ranking Facebook managers who reported directly to Zuckerberg. Negotiations ensued, the confidentiality of which earned the endeavour the code name *Project Gold*. Facebook's requirements were inconceivable; the scale of its project, extreme. The whole thing seemed preposterous. Yet the prospect of having Facebook set up in the middle of Lapland was so appealing that 'we were prepared to do anything to host them,' says Engman.[27] Subsidies and tax cuts were part of the welcome package, and there was talk of the king of Sweden hosting a reception in the company's honour.

Word got out in the kingdom. 'We thought something important was happening, but we didn't know exactly what it was,', says Niklas Österberg, an executive at a local company in

the industry.[28] In October, the news broke: Facebook announced
that it had chosen Luleå, a city flanked by the Arctic Circle for
100 kilometres, to accommodate the most formidable migration
of cat videos and holiday snaps in history. Construction began
almost instantly in an industrial area north of the city. For two
years, 120 companies were contracted to build—confidentially—a
building spanning nearly three hectares. Hundreds of American
sub-contractors invested in Luleå. The comings and goings of
heavy vehicles were constant. The work, costing around 500
million euros, proceeded without any major problems.[29] In
March 2013, as construction was reaching an end, 2,500 residents
gathered on the frozen lake of Luleå, forming a giant thumbs-
up—the Facebook 'like'—as a welcome sign.[30] On 12 June 2013, the
data centre was finally up and running. Engman remembers it
well: that day, internet traffic between Sweden and the rest of the
world doubled in less than a minute.

Today, all the data produced by Europeans on the social
networks owned by Facebook—starting with the messaging
application WhatsApp, and the photo and sharing application
Instagram—is concentrated in Sweden's far north. Not forgetting,
of course, an incalculable number of 'friends'.[31] John, Rebecca,
Enrico, and especially those of us who have a Facebook account
are hosted around 2,000 kilometres from 'continental' Europe. It's
both far from and near European users, as it takes only thirty
milliseconds—three times slower than the blink of an eye—to
become accessible to every single member of our network between
the continent and Luleå.

It was time to 'meet' these friends ...

The aesthetics of the immaterial

Winter 2020. If I have chosen to board the 560 train to Luleå from Stockholm station on this icy, snowy morning, it is to stretch time. For hours, I watch as the landscapes of Lapland slide frame by frame past my train window. To my right are the rounded outlines of the Gulf of Bothnia; to my left lie vast, unaltered plains, rivers muted under layers of ice, and pine forests. No matter how much the social network flares up with tirades and abuse, the Swedish landscape—its chosen domicile—remains tranquil, impassive. Past the city of Kramfors, 500 kilometres further north, the ceiling of clouds shifts, releasing shafts of light. The double-way railway track becomes a single track. Every now and then, the convoy makes a stop to shed a locomotive towing spruce logs. My carriage gradually empties. The sun's pulse begins to slow, its final beats lighting the landscape with a clear, yellow glow. 'What brings you here?' asks a passenger. I venture the most rational explanation possible, and then she stares at me with eyes as big as globes. Apparently, the purpose of my journey here is beyond all comprehension. I am now 900 kilometres north of my starting point, and a final stream of light flows above Luleå as the train draws to a halt.

'How do I explain that, all around me, the photos posted on a billion Facebook accounts are not on their telephones, but here in my hometown, 300 metres from this office, at minus-30 degrees?' says Niklas Österberg. He may well be a veteran of the information-technology industry, but the mere mention of the social network's data centre pitches him into an abyss of both fascination and bewilderment. 'I still can't get my head around the complexity of the world around us,' he continues with emotion and bemusement.[32] Those who have visited the data centre describe it as huge and impressive. 'It's like slipping under the keyboard of your laptop computer and walking around the inside', says researcher Karl Andersson.[33] It is rare to be invited to visit the facility. Thinking it would be a lost cause, I confess that I hadn't even requested a press pass.

Braving the biting cold and navigating perilously through thick powder snow, I settle for just surveying the surroundings on foot. Ahead of me, a light-green hangar around thirty metres tall and the length of three football pitches looms large and silently. Nothing about it—save three discreet flags nearby, bearing the famous logo—provides any clue that it is host to one of the most popular companies in the world. Security cameras and fences set the tone, not to mention the attentions of a thirty-something-year-old, bland-faced security guard who asks for my identity and why I am here. 'Can I take a photo?' I ask. 'I can't stop you!' he replies, clearly frustrated. I look at the building for fifteen minutes or so while, through the window of the security command post, a second guard speaks into his walkie-talkie, requesting a car patrol. As he insists on his request, I decide it's best I leave.

Is the data centre operating as planned? Has Facebook managed to attract the talent it hoped for to such an inhospitable part of the world? And what of the other two data centres it has since built in the same industrial area? The few Americans (no doubt employed by the same social network) I met in the bars in Luleå were not very forthcoming.

'I don't know how to explain this culture of secrecy around Facebook', says Karl Andersson. 'These people are really paranoid.'[34] On the web, the company is everywhere, but in the physical world it is invisible. With its insipid buildings and minimalist communication taking place under Pinnacle Sweden AB—a subsidiary that serves as a screen—Mark Zuckerberg's gamble may have paid off: to be forgotten in a way that 'the residents of Luleå are no longer interested in Facebook,' says Niklas Österberg.[35] Researcher Asta Vonderau has analysed the outcomes of what clearly looks to be a deliberate strategy to render the Californian company's physical presence invisible, 'with the aim of minimising friction and contestation [...] which could disturb free data and profit flows'.[36]

This strategy of frictionless profit is not new. It draws from what the American researcher Jeffrey Winters in 1996 coined 'zonal capitalism': 'a special economic zone—sometimes walled, but always clearly bounded—in which an intensified effort has been made to create a climate favourable to business'.[37] We find the same with oil companies: despite their frequent involvement in the economic and political life of numerous African countries, their industrial activities are obscured. In the case of Equatorial Guinea, there is a good reason for this, as the country's geology is such that mining and refining operations take place on offshore platforms located far from the shores of the continent. This is a boon for oil companies: it limits any protest movements that could disrupt operations.[38]

The FAANGs are seeking the same outcome by wanting to disassociate themselves from the material world. Accordingly, Google, which owns some fifteen data centres around the world, often uses shell companies so that its name is only associated with these infrastructures once the builds are approved.[39] In the US, the search engine also imposed strict confidentiality clauses on the municipalities where it set up in order to bypass any public discussion about the water and electricity consumption of its data centres.[40] Likewise for Apple's immense 4.6-hectare data centre in Maiden, North Carolina, which only appeared on the satellite images of the Google Earth application when its commissioning was announced in 2009![41] As for Amazon, a document leaked on Wikileaks revealed that the company was discreetly multiplying its data centres under innocently named companies such as Vadata Inc and Vandalay Industries.[42]

In the decades ahead, this unbearable lightness of the net will put labour unions—the existence of which is historically tied to the concentration of the workforce in tangible places of production, such as factories—face-to-face with existential challenges. How do you establish a picket line at a workshop designed 'not to exist'? How do you block access to a workplace that has migrated online? Protest movements will increasingly invest in cyberspace by diverting the tools of the new digital aristocracy to their advantage. This is what American researcher Tung-Hui Hu thinks, stating that 'electronic problems should be opposed electronically'.[43] The labour unions of the future could be goaded by artists and 'hacktivists' to multiply cyberattacks against e-capitalism websites by blocking access or leaking sensitive information. Until new forms of protest emerge, 'the big internet companies want to maintain this aesthetic of the immaterial', by Asta Vonderau's account, for it is also 'a way for them to obscure the impact of their infrastructure on the environment and natural resources'.[44]

The dam of contention

A case in point is the Luleälv river and, more specifically, its 460 kilometres of 'liquid gold', as some local residents call it. The fifteen or so hydroelectric power stations running along its length generate abundant, inexpensive, and decarbonated electricity for the dozens of data centres operating in the region—two of which belong to Facebook, which alone consume 1 to 2 per cent of the energy generated in Sweden. Along the 130 kilometres separating Luleå from the town of Vuollerim runs a sinuous road hemmed in by the dark pelt of pine forests. The river, petrified in sediments of ice, blends into the sky, down from which tumble avalanches of thick crystals.

In a parking lot at my destination, I meet Roland Boman. It was not easy convincing this man well into his sixties to speak with me. He is an introvert, taciturn ... that is, until a few kilometres later, further west down the road, when he gazes mournfully at an eighty-metre-high wall, higher than the first level of the Eiffel Tower. We are standing in front of the Letsi dam, built in the 1960s to provide hydroelectricity for the region. Upstream, the valley was flooded over a distance of six kilometres. And downstream, the destiny of the Lilla Luleälv (Little Luleå river), a branch of the river, was changed forever.

Taking refuge in a restaurant in Vuollerim, his hands wrapped around a cup of boiling-hot tea, Roland Boman shows me old photographs of the little river before the dam was built. Fifteen kilometres of raging waters used to wash up against pine and birch forests, and, more importantly, he tells me, it was one of Sweden's best-known spawning grounds for salmon. 'It was paradise!' says Roland, who lived a stone's throw from the shore at the time. The life of Vuollerim's 3,000 inhabitants gravitated around Lilla Luleälv ... as did the lives of their children. 'Every spare moment we had, my friends and I would jump on our bikes to come here to swim, bask on the rocks, and fish. It was like the river had a soul.' But soon the government began to build hydroelectric power stations across the country to support Sweden's economic development. Luleå's river had great potential, as it would ultimately meet up to 10 per cent of the country's electricity needs. And so the decision was made to build several dams, including Letsi.[45]

For three years, hundreds of workers and trucks were mobilised to build a retaining wall of concrete and stone. And one day in the summer of 1967, the hydroelectric power station operated by the utility Vattenfall AB was ready for commissioning. Boman remembers the day very clearly: 'I was twelve years old, and as usual I came to the river to fish with my friends.' But something had changed. All of a sudden, the water level upstream was dozens of metres higher. A seven-kilometre tunnel had redirected part of the stream to the main river. And downstream, the Little Luleå river had suddenly dried up. Boman didn't have the time to watch the last pair of salmon escort away the last flow of fresh water. A dull foam had already exposed the river's stones and algae, and a deathly silence fell over the small vale. 'The stream was gone', he says, his throat tight. Dried up over some fifteen kilometres, the Lilla Luleälv remains the longest river in Western Europe drained at the hands of humans.

'The adults didn't understand right away that their stream had just been taken away from them', said Boman. 'There were no complaints, not a single protest. Then they had to face up to the fact that the Lilla Luleälv was gone forever.' What remains is ineffable grief and long-lasting mourning. A mourning for water. 'We immured ourselves in silence to come to terms with it. It was too painful. The river became a taboo topic. It stayed that way for twenty years.'

I interrupt: 'Twenty years of silence?'

'Absolutely, twenty years of silence. Only in the 1980s did

tongues begin to loosen. We began to refer to the dam as "a massacre of the environment", a facility that got the better of an extraordinary biodiversity; that "not the slightest impact assessment" of the hydroelectric power station was carried out.[46] Boman talks to his children about the missing river as if talking about a loved one lost too soon. For the last five years, he has been holding talks, and meets with the press and members of parliament. There is also a Facebook page where people can post photos of former days.[47]

Of course, in no way is the social network responsible for the construction of the Letsi dam, and no one's to say that nature hasn't adapted to this mineral tourniquet. But Facebook has helped to perpetuate the presence of a power facility that meets its energy needs and props up its image as a sustainable company, whereas, as pointed out by a Swedish activist, 'hydroelectric power plants have a much heavier impact on biodiversity than any other green electricity'.[48] Roland Boman ruminates on his ambivalence towards the Californian company. On the one hand, 'I love Facebook', says our man of few words. 'It's a place where I can express my emotions!' Yet the very mention of the company vexes him: 'I don't think it knows where the electricity for its data centre comes from. What happens in Vuollerim is far away from Luleå, but here, energy comes from the river! And we're talking about a river that is dead.'

Las Vegas in the far north

The arrival of Facebook brought a breath of fresh air to the local economy, transforming Scandinavia within a few years into a promised land for the likes of Amazon Web Services, Google,

Etix Everywhere, and Microsoft.[49] In 2017, the ever-enterprising American-Norwegian company Kolos created a sensation by announcing the construction of the world's biggest co-location—a shared data centre—in the city of Ballangen in Norway's extreme north.[50]

I leave Luleå aboard a new snowpiercer. It charges towards the North Pole, traversing vast plains awash in a diluted, pale light, as it enters the Arctic Circle.[51] After passing the mining town of Kiruna, the train reaches Norwegian territory, snaking along the flanks of mountains that overlook the first fjords, their depths dense and unfathomable.

The world is truly remarkable.

'Kolos? You won't meet a single person who hasn't heard of it. What a mess!' says a Norwegian as I drop off my suitcase in Narvik, a neighbouring city of Ballangen. She's not wrong: barely had the first stone of the data centre been laid when the cloud company was bought for close to $10 million by the Canadian firm Hive Blockchain. The data-centre project was then morphed into a centre for cryptocurrency 'mining'—a booming, energy-intensive industry.[52] The world's best-known cryptocurrency, Bitcoin, itself guzzles 0.5 per cent of the world's electricity, or the equivalent of Denmark's energy requirements.[53] But such considerations have little bearing when the key premise is to 'make money fast', a local journalist told me.[54] This didn't stop the barrage of criticism against what was perceived as a purely speculative transaction.

Meanwhile, the authorities were discontinuing a number of tax breaks for cryptocurrency companies, at which point Hive Blockchain ceased all communications. In May 2021, it paid the municipality of Narvik $200,000 to take Kolos off its hands. All you can see now on the piece of land acquired at the price of gold are herds of reindeer, and no one believes the project will go anywhere. Although not everyone came up short: the directors of Kolos 'pocketed loads of money in exchange for a basic concept! The whole world was watching Ballangen, whereas there was nothing, just an idea,' Knut Einar Hanssen, a former civil servant in the Ballangen municipality, says in disillusionment. In Kolos' defence, it's easy to fall into the trap of the siren song. 'It was a race for cash, the Las Vegas of the far north! The data casino!' agrees Hanssen with disarming frankness. 'And we were all blinded by what the deal promised.'

Ballangen may be the only place on the planet where something that didn't exist went up in smoke. Where out of nothing came naught. 'This event symbolises the kinds of difficulties faced by cloud companies setting up data centres in the far north', says Hanssen. Ultra-fast fibre-optic cables for linking Asia and Europe via the Arctic (see chapters nine and ten) could indeed make the Nordic countries a 'natural' choice for data storage.[55] But claims for digital sovereignty by a growing number of states could rearrange the cloud's geography. This desire to control their own information flows gives rise to a new power paradigm, whereby it is more important for them to consolidate their infrastructure on home soil than it is to scatter it around the globe. Since 2015, Russia requires all its citizens' personal data to be located on its territory.[56] The European data infrastructure project Gaia-X also seeks to establish a sovereign cloud on the old continent, bypassing the services of the American platforms. Africa, too, is challenged: it 'concentrates 17 per cent of the global population, but hosts only 1 per cent of the world's data', says an expert at Cap Ingelec.[57] There are hubs across the continent, including at Johannesburg, Dakar, and Accra.

In winter 2020, I went to another hub, in Casablanca. 'Morocco's strategic position between Europe and Sub-Saharan Africa means European companies can store the data of their African clientele, and gain a few milliseconds of latency,' says a colleague from the same company.[58] Here, again, we see the demand for speed. Indeed, several data-centre experts believe that hosting data so far away from hubs results in a latency that is barely acceptable in the internet ecosystem. Alongside hyperscale infrastructure, the future therefore lies with edge computing—a network of micro data centres spread out in close proximity to users. These 'short information circuits' also require less energy for data transfers—an operation reputed to consume more energy than data storage.[59]

Imagine just how different the world would be—the geography of cables, data centres, power stations, and digital hubs turned on its head—if internet users could wait just one second longer! What we have at the moment is a digital geography of urgency, of impatience, while we condemn the industry to a perpetual—absurd even—quest for performance and immediacy. Walking down the rows of Hydro66's servers in Boden, Sweden, Fredrik Kallioniemi told me that the migration of data to Swedish Lapland has decreased by 15,000 the pollution generated by a 'like' on Facebook. Such impressive, often unverifiable, figures need to be counterbalanced with the ever-increasing production of data. 'Servers are much more efficient, but the multiplication of data is even more so', says an executive of a major power utility in Quebec.[60] It could result in data centres consuming up to 15 per cent more electricity every year.[61] Others state the opposite, suggesting that the two trends balance themselves out. 'The [data storage] centralisation paradigm is efficient. We are managing the grid better, and perhaps we'll continue to do so going forward', says a digital infrastructure specialist.[62]

Ways to curb our digital appetite

There are already countless solutions recommended—even applied—so that all users produce and store less data. One of the most relevant of these is Digital Cleanup Day, launched in 2020 by a group of activists led by the Estonian Anneli Ohvril.[63] The first edition took place in April 2020, and was joined by hundreds of thousands of internet users in eighty-six countries. The concept is simple: participants are invited to spend one day cleaning up their various storage spaces (email, Google Drive, Dropbox) so as to reduce their environmental footprint. It applies to all kinds of data: 'useless emails, as well as old photos and videos stored on your mobile phone', says Ohvril, whom I met in Tallinn in summer 2020. With this movement, she is targeting, in particular, iCloud, the data-storage platform for Apple devices (such as iPhones, iPads, and MacBooks). 'In Estonia, people use their iCloud accounts like a rubbish bin, and forget what they have in there', she explains. 'A lot of people who join Digital Cleanup Day aren't even aware of the energy impact the service represents.'[64] It is difficult to put a precise figure on the ecological gains reaped by such an operation, but for Ohvril its effectiveness needs to be looked at from a different angle: 'The campaign is not about the number of gigabytes saved, but about the change in mentality.'[65]

There are other beneficial practices with astounding effects that we can all adopt every day without even getting off the couch: watch videos using WiFi, which uses twenty-three times less electricity than 4G; switch off the internet box when you're not at home—an old one can use as much electricity as a large refrigerator; connect to a website without going through Google, whose every search request uses as much electricity as a lightbulb switched on for up to two minutes; watch movies at low definition rather than high definition, and consume four to ten times less electricity.[66] In fact, if 70 million streaming subscribers were to lower the video quality of their streaming services, there would be a monthly reduction in 3.5 million tonnes of CO2e [...] or approximately 6 per cent of the total monthly coal consumption in the US.[67]

Using online services that respect users' privacy also limits the harvesting of data and its energy-intensive storage. This involves opting for messaging apps such as Signal or Olvid, opening an email account with ProtonMail, and using the e Foundation cloud service, and while you're at it, paying in a few euros or making a donation.[68] For looking up information, why not try DuckDuckGo, an American search engine that doesn't record its users' search history?[69] Such advice can be multiplied endlessly, and shows how many concrete and simple steps we can all take for a cleaner internet through digital sobriety.

This policy of small actions does not subtract, however, from these deep and systemic questions:

- Is moving towards a freer internet a desirable income? The question seems absurd, especially since the web was built on the ideals of openness and universality. But without undermining this sacrosanct principle, we could think of ways of setting a fixed price based on the volume of data used.[70] Basic access could be guaranteed across the board, while users with bigger data appetites paid a subscription price by volume. Having a pricing policy would help regulate our data consumption.

- That question automatically raises another issue: that of the neutrality of the internet. Not all digital uses are equal, and some should take priority (reserving bandwidth for a smart hospital, rather than TikTok). But such thinking goes against the cardinal principle of equal access to the web, guaranteed to all senders and recipients of content, no matter who they are. It also assumes that the internet will become a rare and finite resource, and that access to it should be rationed.[71] It's a fascinating debate, but far from clear-cut, as we shall discover, as the web's engineers begin to make superb progress so that the network can withstand the imminent tsunami of data.

- Taking a more radical angle, there are those advocating that we dispense with the internet entirely or partially. Like the Luddite artisans in nineteenth-century England who were opposed to companies that used looms, 'disinformation' civil movements, more or less underground, have begun to surge. They urge us to ward off the soothsayers of the digital world who boast an even more connected future, in favour of a more habitable future without it.[72] At the very least, the 'slow web' movement invites us to decrease the network by lowering broadband speeds.

Our digital diet will also depend on the circular economy of data centres. The next part of the story: certain data contained in servers nearing end-of-life has by that stage become so sensitive that the hardware must be destroyed at all costs. A Dutch recycler speaks about how many major banks and government bodies hire armed guards to transport servers back to the factory to be scrapped ... Some companies even film it happening to prove that their clients' data has been destroyed.[73] 'The circular economy of data centres will be absolutely crucial, but it won't be enough', says Philippe Luce. 'At some point, we will need to move towards an awful thing called [digital] sobriety.'[74]

Which would mean upending the hierarchy of priorities displayed by corporations to address the accumulation of data: switch to 'green' sources of electricity; improve storage technology; and then reduce our data consumption. Instead, we need to tackle digital obesity at the source before optimising processes and power grids. Failing that, corporations will continue to talk—schizophrenically—in the same breath about the explosion of data, environmental responsibility, processing power, and carbon-free electricity from rivers.

Let's not fool ourselves: very few people are ready to change. Not least because the way we use digital is about to evolve as we brace ourselves for the vertiginous world of the internet of things. After the internet of the eyes and ears, the internet of the body. The internet of everything, even. Such an entirely connected future could completely sterilise the energy gains made at the Earth's poles.

CHAPTER SEVEN

Expansion of
the digital universe

IN 2017, STEVE CASE, THE FOUNDER OF AMERICA ONLINE (AOL), one of the first global internet service providers, left a deep impression with his book *The Third Wave: an entrepreneur's vision of the future.*[1] During the internet's first wave, he explained, web companies, including AOL, IBM, and Microsoft, built the infrastructure that allowed computers to connect to one another. During the second wave, companies such as Google and Facebook created search engines and the social networks that connected users to one another. In this third wave, Case predicted, we will connect everything, both animate and inanimate, that can be fitted with a sensor. He calls it 'the Internet of Everything'.[2]

Around the same time, fellow technoprophet Kevin Kelly, founder of the American magazine *Wired*, made a similar prediction in his book on the '12 technological forces that will shape our future'.[3] In the future, he wrote, every surface will have become a screen, personalised e-services will anticipate our every whim, there will be complete surveillance of consumers and citizens, and we will have constructed 'a planetary system connecting all humans and machines into a global matrix'—a superorganism called *holos*. In 2025, humans will not be 'on' or 'in' holos; they will be holos itself.

This generalised connection to the internet 'has already begun', said Kelly.[4] Today it is called the Internet of Things (IoT)—a term coined in 1999 by researchers at the Massachusetts Institute of Technology (MIT) in reference to the ability of objects, of things, to transmit and receive information via an RFID chip, for instance.[5] From mobile phones, tablets, thermostats, watches, lighting, to air conditioning, IoT has grown so fast that there are some 20 billion connected objects in the world today.

IoT is consolidating and moving to the next level. Take smart glasses: German writer Byung-Chul Han describes them as being close enough to the body to almost be part of it, as the ultimate achievement of the information society by merging the being and information.[6] Then there are medical applications for analysing data from deep within the human body. 'My daughter is diabetic', explains Fredrik Kallioniemi. 'When her blood sugar is too low, I get an alert on my phone, followed by her health metrics a few seconds later. This is where the Internet of Everything starts.'[7] Next, whole forests and animal species could be equipped with chips to better monitor and protect them. Humans could wear headsets that read their minds, and smart contact lenses to see in the dark—the 'Internet of Bodies' (IoB).[8] There is a good chance that our descendants will regard us as ersatz Australopithecus when, by 2030, humanity as a whole will live with 50, 100, even 500 billion such devices connected to the information superhighways.[9] But an all-encompassing interconnection of animal, vegetable, and digital matter is contingent on an ultra-high-performance network that can transmit extraordinary quantities of data.

It is a network that is gaining ground, and it is called 5G.

High frequency for emancipated machines

It is spring 2021. Splinters of light scatter over Monaco, catching the hulls of the yachts moored in the Port of Fontvieille, the bay windows of luxury apartments leaning into the sea, and the bonnets of the racing cars tearing through Monte-Carlo. The principality has always benefited from the distilled radiance of its tiny territory (two square kilometres). A tax haven, it attracts the fabulously wealthy. It is now also one of the very first countries to boast full coverage of 5G—the latest generation of mobile phone networks, replacing 4G. The ninth of July 2019 marked an important day in the country's history. After two years of installation, and 30 million euros of investment, some 40 5G antennas went into service. Monaco Telecom's majority shareholder, Xavier Niel, and Ren Zhengfei, the CEO of Huawei, which provided the technology, went to Monaco to mark the occasion at a five-star palace. The president of China, Xi Jinping, even made a state visit to Monaco a few weeks earlier to promote Huawei.

If 5G has become a priority for the principality, it is because it can transfer 10 times more data 10 times faster than 4G. It takes less than 10 seconds to download a two-hour film, instead of seven interminable minutes on 4G.[10] But who needs this kind of speed for uses as banal as sending a lousy email or looking at holiday photos? 'Only 5 per cent of our subscribers have a 5G contract, because it's not actually that useful', says Monaco

Telecom's managing director, Martin Péronnet.[11] But perhaps it's just a matter of time. In South Korea, the fifth-generation mobile network has been rolled out on a massive scale, and has already been adopted by 13 million people—nearly 20 per cent of all mobile phone contracts.[12] There, the prospect of a faster connection was enough to arouse consumer curiosity and trigger the buyers' reflex.[13] And the technology will undoubtedly revolutionise uses, allowing new modes of bandwidth-hungry digital consumption to flourish, such as virtual reality games and live-streaming videos on platforms such as Periscope or YouTube Live. That is, if recent history is anything to go by: 'When 3G arrived, we never thought watching football matches on a 3-centimetre screen could work. Clearly, we were wrong about that!' recalls an activist from the French non-profit Agir pour l'environnement.[14]

Monégasque companies stand to reap the most tangible rewards of this new generation of mobile network. As Martin Péronnet explains, 5G is much easier to install than fibre, and its lower latency opens a world of remote-controllable objects and infrastructure—drones, ships, hospitals, vehicles. Ultra-high-speed digital technology will ignite the economy of the country already nicknamed 'the smart principality': 'A wide array of sectors will be able to use 5G: energy, health, media, transport, manufacturing', says a French government report.[15] A greater capacity to handle more copious volumes of data could also, on a global scale, optimise road traffic and electricity-distribution systems, and make for more autonomous robots in the future factories of the fourth, ultra-connected, industrial revolution. Used properly, 5G will spur extraordinary social and human progress that we can all look forward to. But when will that future be? In the shorter term, business leaders are sceptical: 'At the end of 2019, technicians from the operator Orange approached me to ask me what applications would need 5G', reports a researcher at Belgium's Leuven university. 'They were stumped and kept saying: "We don't see where there's a market for it today." We were completely in the dark'.[16]

The geopolitical situation certainly explains how the horse was put before the cart. China was one of the first countries to make the roll-out of 5G a national priority.[17] Thanks to telco equipment manufacturer Huawei, Beijing acquired a major technological head start with the installation of thousands of 5G antennas countrywide, overtaking the US and Europe. Both sides of the Atlantic shuddered at the idea that China's progress could spell the end of Western domination. In late 2020, the then chancellor, Angela Merkel, expressed her concern at seeing Germany fall behind in the digital revolution, and called for the country to pick up the pace, otherwise it would 'come in last'.[18] Three years prior, the chancellor was already worried that the country 'would soon be at the same point as developing countries' in the digital arena.[19] This context has long pushed the ecological impacts of 5G down the list of priorities. And yet deploying 5G requires installing more antennas; they may be more powerful, but their range is more limited. 'The UK already has 26,000 3G and 4G antennas. 5G has half their wave spectrum, which means having to install twice as many just for England', predicts a consultant at Green IT.[20]

The much-overlooked ecological threats of 5G

Measuring a few dozen centimetres, these antennas laden with rare metals such as gallium and scandium will be installed every 100 metres or so, on bus stops, streetlights, and even billboards.

How will they be recycled?[21] And what about the additional wired fibre-optic connections needed to relay data? In the US, the Fiber Broadband Association already estimates that providing coverage to the 25 biggest metro markets in the country will require pulling 2.2 million kilometres of wired fibre—55 times the circumference of the Earth![22] What will be the multiplication factor of these numbers when, by 2026, 60 per cent of the world's population has access to the new network?[23] And then there are the device upgrades to get the full benefit of 5G ... In 2020, some 278 million 5G-compatible smartphones were sold.[24] Were they bought to replace genuinely defective devices? Or were consumers driven by the promise of getting even more from digital? What is the true ecological cost of this technological enterprise? It must be said that no one really knows: 'no environmental impact assessments were carried out', grumbles a member of the European Parliament I spoke to. 'One can't help but wonder whether the premise of the 5G roll-out is "zero precautions."'[25] This absence of information stokes irrational, unfounded fears, with people scared that the new antennas emit harmful electromagnetic waves.[26] Any impact assessments carried out at a later stage were lightweight. Municipalities across Europe decreed moratoriums, and citizen committees formed to open the debate were swept under the carpet by government authorities.

This doesn't stop service providers from extolling the undeniable environmental benefits of 5G. For the same amount of data, they say, the technology is 10 times more energy-efficient than its predecessor. But that's forgetting that with 5G our internet and data consumption will explode. We can all agree that the objective of new technology entering the market is not to make us consume less ... but even more. It's a simple truth, the effects of which were first addressed in 1865 by the British economist William Stanley Jevons. At the time, the improved performance of steam engines was predicted to lead to a decline in the use of coal. However, as Jevons demonstrated, the energy gains generated by the technological progress were negated by the increased use of the machines, and with it, increased coal consumption—the very opposite of the desired outcome.[27]

Known as the 'rebound effect', this paradox can be applied to myriad technologies—the internal-combustion engine (ICE), for instance. Between 2005 and 2018, the fuel consumption of the average ICE car decreased from 8.8 litres to 7.2 litres per 100 kilometres, a 22 per cent energy gain.[28] But the annual sale of new cars worldwide increased from 66 million to 96 million, a 44 per cent rise.[29] Another example comes from the civil aviation sector. In 2019, one passenger emitted 12 per cent less carbon dioxide per kilometre travelled than in 2013. But over the same period, the sector's carbon emissions jumped 29 per cent, and by 2050, emissions are expected to be seven times higher than in 1990.[30] Then there is the use of light-emitting diodes, more commonly known as LEDs. Research shows that their energy gains do not cancel out the fact that more energy is consumed because of their increased use.[31]

Digital technologies are no exception. Recent smartphones generally have a shorter battery life than the previous generation, despite the capacity of their batteries increasing 5 per cent per year on average. But this doesn't measure to how much more energy the newer models consume.[32] A report published in 2019 by the telco company Ericsson concluded that by 2025, 20 per cent of internet users will use 200 gigabytes on 5G devices every month—10 to 14 per cent more than what they were using on 4G.[33] That's excluding the advent of the Internet of Everything, to which 5G is already contributing—yet another trend entirely at odds with the goals of the fight against climate change.

While the players of the digital economy are aware of this boomerang effect, they are the first to point their fingers at the consumer. 'Everyone is free to not participate in digital overconsumption', Stéphane Richard, the then CEO of the French telecommunications giant Orange, said in 2020.[34] And, in the same breath, Orange runs advertising celebrating the new uses offered by 5G—a paradoxical attitude, to say the least.[35] Says one academic, 'digital players know full well that these new technologies will increase our digital consumption and that, far from solving the problem, it is energising it'.[36] 'Everyone plays the blame game', adds the founder of Green IT, Frédéric Bordage. 'No one is interested in going beyond their legal scope of responsibility to look at the system as a whole.'[37] Some of the trade unions at Orange nevertheless concede being 'aware of the contradictory messages' to which consumers are exposed.[38] Perhaps this explains why hundreds of the operator's employees—particularly the younger among them—openly disapprove of the group's strategy. 'On the intranet network, people ask: "Why are we heading into this madness?" For the first time, we're seeing comments like: "We must be crazy, instigating more energy consumption and mining for minerals"', says an internal source.[39]

With these rebound effects come other, indirect, effects. Time savings and increased buying power afforded by digital technologies means changes in consumer behaviour. 'Thanks to the internet, I could work from home, saving myself 1,000 euros in petrol. What am I going to do with the money?' asks a close source. 'Winter is long in northern Europe, so I'm going to fly to the Canary Islands.' An IT engineer adds, 'Digital has a tremendous impact on the way society is organised, and on the flow of goods and services. Things like trading instantaneously on the stock market or ordering a product on Amazon did not exist before digital.[40] In other words, digital works as a catalyst for the astounding economic and technological acceleration to which we are witness. And while these indirect effects have not been calculated, we can be absolutely certain that they do not contribute to the virtualisation of our existence. After analysing 57 inventions designed since the 1930s in the sciences of materials, digital, and energy, researchers have in fact concluded that none resulted in a decrease in resource consumption.[41] By burying our heads in the sand of an allegedly ethereal world free of all physical shackles, we are evading the reality that will eventually catch up with us: a dematerialised world will always be a more materialistic world.

This is where the debate takes an ideological turn. The rebound effects can be equally feared and celebrated, depending on where you stand on the increase of wealth, the globalisation of trade, and the mixing of cultures. This is how the expansion of the digital world puts us face-to-face with our most intimate convictions ... it is neither a good nor bad thing; it just depends on what we do with it.[42] The internet will allow children in the furthest regions in the world to educate themselves remotely; it will also be used to spread conspiracy theories that undermine our democracies. It will treat rare diseases; it will also allow Ryan Kaji—a child famous for unboxing presents every day on camera in Texas—to continue to be the highest-paid YouTuber in the world.[43]

Either way, digital's economic, social, and psychological repercussions should not be confused with its ecological function. While it stimulates the emergence of incredible initiatives aimed at protecting the climate and biodiversity, it was not designed to 'save' the planet, and claims about the resilience of life on Earth being connected to the performance of digital tools is, I believe, a myth, a fantasy. As a digital technology expert told me, 'ICT [information and communications technology] has really made the world a better place, but in terms of environmental impact, it is the worst thing that could have happened.'

Are we heading for a 'connected gate'?

If there is one technology that 5G will help to mainstream, it is the connected car, because of its capacity to relay huge amounts of data about the surrounding environment. Today, a vehicle with onboard GPS navigation is already 'connected'. And that's just the start. Driver-assistance systems are increasingly prevalent: warning signals in the event of a risk of collision; emergency brake assist; electronic steering assist; sensors that monitor blind spots, etc. The advantages in terms of road safety are unquestionable, and over 500 million connected cars are expected to be on the roads worldwide by 2025.[44] With onboard GPS suggesting shorter and, therefore, cleaner journeys, this digital revolution also addresses environmental concerns. Another breakthrough in electronic systems is 'eco-navigation', which allegedly reduces a vehicle's carbon dioxide emissions by 5 to 20 per cent.[45]

But capturing the necessary information requires myriad cameras, radars, and sonar. A connected car is embedded with up to 150 electronic control units, producing, by the most conservative estimates, 25 gigabytes of data per hour.[46] Its onboard computer therefore needs as much processing power as 20 laptop computers, and a total of 100 million lines of code to run its software.[47] While the number of lines of code alone does not reflect the complexity of the software, we can nevertheless draw comparison with a spaceship, which requires 400,000 lines of code; the Hubble space telescope, which requires two million lines of code; a military drone, 3.5 million lines of code; and a Boeing 787, 14 million lines of code. (See appendix 8.) In other words, a connected car's software is as bloated as 250 spaceships put together, or 50 Hubble space telescopes, or seven Boeing 787s. A report by US consulting firm McKinsey & Company states that by 2030 a driverless car will require some 300 million lines of code to function.[48]

The final frontier of the connected car is the driverless car, even if nothing suggests that they will one day find their way onto the road in their millions. 'Everyone realised that it's more complicated than we thought. Even Google and Uber keep postponing [the roll-out of these vehicles]', says Mathieu Saujot, a researcher at IDDRI, a sustainable-development think tank.[49] But if driverless cars do one day go mainstream, they will produce, on account of their lidars and ultra-high-definition cameras, up to one gigabyte of data per second.[50] In the words of the head of a big tech company, 'A million autonomous cars represent as much data as the entire world population connected to the web.'[51] And what will these vehicles use to communicate with? Road signs, smart roads, and other driverless cars connected to 'edge data centres' that offer the lowest possible latency. Paradoxically, the more 'autonomous' the car, the more it will depend on the surrounding infrastructure ... There is nothing less autonomous than an autonomous vehicle. 'It's an oversight in terms of innovation', says Mathieu Saujot, 'and that's the physical reality in which they'll find themselves.'[52]

Some observers reassure us that only shreds of the data

produced will leave the vehicle to communicate with the outside world.[53] Others add that the driverless car is meant to be a shared vehicle, which should limit the number of cars on the road (a point that is indeed up for debate).[54] One thing we can be sure of is that it will use far more electricity—up to 1,500 additional watts.[55] How will that affect the range of the electric car? Will the volume of its battery need to be increased, or will hybrid engines be the key to compensate for the surplus in energy consumption?[56] Furthermore, the data produced by a driverless car will result in carbon dioxide emissions from the infrastructure used to transmit, store, and process the data needed to better understand our consumer behaviours, to propose adapted car insurance plans (known as 'pay as you drive'), and to design targeted advertising. Accordingly, every kilometre travelled by a driverless car could indirectly increase average car emissions by over 20 per cent ... at a time when, worldwide, vehicle-emission standards are becoming stricter and more widespread.[57]

Who's to be held accountable? 'For manufacturers, it's in their interest to blame IT contractors for this pollution. As for drivers, they'll never see the additional energy cost on their bill', states an engineer from the automotive sector.[58] It is difficult to quantify the pollution. 'Manufacturers are sensitive to the ecological issues, but their first priority is to work out their survival in this world of technological disruptions', explains Mathieu Saujot. 'It's too early for them to think about lifecycle analyses.'[59] Manufacturers can also plead ignorance and good faith: after all, it's not their job to build and manage digital infrastructures.

But let's be clear: by not making the driver take responsibility for digital pollution that is directly linked to the use of a connected or driverless car, manufacturers are, in the same way as for electric cars, preparing to displace yet again part of the impact of these vehicles on the environment—from roads to the areas where the data centres and power stations that power them are piling up. The impact will therefore be borne by tech companies (such as FAANG, cloud companies, and interface manufacturers), propping up the illusion that our driving habits are cleaner and more responsible. A disturbing question, therefore, is whether we are already unwittingly sowing the seeds of the next 'connected gate'—the day when the environmental fallouts of these new modes of transport will have to be assumed by motorists.

16,777,216 shades of blue

The driverless car will be like a lounge on wheels, an entertainment area where, our hands off the wheel, we will consume ... even more digital services on social media, Google, or Netflix. So for the key players of the digital economy, the automobile will become a new front in the strategy to capture our attention, and therefore expand the digital universe. From the turn of the millennium, they pinned their ambitions on techniques such as 'design for attention' and 'captology' to make consumers more and more dependent on digital tools. One of the first authors to reveal this new science to the general public was the American consultant Nir Eyal in his bestseller *Hooked: how to build habit-forming products*.[60] It unpacks the 'manipulation matrix' perfected by developers to make us consult our phones no less than 150 times a day: 'triggers' (sensory stimuli or negative emotions that encourage the user to connect) lead to the 'action' of browsing a website, with the expectation of a 'reward' (social recognition, enrichment, satisfying the ego).

This then drives the user to 'invest' more into the digital product to maximise the benefits (personalised recommendations, better-targeted content). Yet at no point does Nir Eyal mention what has made captology even more formidable: the colour blue.

The date is 28 May 2009, and Steve Ballmer is feeling confident. He is announcing the launch of the search engine Bing, developed by the company of which he is the CEO: Microsoft. Ballmer is armed with information anticipating the future performance of Bing—a piece of information worth $80 million. For months, Microsoft's engineers, headed by Bing's user experience manager, Paul Ray, had been pondering what colour to use for displaying the results of its future users' search requests. They'd been leaning towards blue, the colour traditionally used for hyperlinks.[61] But which blue? Paul Ray wanted to find the best blue, one that he hoped would increase Bing's user fidelity, and the number of clicks it prompted. Essentially, Paul Ray believed in the existence of a perfect colour, one that could increase the influence of the one of the world's most powerful multinationals on the subconscious of millions of individuals. But it was a daunting task: there are 16,777,216 shades of blue. The engineers turned to an information-analytics procedure—A/B testing—to assess with consumer panels the appeal of different shades.[62] Soon the tests identified a dark blue that yielded a particularly satisfactory level of engagement. In fact, based on preliminary estimations, Paul Ray was confident that it could generate an additional $80 to $100 million in annual profit.[63] That blue is hex #0044cc.

Was this a stroke of marketing genius, or a publicity stunt orchestrated by Microsoft to get people talking about its new web application? There are diverging opinions. Either way, around the same time, other companies in Silicon Valley were on a quest for the perfect blue. For its email service, Gmail, Google selected a very similar colour to that chosen by Bing, and evaluated its additional annual revenue as $200 million ... again, thanks to A/B testing![64] Perhaps it is not an exaggeration to say that you and I are even more susceptible to monochromes than Patrick Süskind's French men and women were to the fragrance of love in his world-famous novel *Perfume,* and that our emotions have now been taken over by a new generation of the book's main protagonist, Jean-Baptiste Grenouille: the computer.[65] But all these efforts have little impact against the incommensurable power of another colour that has invaded our screens: red.

The mechanics of red

Since the 1970s, scientists have known that red stimulates those exposed to it. 'For humans, it is the most eye-catching of the primary colours because it's the one that is the least found in nature', explains an information-science engineer.[66] It is also a colour traditionally associated with traffic lights and other signals requiring our attention. In that respect, we are socially conditioned to react to red.[67] From 1997, a specialist manual advised developers to make alerts red—and, more specifically, 'high chroma red'—as the contrast with the background colours 'seems to aid a faster response than yellow or yellow-orange'.[68] This claim was later confirmed by a study that demonstrated how a red button on a screen increased the user engagement rate by 21 per cent compared to a green button.[69] Pure coincidence? Apple (in 2000), BlackBerry (2006), and WhatsApp (2009) would soon make red their colour of choice for on-screen notifications that a new message has come in, for instance. Facebook took a similar route in 2010, followed in 2016 by Instagram and Netflix, both of which also changed their logo accordingly.[70] Indeed, red 'is such a harsh colour', explains a Netflix employee anonymously, 'that it's used everywhere to grab attention'.

The mechanics of red are the very same analysed by Nir Eyal: visual stimuli that trigger the user to open a given application in exchange for a reward. This action results in the release of dopamine—a chemical substance called the 'pleasure molecule' because it pushes us to repeat the same action over and over in the hope of continuing satisfaction. Scientists understand this feedback loop perfectly. It stands to reason: armadas of researchers had been observing similar behaviour patterns with mice in laboratories for years before suggesting that companies could do the same with billions of humans to squeeze out more attention ... and more money. And it's not going to change anytime soon. 'Programmers work very hard behind the screens to keep you doing exactly that', explains a neurobiologist.[71] Many a priest may well have presented *Sapiens* as a creature modelled in God's image; as it turns out, we are scarcely more intelligent than rodents.

What are the colours of the future? Everyone has their opinion. Some say that white will be the favourite for developers seeking clean, uncluttered interfaces. Then there's green, nature's signature. What about increasingly fashionable purple? One certainty is that, for a long time to come, colours will remain the links of a vast network of stimuli (such as ringtones, vibrations, and jingles) aimed at insidiously capturing our attention. 'Social media applications are hacking our brains, and we're giving them permission to do it', says a 'sustainable IT' expert.[72] The key to this is that the more time we spend on our screens, the more data we produce ... and the more energy we use. Consider that for videos, high-definition will soon be overtaken by 4K (number of pixels) video resolution, even 8K video resolution, which 'uses 32 times more data than high-definition', according to one report.[73] Another staggering statistic is put forward by a researcher for the magazine *The Conversation*: 'A 10% increase in 4K video in 2030 alone would produce a 10% increase in the overall volume of electricity used by digital technology.'[74] The CEO of Digital For The Planet says that the intellectual and social pollution generated by captology techniques causes environmental pollution: 'These three forms of pollution are interdependent, and so we cannot tackle one without addressing the others.'[75]

How do we resist such strategies? First, we must call out, as did the former engineer at Google, Tristan Harris, the manipulation techniques developed by the big tech companies. The next step is to act. There are a number of solutions aimed at giving users back control of their existence: deactivating notifications, deleting the most addictive applications (Facebook, Snapchat, TikTok, and Instagram), distancing ourselves from social media whose algorithms provoke user indignation (and create traffic on the application), banishing smartphones from the bedroom, or switching off one day a week.[76] There are associations that list bars and restaurants where using a smartphone is forbidden. In Taiwan, any parent caught exposing a screen to a child below the age of two is slapped with a US$1,500 fine. It's simple; 'the Taiwanese see it as a form of abuse', as a neuroscientist explains.[77] Researchers and web designers with the association Ethical Designers propose 'slimming down' the most bandwidth-hungry websites into clean, crisp websites.[78] One such website is Wikipedia. Scrubbed of all energy-intensive video content, the entire website, with its millions of articles, weighs only a few dozen gigabytes—as much as a portion of the memory of a laptop computer. Adopting the Ethical Designers' philosophy of 'ethics by design' also means suggesting fewer 'animations' (such as advertising and videos) on the websites, fewer content recommendations, and disabling the 'like' function, used to grab attention and increase traffic.[79]

Because of the effects of colour, some even advocate the return of black-and-white screens. In 2017, a group was formed under Rehman Ata, a student at Ryerson University (Toronto) and initiator of the aptly named website gogray.today. The digital universe in greyscale seems to foil certain pernicious effects of addictive design, and reintroduces the notion of choice in our daily actions ... and perhaps even claws back some of the control that the FAANGs have taken over our existence by saturating our retinas in blue and red.[80] Apple didn't need much convincing: in 2014, it introduced a feature allowing users to switch their iPhone screen display to black and white.[81] Is this a way to short-circuit social media's lack of enthusiasm to change their practices? Even if a growing, but hard-to-estimate, number of users are choosing greyscale for their screens, this ecology of small actions will fall short of reversing the trend. 'Developers will make sure that this type of scenario doesn't happen', confirms the co-director of Ethical Designers. 'They don't like the kind of features that can wipe out their work in two seconds flat.'[82]

The expansion of the digital universe is about connecting everything and everyone, everywhere and all the time. By pushing, without consideration of ethical questions, individuals to spend more time on the internet; by enhancing bandwidth and image quality; and then, by making billions of internet users interact with connected devices, the digital gurus are ushering in the dawn of the Internet of Everything predicted by Steve Case and Kevin Kelly.[83] But they are going further still. 'Unlike 4G, 5G will change our nature: it is nothing short of the colonisation of man by machine', warns an academic.[84] For humanity is preparing the advent of a largely robotic internet that is already dispensing with human intervention.

And at what cost for the planet?

CHAPTER EIGHT

When robots
out-pollute humans

COLLABORATIVE ROBOTS, DRIVERLESS CARS, COMMUNICATING devices, smart homes, connected infrastructure, digital supply chains, digital clones ... 5G heralds the gradual emancipation of billions of objects and other machines destined to live with—and independently of—humans. This is on the right side of history: in the early-twentieth century, humans talked to other humans; then they began to talk to machines; which then began to talk back. 5G allows more and more machines to talk to one another without any human intervention. Their purpose is to serve *Sapiens*, but the internet is fashioning a world where the digital universe is run not only by human activity. 'Computers and objects communicate with one another without human intervention. The production of data is no longer the domain of our action', confirms Professor Mike Hazas of Lancaster University.[1]

Of course, this phenomenon has an environmental impact, but one we are incapable of calculating, let alone controlling.

This raises a disturbing question: given their digital activity, could robots one day leave an even deeper environmental footprint than humans?[2]

The exponential digital lives of robots

The question is all the more serious when we know that we are responsible for less than 60 per cent of measured global activity on the internet. The remainder is 'artificial attention, produced by robots or by humans whose job it is to do so', writes an author of a book on the attention economy.[3] The internet is effectively a battlefield where 'trolls', 'botnets', and other 'spambots'—often automated—are put to work to dispatch spam emails, inflate rumours on social media, and exaggerate the popularity of certain videos. In 2018, YouTube even deployed tools to detect 'fraudulent' views of videos.[4] IoT has only accelerated such non-human activity: machine-to-machine (also called M2M) connections, especially connected homes and cars, are already expected to account for 50 per cent of connections to the web.[5] As for data production, non-human activity overtook human activity in 2012.[6]

This is only the start, for robots are now answering back ... to other robots. Since 2014, 'generative adversarial networks' have been allowing software to produce so-called deep fakes—videos where a person's face or words are replaced with those of someone else. But there are algorithms in place to destroy these networks. 'No human wrote the codes to produce this content, and machines are running to unmask these deep fakes', says Liam Newcombe, a British engineer specialising in the internet.[7] Another example comes from New Zealand: to ward off spammers (often robots themselves), an association created Re:Scam—a bot that starts a never-ending conversation to waste scammers' time instead of yours.[8]

'The dynamics driving the increase in data production are becoming less to do with the attention of individuals and the time they spend consuming content', says Professor Hazas. FAANGs work to make sure that ever more people spend ever more time on the net, thanks to the explosion of computers, algorithms, and other communicating objects that together have blown apart the physiological limits of online human activity. We are switching from a network used by and for humans, to one used by—if not for—machines. Which means, concludes Professor Hazas, that 'there is no ceiling [on data production]'.[9]

What will be the ecological impacts of a world where swarms of empty, driverless vehicles cruise through slumbering cities, and where armadas of software programs pick through the web, 24 hours a day, while we attend to other pursuits? It's safe to say that the impacts would be colossal, possibly exceeding all digital pollution since the origin of humankind. An example: researchers recently calculated that the massive inputs of data into artificial intelligence could be emitting as much carbon dioxide as the entire lifecycle of five cars.[10] And 5G has changed the rules of the game to the point that our focusing on the repercussions of our digital habits may prove vain and illusory. We are now reaching a new level of digital pollution, a paradigm shift. Let us face the facts of the future: what we are experiencing today is only the start of the digital age—a robotics revolution (or 'robolution') that is accelerating the hybridisation of man and machine.

It is impossible to fully quantify the future pollution of robotics. I nevertheless turned my investigation to a sector of the economy where the explosion of algorithms is already having a dire impact on the environment: finance.

The strategy of planned human obsolescence

The date 23 March 2020 probably does not mean much to most of us, and yet it would come to symbolise a change of era. In the wake of the coronavirus, the world's biggest stock market, the New York Stock Exchange, opened to an empty trading floor, with not a single trader in the ordinarily bustling 'pit'. With no end to the pandemic in sight, listings became entirely automated—a first since Wall Street opened its doors in 1792.[11] This episode exposed the growing role of algorithms in the global financial system. Software is used for its simplicity, its cost efficiency, and the speed at which it can place orders, as evidenced by the increase of trading bots that execute trades in microseconds. 'High-frequency trading is a high-tech, super-quick speculation system', explain the authors of a documentary on the subject.[12] As proof of its efficacy, trading bots perform close to 70 per cent of trades worldwide, representing up to 40 per cent of the value of all traded securities. So it's not surprising that humans have deserted stock exchanges where high-frequency trading is used, for they simply cannot compete with these 'money bots', which, the documentary makers conclude, are now at war with one another.

This has disrupted all players in the financial markets, from investment banks to hedge funds. 'Algorithms were developed from the 1980s. Today, a large part of the 10,000 hedge funds in the world uses algorithmic techniques', explains a macro-economics strategist.[13] To be clear, 'The vast majority of algorithms are very simple', says Juan Pablo Pardo-Guerra, professor of science, technology, and economics. 'Most of them look at the number of people willing to buy a share versus those willing to sell the share; they try to predict short-term profits within a minute.'[14] This is confirmed by an employee of a brokerage firm: 'It's very basic. The machines set out to beat a series of statistics, and 80 per cent of the time that's as far as it goes.'[15] But some of the more sophisticated funds use more powerful computerised tools that can perform far more complex analyses than humans could. These funds are called quantitative ['quant'] funds.

Very few observers could have predicted the emergence of quant funds in the 1970s—a decade dominated by 'fundamental funds' whose investment strategies drew on human intuition and a practical understanding of fundamental economic mechanisms. It was a time when 'everyone was trying to understand the markets, rather than model them', says a former analyst at HSBC Bank.[16] But in 1982, James Simons, a former mathematician at the National Security Agency, created a revolutionary fund called Renaissance Technologies. 'Simons wanted to automate the processing of signals that traditional hedge funds look out for', the analyst explains.[17] It involves lines of code that inject large volumes of data into statistical models in order to identify combinations that best predict profitable market activity. Today, these processes include increasingly advanced non-financial information (such as real-time monitoring of industrial supplies, and logistics flows via satellite images, or market sentiment as expressed on social media).[18] All this can be bought or sold with a time advantage.

With the help of the digital revolution, quants assimilated an increasingly phenomenal quantity of variables and information. Their processing power has surpassed all existing human capacity:

they began, in the 2010s, to outperform traditional funds.[19] Today's hedge funds that continue to resist algorithms could find themselves outclassed, pure and simple. One of the multinationals to have perfected this quantitative-analysis strategy is none other than BlackRock, the biggest asset manager in the world. Since the end of the 1990s, the firm has been using a computerised platform for its forecasts that 'combines sophisticated risk analytics with comprehensive portfolio management, trading and operations tools'.[20] Known as Aladdin, it has around $15,000 billion in assets under management (7 per cent of assets worldwide), and today has developed exceptionally powerful and refined quantitative analytics. The machine can perceive positive market correlations like no human can, and is able to suggest detailed investment strategies adapted to a given market environment.[21] 'BlackRock is better off spending money on a machine than on the salaries of analysts, who are expensive and less efficient', says Juan Pablo Pardo-Guerra matter-of-factly.[22]

Thus the world of finance is finding itself increasingly emptied of humans facing off each other to make the biggest profit.[23] As recently asserted by an academic, it is a world where 'individual personalities play a partial role at best'.[24] It follows, therefore, that in 2020, BlackRock announced that it was laying off several thousand of its employees—increasingly, financial analysts—who had become obsolete because of the superior performance of algorithms.[25] 'The ultimate fantasy of quants is to have employees only to turn a few buttons every now and then to make sure everything works', says the same former analyst.[26] We can guess what happens next. 'Once all the infrastructure works, it doesn't take a lot of imagination to then say: "Perhaps the computer can make [investment] decisions on its own"', postulates Michael

Kearns, a professor of computer and information science.[27]
This was the case of funds such as Two Sigma at Renaissance
Technologies, which has already taken automation a step further
with tools so powerful that they are often associated with the
somewhat catch-all term 'artificial intelligence' (AI).

A multinational on a quest for passive investments

And so alongside 'active' funds, where investment decisions are
made mostly by humans, are a growing number of 'passive' funds,
whereby financial transactions are increasingly put on autopilot.
These are often index funds that track market indices—such as
the S&P 500, based on the 500 biggest companies listed on the US
stock exchanges—and long-term investment in these companies.
This lowers operating costs, resulting in bigger profit margins.
This is the sweet spot for BlackRock, Vanguard, Renaissance
Technologies, and Two Sigma. Passive funds are huge, and in
the US today they invest more than active-management funds.[28]
Quant funds are only the tip of the iceberg. The entire financial
sector is following suit by increasingly becoming a business of
coding, algorithms, and computing.

 Enter the multinational corporation Encana. Long operating
out of Calgary, the largest city in the Canadian state of Alberta,
it is one the biggest producers of Canadian natural gas. In fact,
since 2014 it has been on the Carbon Underground 200 list as
one of the 200 largest owners of hydrocarbon reserves in the
world, giving it the highest carbon dioxide emissions potential.[29]
Featuring on this unhappy list of 'top performers' is not a good
thing for a company, as investors sensitive to climate change tend

to withdraw their capital. Could this situation at least partially explain the sharp decline of Encana's share price in 2018? It's hard to know. Either way, in August 2019, the company's CEO, Doug Suttles, announced the imminent relocation of its head office to Denver in the United States. American stock exchanges were far more advantageous in terms of market capitalisation compared to their Canadian counterparts, Suttles said, as Encana would have access to a broader panel of investors. But not to just any investors: passive funds. 'When we compare ourselves to our US peers, we're about 10 per cent passively held, and they're more than 30', the CEO said. 'So, you can imagine how important that [an increase in passive investing] could be. And, of course, you also know how significant the growth is in passive investment.'[30] Despite some internal resistance, Encana's move (and subsequent renaming to Ovintiv) was sanctioned by the group's shareholders in 2020.[31]

But there is another, more shameful, reason for Encana's relocation. Too bad for its deplorable environmental footprint and the reticence of its investors to take the Carbon Underground 200 seriously. So long as it's listed on the US indices tracked by passive funds, the company can raise funds to finance its growth more easily. In summary, one of the biggest polluters in the world therefore chose to increase its exposure to algorithmic finance that is disposed to supporting industries that exacerbate the climate crisis.[32] It must be emphasised that investment funds run by machines are today contributing to the destruction of the environment more than are funds managed by humans. It's a startling premise, but it is also the conclusion reached by the researcher Thomas O'Neill in his 2018 study *Who Owns the World of Fossil Fuels?* for the British organisation Influence Map.[33] He identified the asset-manager firm BlackRock as the biggest backer of coal amongst its peers: for each million dollars invested in 2018, its passive funds were responsible for the emissions of 650 tons of carbon dioxide (expressed as thermal coal intensity), while its actively managed funds showed a much lower TCI of 300 tons.[34]

O'Neill concluded that passive funds the world over are notoriously overexposed to fossil fuels, much more so than active funds. Today, there is an alliance between robots and the biggest industrial polluters that is systemic.

Why? Because algorithmic funds are configured to seek out profit above all, not to predict melting icecaps. The consequences are grave. First, easy access to liquidity stimulates the market value of companies in the gas, oil, and coal sectors. It even allows them to artificially inflate their market value, even if they underperform.[35] BlackRock, Vanguard, and State Street also hold a quarter of the shares on the S&P 500. Other than these funds being somewhat reluctant to oppose strategies led by the companies in which they are shareholders, their weighting obstructs any vague desire that more environmentally conscious shareholders might have to influence the policies of top management. Evidently, the wave of passive investing is accelerating the climate crisis more than it is resolving it, for it is 'pumping capital into carbon-intensive companies', according to the Sunrise Project report.[36]

Active funds, however, are managed by human beings, who are better able to reconcile the quest for profit with their ecological convictions. Flesh-and-blood investors prove much more agile than algorithmic funds that bet blindly on an index: traditional funds can constantly adapt to the specificities of each sector, 'making a quick exit' where necessary, says a strategist with the Sunrise Project.[37] This goes to explain the sizeable gap between the ecological performance of BlackRock's 'human' investments and its automated investments. And yet there are solutions: passive funds can quite easily offer investments in green stocks by default.[38] 'It's actually quite easy to change the current trajectory', explains our strategist. 'It could be as simple as changing a line of code.'[39]

But passive fund managers argue that their hands are tied by the indices and the algorithms that track them. There is also potential for conflict with their commitments to their clients who, they say, are responsible for their investment choices. So, while managers and investors evade their responsibility, the machine emerges as the champion of fossil fuels. With the intrusion of algorithms, we have placed the 'marketplace on autopilot with no one capable of taking hold of the wheel and steering us down a different path', according to the Sunrise Project report.[40] In 2017, the Hong Kong fund DKV (Deep Knowledge Ventures), went as far as appointing a robot named Vital to its board of directors, announcing that its analysis would need to be collected for all decision-making.[41] The American company EquBot now offers services using artificial intelligence that surpasses the 'inherent emotional and psychological weaknesses that encumber human reasoning', says the company's founder.[42]

Let's not be naïve; there is much grandstanding in these announcements. Nevertheless, they do reveal our fascination with algorithmic perfection. A super-intelligence will never take over global finance: circuit-breakers exist, and central banks have become too powerful and interventionist to be overrun by machines. But our gradual surrender to the power of algorithms is undeniable, and the refusal to change the codes that govern passive funds is highly symbolic ... 'Delegating our decisions to algorithms tends to disempower us', says professor Juan Pablo

Pardo-Guerra.[43] Case in point: the Two Sigma fund, which has made its prodigious IT infrastructure the cornerstone of its success, warns that software errors that could lead to poor investment decisions 'are entirely beyond the control' of the fund![44] If the burden of responsibility shifts from creator to creature, it must itself be assigned, de facto, a part in the fight against global warming—including accountability for possible failure.

This heralds a new world: one where the fight for the survival of humanity can take place without humanity ... Some take this conviction even further, and predict the advent of a super-powerful artificial intelligence with an environmental conscience that can make decisions in the place of humans for the good of the planet: an 'eco-responsible artificial intelligence'.

A super intelligence at work for the planet

In July 2014, the information-technology multinational IBM launched Green Horizon—an initiative designed to help China reduce the pollution in its conurbations where the urban population is ballooning. Researchers were given the core task of developing an IT system capable of predicting 72 hours in advance how bad pollution would be in Beijing.[45] The tool is a source of pride for its developers, for in the first three quarters of 2015, boasted IBM, Beijing's authorities managed to reduce particle emissions by 20 per cent in the Chinese capital.[46] Better still, the company continued, other than predicting pollution levels, Green Horizon could 'eventually offer specific recommendations on how to reduce pollution to an acceptable level—for example, by closing certain factories or temporarily restricting the number of drivers on the road'.[47] We are therefore in the presence of one of the first tools capable of furnishing an environmental strategy, with temporal and spatial scalability, using vast amounts of parameters beyond the processing capacity of one human brain. The tech giant was unequivocal, and called Green Horizon nothing short of AI, artificial intelligence.[48]

This trendy catch-all phrase covers a variety of definitions. 'Strong AI' is a super intelligence so powerful that it can supposedly experience 'emotions, intuitions, and feelings to the point of becoming aware of its own existence', says the Dutchman Lex Coors, one of the stars of the data-centre industry.[49] The more optimistic believe that such an entity will become a reality in the next five to 10 years, once humanity has produced 175 zettabytes of data—enough for an AI to learn and perfect itself by processing data itself through 'deep learning'. Seth Shostak, a senior astronomer at the Search for Extraterrestrial Intelligence Institute with NASA (the National Aeronautics and Space Administration), has even put forward a theory that is equally fascinating and disturbing: the main form of intelligence in the universe is already electronic in nature. Our intelligence, in essence animal, is but a 'transient phenomenon', a step in a process of evolution culminating in the emergence of a post-biological life constituted by machines.[50]

The sceptics belittle this as forever remaining in the realm of science fiction or fantasy. It is for this reason that many people think that our species will more likely live alongside 'weak AI', one that is narrowly gifted for specific tasks that exceed human capacity, but that remain within our control. Until recently, the terms 'AI' and 'environment' were associated in relation to 'green artificial intelligence'—a computerised platform requiring few resources and little energy, and whose environmental impacts are outweighed by the benefits it generates. Now, a new term is entering the debate: 'artificial intelligence for green'.

The fight against climate change is proving to be a wildly complex undertaking. Mitigating the dangers demands a holistic response that can simultaneously tackle sectors ranging from electricity generation, transportation, and housing to farming.[51] It will take formulating long-term strategies and maintaining a constant course of action over decades, whatever the future holds, to reach the desired outcome. This is the price of the planet's salvation. When we see how international communities struggle to lower their global carbon dioxide emissions, we might rightly question our own ability to take on such a challenge. Thus, some scientists are considering the hypothesis of a superhuman, or even strong, AI that alone could undertake such a mission.[52] It would be the ultimate phase of the 'sustainable digital' order discussed at the start of this book: 'green IT' in its purest form. Entrepreneurs have already declared their ambitions. One of them is Demis Hassabis, chief founder of the UK company DeepMind, whose mission, he says, is twofold: 'Step one, solve intelligence. Step two, use it to solve everything else'—that 'everything else' includes climate change.[53] A report published in 2018 by the consulting firm PricewaterhouseCoopers (PwC) puts it plainly: 'It's time to put AI to work for the planet.'[54]

Overconfidence? Quackery, even? Either way, this eventuality—albeit a theoretical one—poses fascinating ethical, philosophical, and democratic questions. How would humanity effectively benefit from a super intelligence that cares about the climate and biodiversity? What dangers would we face as a result? And would we need to build in safeguards to manage—if not stay clear of—the bounds of strong artificial intelligence? 'We're investing billions of euros to improve this technology, progress is fast, and people are starting to wonder: "What happens if we succeed?" That's the question we need to ask ourselves', says Stuart Russell, a British computer scientist known the world over for his work in artificial intelligence.[55]

What would such artificial intelligence be capable of? Many of the academics I spoke to believe it would, for example, reveal hitherto unknown climate events, and expose the mysterious correlations that govern ecosystems.[56] Another researcher believes that artificial intelligence would have the power to reduce our consumption of products with a high environmental impact (such as meat) by manipulating our subconscious motives as consumers, using highly sophisticated marketing techniques. More importantly, a super machine would enable incalculable amounts of data produced by the climate and ecosystems to be aggregated and then transformed as the basis for a long-term conservation policy: 'We need artificial brains to set up an environmental strategy for the next 200 next years', says Lex Coors. 'I don't think humans can. But with an AI, we as humans will therefore be able to be way ahead in terms of planning an environmental strategy.'[57]

This outlook comes with risks: given strong AI's consumption of mineral and energy resources, it could actually do more harm than good to the planet. '[L]eft unguided, it also has the capability to accelerate the environment's degradation', confirms the PwC report.[58] According to pessimistic scenarios, by 2040 AI could monopolise half of the world's energy production.[59] And surely placing all our hopes in AI is tantamount to passing on the responsibility for climate action to future generations? 'We need major political change over the next 10 to 20 years, but strong

AI won't be ready by that time', warns a researcher.[60] Moreover, the fight against climate change would give internet companies an excellent argument to ramp up their AI research. How would we ensure that this tool would be benevolently configured and governed? Not everyone would look kindly on a super intelligence that embraces the philosophy of 'deep ecology'—a radical ecological philosophy founded by Norwegian thinker Arne Næss in the 1970s. According to Næss, '[T]he flourishing of human life ... is compatible with a substantial decrease' in the number of people on the Earth, and '[t]he flourishing of nonhuman life requires such a decrease'.[61]

A 'green leviathan' against humanity

Here I consider the most colossal—and worrying—challenges that come with the advent of strong AI: to what extent could the decisions it would make for the good of the planet turn against humans? Would it deprive us of our freedoms by initiating a curtailment of democracies, for instance? Already today, numerous restrictions are justified as being in the interests of protecting nature (such as refraining from eating meat, not taking the car when pollution levels peak, or travelling by plane). What would happen if a super machine extended or deepened such dictates? Questions such as these should be enough to convince us that this 'green leviathan' would need to share our values—including the most basic humanistic moral standards. For another premise comes into play: there is the possibility that the objectives we assign to an AI would lead it to wipe out the human species.[62] This is a risk taken seriously by some scientists, who say that the best decision an AI would make would be likely be to protect the environment by eliminating those who harm it.[63] Protecting nature would not necessarily go hand in hand with protecting humans in nature. The two goals, far from being compatible, could prove to be diametrically opposed. We could potentially design a hostile AI: Earth-friendly, yes, but not human-friendly. That is why Stuart Russell is opposed to the school of thought that proposes conferring a moral status on nature. Such an approach could legitimise emptying nature of those foreign and harmful to it.[64]

Far from these conjectures, either way we would risk being intellectually surpassed by the solutions that the green leviathan could offer. By surrendering all, we would cede exceptional powers of decision to it. We would subject ourselves to its goodwill in the name of a just and undisputed objective, while being incapable of understanding the decisions it would dictate to us. Will a century governed by an eco-responsible AI still make sense to us? In his fascinating op-ed in a special AI edition of the monthly US magazine *The Atlantic*, Henry Kissinger, the former secretary of state for the American presidents Richard Nixon and Gerald Ford, writes that during the Middle Ages, religion enabled us to structure our understanding of the universe. Then in the eighteenth century it was the Enlightenment; in the nineteenth century, history; and in the twentieth century, ideology.[65] In the twenty-first century we would be unable to decode (in the true sense of the word) any part of our journey to a greener, more sober world. Hence this paradoxical thought: would a world that is entirely based on information be even more mysterious?

But enough philosophical reflection. Far more down-to-earth matters are weighing on the mind of digital players: will we be able to support, technically speaking, the exponential increase of data produced, shared, stored, and processed? Given how much energy and resources digital infrastructure needs, will power grids be able to handle the immaterial tsunami caused by 5G and the internet of everything? Our overconnected society is delivering a radical change of paradigm: the challenges of a world drugged on abundance are now even more colossal than those of a world enslaved to scarcity. Accumulating is in the process of becoming more lethal than lacking. Luckily, some decades ago, the human brain came up with a brilliant invention that promises to stretch further still the limits of the grid, our attention to red and blue, driverless cars, passive funds, and artificial intelligence.

That invention was the undersea cable.

CHAPTER NINE

Twenty thousand tentacles under the sea

NEITHER TECHNICAL LIMITATIONS NOR PHYSICAL boundaries today seem able to impede our quest for virtuality. The production of data may well explode; armies of engineers will retaliate with astonishing innovations. The most arresting illustration of this technological 'solutionism' is in a comment made popular by Al Gore in 1993: 'Well today, commerce rolls not just on asphalt highways, but along information highways', declared the US vice-president in an address that would go down in history.[1] And it was no metaphor; for decades, humans have been building physical routes to consolidate the internet's architecture and to support its formidable expansion so that more and more data can be exchanged at ever-increasing speeds. This escalation is driving the proliferation of the fibre-optic cables to which Al Gore refers.

My first encounter with these threads of the web takes place on the morning of 11 March 2020 on Parée Préneau beach near

Saint-Gilles-Croix-de-Vie in the Vendée department on France's west coast. The clock has not yet struck eight, yet this long stretch of sand, restrained by the rolling waves of the Atlantic, is unusually lively. A group of some 15 people in hardhats and hi-vis safety vests stand looking out to the roiling sea, the sky the colour of anthracite. Bobbing a few hundred metres offshore is a cluster of small boats. Aboard one of them—the unsteady *Miniplon*—four commercial divers await orders from the shore. Also on the beach is Laurent Boudelier, the mayor of the neighbouring town of Saint-Hilaire-de-Riez. 'Dematerialisation is a physical reality', he tells me. 'To send and receive data there needs to be a connection'.

This connection is what brings the local official to Parée Préneau beach, for preparations are underway for a unique event: the 'landing' (installation) of Dunant, Google's second intercontinental internet cable.[2] A 12-fibre-pair cable with a capacity of nearly 300 terabits per second, Dunant is one of the most powerful cables ever commissioned. In a few months, it will cover a distance of 6,600 kilometres to connect the American city of Virginia Beach, south of Washington, to a Google data centre built in the Belgian city of Saint-Ghislain. The cable will cross the French coastline, and it is this first section of the cable, measuring 5 kilometres, that is about to be deployed. 'It's not every day a cable crosses the Atlantic!' confirms Richard Brault, project manager at the company Merceron, which has mobilised two excavators for the job. It's a first in 20 years, in fact ... What will it be used for? 'YouTube, online gaming', explains a member of the team, waiting on the beach, and then 'virtual currencies, which are booming', adds the mayor.

But until the churning, foaming swells of the ocean beating relentlessly against the coast calm down, the operation is on hold. 'We're raring to get out there!' says a worker. But the divers dispatched by the company Atlantique Scaphandre to lay the cable underwater have the final say. The operation would be dangerous if conditions were extreme, and they have been instructed not to take any risks. The weather doesn't show any sign of letting up. If anything, 'It feels like it's getting worse', says Olivier Ségalard, looking up at the clouds. A project manager with the French operator Orange, he is in charge of overseeing Dunant's landing in France.[3] Nine o'clock. It's time to admit temporary defeat: the mission is postponed. The *Miniplon* heads back to the harbour of Saint-Gilles-Croix-de-Vie, while TravOcean's ship, transporting the cable, returns further south to Les Sables-d'Olonne. The work has been held up for two weeks, and for Isabelle Delestre, press attaché for Orange, 'It's starting to become really annoying—every day lost costs us 30,000 euros for the boat and the equipment.'

But there are bigger worries. Google must respect the activities of the Kentish plover. This small, protected shorebird with grey-brown plumage, measuring around 15 centimetres high, has the good sense to nest from mid-March on the beaches of the Vendée—directly along the cable's route. With the nesting season fast approaching, and with administrative opposition to new technologies in its favour, the shorebird prevails. In a few days, Google, one of the most powerful companies in the world, will not be allowed to deploy Dunant until the Kentish plovers' chicks have safely hatched—leaving hundreds of millions of internet users hoping for more bandwidth to chomp at the bit. 'All this for cat videos!' sighs Ségalard. 'Still today, when we give talks at high schools, most pupils think satellites are responsible for communications, when in fact everything transits via cables.'

Illuminating the bowels of the internet

The internet is a gigantic amphibious network. Close to 99 per cent of the world's data traffic travels not though the air, but via the cables deployed underground and at the bottom of the sea. My geopositioning data and meetings on Zoom bear traces not only of the mines of Heilongjiang, Scandinavian rivers, and the Taiwanese sky; they also criss-cross abysses, pass by straits, and traverse deltas. Every passing day, we use hundreds of cables spread over thousands of kilometres. Yet the vast majority of us believe that our calls, photos, and videos fly over our heads—perhaps because antennas (3G, 4G, 5G) come first to mind regarding our digital activity, before the data is passed on to wired networks. After all, says Olivier Ségalard, 'a rocket at take-off is more impressive than a smoking ship!' There's also the fact that, in the 1970s, cables and satellites competed for data traffic, then still in its infancy. 'Back then, the debate was over which of the two technologies were best suited', recalls a former telecommunications cables engineer.[4]

That was before these lines were written; before big data entered the fray ... Given their outstanding transmission capacity and competitive prices, the ocean highways would prevail over space. To fully appreciate this infrastructure, let us dive into the appropriately named 'bowels of the net ... the parallel with sewers is interesting: not terribly glamourous, barely visible, and yet indispensable', explains a telecommunications professional.[5] The undersea cables are made of fine metal encased in polyethylene (plastic), and these enclose the fibre-optic pairs—that is, glass-fibre strands—through which coded information in the form of light pulses (see appendix 9) transit at a speed of around 200,000 kilometres per second.[6]

While the ability to maintain the signal over very long distances is a recent innovation, it relies on an age-old principle. In ancient times, the Amerindians, Greeks, and Chinese sent messages using torches, smoke signals, and fires. Then, in 1690, the French physicist Guillaume Amontons came up with the idea of using semaphores. 'The secret consisted of placing in several consecutive posts persons who had perceived through a telescope certain signals from the preceding post, transmitted them to the following ones, and so forth', explained the French scientist Fontenelle.[7] In 1794, Claude Chappe would refine and apply this system over hundreds of kilometres, a system that would be called the 'Chappe telegraph'. Almost a century later, in 1880, Alexander Graham Bell designed the photophone with which, as he explained so vividly, 'it would be possible to hear a shadow'.

Thus, for millennia, humans have in one way or another come to understand that light is information. 'An email is light. A cat video is light. To bring a cable into service, industry professionals in France even talk about "lighting a cable"', says the director of a telecommunications equipment company.[8] In other words, the internet is no more than a glorified network of semaphores! It is no exaggeration, therefore, that we internet users are literally 'illuminated'... Exceptional progress has been made in fibre technology since the first optic cable, TAT-8, was laid between the United States and Europe in 1988, and which allowed over 40,000 telephone calls to be made simultaneously. Today, Dunant can handle five billion telephone calls, or three times the information contained in the US Library of Congress, per second.[9] This helps to understand how these poetically named 'hairs of light' have conquered the planet, weaving vital infrastructure for our connected lives.[10] Perhaps no one knows this better than the

100,000 inhabitants of the island nation of Tonga, isolated in the middle of the Pacific, who, in 2019, were plunged into a digital blackout after the archipelago's one-and-only undersea cable was severed. The country was 'cut off from the rest of the world', recalls a specialist.[11] For some, never had the expression 'life hanging by a thread' been so meaningful ...

Some 450 'illuminated' tentacles totalling 1.2 million kilometres, or 30 times the Earth's circumference, could potentially refloor the ocean bottoms.[12] This backbone of the net thrives particularly in water. Laying an undersea cable may well cost hundreds of millions of dollars, but it is still 10 times less expensive than digging trenches on land. An atlas of information highways (see appendix 10) maps out an uneven network, from well-serviced hubs such as Djibouti, the Suez Canal, and the strait of Malacca, to deserted areas, such as the Arctic and the waters of North Korea. Some cables are very short, such as Amerigo Vespucci, which spans just over 85 kilometres between the islands of Curaçao and Bonaire off the coast of Venezuela. Others, such as SEAME-WE-3 (standing for South-East Asia, Middle East, and Western Europe), span 39,000 kilometres between Northern Europe and Australia. The network is growing, and it is unstoppable.[13] While these lines were being written, dozens of undersea cables were in the process of being laid on the ocean floor. At this rate, there could be a thousand in operation by 2030. Hence this paradox that didn't escape curator Elizabeth Bruton, as we strolled through the Science Museum of London's cable gallery: 'People think we live in a "wireless world", when in fact we have never been more connected by wires than we are today!'

Cables, white sand, and beach towels

Needless to say, the Atlantique Scaphandre divers will be kept busy for a long time to come. But first, Dunant needs to make landfall. Two days later, on 13 March 2020, at dawn, they are back at work on Parée Préneau beach. The weather is clear; the time is right. A diver pulls a messenger rope from the TravOcean boat to the beach. From the ship, the cable is attached to the end of the rope. On land, a winch gently hauls in the rope, pulling with it the Dunant cable, kept afloat by a procession of yellow buoys. The atmosphere is jovial as we watch the manoeuvres. Then we hear: 'We've got the cable!' Excitement takes hold; voices become animated, and the jokes come thick and fast. 'Let's take a photo!' one person says. Olivier Ségalard sticks the Orange company logo onto one of the buoys, and poses for the photo, grinning ear-to-ear. 'We pulled the cable!' The time is 8.15 am.

Next, it's over to the excavators to dig a 75-metre trench from the sea to a concrete conduit installed below the dune into which the precious cable—just thicker than a hosepipe—is inserted. Workers move quickly to cover it in a cast-iron casing before the tide comes in. Underwater, the divers make sure Dunant is properly laid on the sand, avoiding any rocks. In the evening, a robot resembling a plough will dig a furrow more than a metre deep into the seafloor to bury the cable. It will be connected to a beach manhole (an underground room) set into the shore, and then tested using an optical time-domain reflectometer. A passer-by, bucket in hand, his face a scowl, walks over to ask what the commotion is about. Hearing the answer, the old man protests: 'How about they clean the sea instead of throwing junk into it?

There's nothing good about it... It's pointless! All that for a load of online twaddle and porn.'

Three o'clock. The operation is reaching its conclusion. On the French side, Dunant will be directed towards Paris, then Belgium, via Nantes and Niort. 'As a precaution, we use two different routes', an engineer explains. 'Everything is "replicated" to avoid any mishaps, such as an excavator severing the cable, shutting down all internet traffic.' In July, a ship will pick up the other end of the cable left off the coast of Saint-Hilaire-de-Riez, and connect it to a new section, and unwind to Virginia Beach.[14] On Parée Préneau beach, temporarily renamed 'gates of America' by the mayor, the excavators have finished filling up the trench. The tide will take care of erasing any remaining traces. The beach is again pristine. 'In a few months, tourists will arrive and put down their beach towels on top of Dunant!', exclaims the mayor. 'I wonder if they'll realise the holiday snaps they're sending are travelling below their feet.'

Some weeks earlier, everyone in the European undersea cable industry, from engineers to sales reps, consultants to strategists, met at a huge conference centre in Islington in the centre of London.[15] Courtesy of big data, the internet of things, and artificial intelligence, the industry is rocketing. Overall turnover worldwide is growing by 11 per cent annually, and is expected to reach $22 billion by 2025. 'The industry is booming!' a participant tells me. 'They're building around the clock.'[16] Over the course of debates, meetings, and keynotes, the experts revel in a secret language. Expressions such as 'capacity growth', 'perfected submarine systems', 'development plan', or 'cost per byte' reflect the frenetic logic that has taken hold of the architects of the net.

The industry prefers to keep a low profile. 'One of the best ways of protecting an undersea cable is to not talk about it', says one of its engineers. But I learn that the sector is structured around the owners of the cables (typically, operators such as Deutsche Telekom, AT&T, Telecom Italia, Vodafone, and Orange), manufacturers (such as Alcatel Submarine Networks, SubCom, and NEC), and ship owners, who install and repair the infrastructure (Global Marine Systems Ltd, in particular). Of note: given their strategy of vertical integration, the FAANGs now have their own undersea cables—a serious disruption for telecom operators. This is the case for Facebook, which has formed its own team dedicated to its subsea foundations. And for good reason: in 2013, within a few hours of the social network launching the video auto-play feature, 'it took up so much bandwidth that their IT infrastructure almost went down', a submarine telecom specialist tells me.[17] As the old adage goes, if you want something done properly, do it yourself. Following this move by Facebook, the cable industry has had to accommodate a growing number of internet giants, such as Google and Amazon, who want to control the conduits of their content. 'On the Atlantic route, the FAANGs had 5 per cent market share three years ago. Today they have 50 per cent, and it's expected to increase to 90 per cent in the next three years', remarks a submarine telecommunications expert.[18]

Overheard in London:

- 'The LV-SE [Latvia-Sweden], installed just after the Cold War between Latvia and Sweden, was the most difficult system to deploy. The sea was frozen, and the insurance companies wanted to have the bottom of the Baltic inspected to make sure it wasn't packed with naval bombs.'

- 'From the first idea to the cable's commissioning, you're looking at 10, 15 years. Some deployment projects have never got off the ground.'
- 'Will future seabed mining operations get in the way of installing fibre-optic cables?'
- 'The price of cables per kilometre hasn't changed in decades, but their initial capacity has increased by a billion.'
- 'We're a population of ageing experts in this sector; we're not managing to attract young people.'
- 'I don't see anything better than optical-transmission technology for the next thousand years.'
- 'The more cables you pull towards the north of the Atlantic, the less resistant they'll be over the long term because of potential damage from iceberg debris.'

The backbone of the internet overall is a robust substructure, but apparently it has some local weaknesses, with up to 150 cases of cable damage reported annually.[19] At the end of 2006, a magnitude-7 earthquake shook Taiwan, damaging and severing most of the fibre-optic cables threading the nearby Luzon strait; it took 49 days and 11 ships to restore the connection between Taipei, Hong Kong, and the rest of south-east Asia.[20] Then, in 2017, a storm got the better of the SEA-ME-WE 4 linking Marseille in the south of France to Annaba, Algeria, knocking out 80 per cent of Algerian internet traffic for two days.[21] A year later, a dozen countries in West Africa saw their connection slow down for 10 days after the ACE (Africa Coast to Europe) undersea cable was damaged by a fishing trawler.[22] According to research, the anchors of fishing boats, and cargo ships, are the number-one threat to internet infrastructure, ahead of offshore windfarms and deep-water drilling activities.[23] Beware of the consequences for a fishing boat that inadvertently severs a thread of the World Wide Web with its grapnel! The vessel's captain (or rather the insurer) must bear the costs of repairs, which can be as much as $1 million.

This means that cohabitation with fishermen is not always tranquil. Take the English Channel. Every day, the world's busiest section of sea is used by 800 vessels ... and the SEA-ME-WE 3. 'The cable is sunk in the sands, but sometimes tidal currents bring it to the surface ... While fishing boats can steer clear of the cable, trawlers leave their fishing gear [nets] in place 24 hours a day, so they absolutely must be warned, otherwise it creates cohabitation issues', said a spokesperson of a French fishing association.[24] And we can't have a sardine vessel cutting the remaining ties between the United Kingdom and Europe! The result is that 'fishermen are fed up, and they're digging in their heels', says one of their representatives angrily. 'They used to be more or less alone on the English Channel, and now there's a very bureaucratic take on things, as if the sea has been divided along property lines.'[25] And watch out for sharks, whose 'bites tend to pierce through the cable insulation', points out a report.[26] 'Once they even found a shark tooth in a cable!', related an expert. Even the increase in the number of hurricanes—a consequence of climate change—could worsen shifts in the seafloor, and compromise certain sections of the web.[27]

Critical internet infrastructure is a regular target for acts of sabotage. In 2009, 'vandals' severed four cables in the San José region, in California.[28] Two years earlier, 'pirates' gained notoriety for bringing to the surface an 11-kilometre section of the T-V-H (Thailand-Vietnam-Hong Kong) cable system off the coast of

Vietnam, with a view to selling the salvaged metal as scrap![29] Consequently, there are 'ocean emergency brigades' constantly patching up cables, and dispatching submersibles that can identify the damaged section, before replacing it and restoring internet traffic. 'If cable ships weren't spending their time repairing them, the world's internet would be down in barely a few months', warned an undersea cable specialist.[30] The worst cable? Perhaps the one belonging to Orange—30 metres deep and keeping close company with the Belgian city of Ostend. 'We're on our 91st repair!', huffed a director at the French telco.[31]

Australia and New Zealand took a series of unprecedented decisions from the 1990s: establishing 17 cable-protection zones where all anchoring and fishing activities are banned in order to avoid damaging the strategically important web for these island nations.[32] The fines are punitive, up to 285,000 euros.[33] Silky sharks, pink skunk clownfish, and big-belly seahorses—all endemic to this region of the Pacific—should be invited to converge on these sanctuaries created by humans out of love for the famous online video game, Fortnite, and the latest season of *The Handmaid's Tale*. A steel and plastic cable unspooled in a spot of the ocean could be their last refuge ...

A quest for time savings

Fishing grounds scraped by the anchors of trawlers, protected marine areas, and submarine volcanos are a few of many obstacles that cables must circumnavigate. It's not all that complicated in the vast majority of cases: since information travels at 200,000 kilometres per second, any twists and turns along the way have virtually no impact on the speed of the network. Not a blip in our 'user experience' on Facebook. But for high-frequency trading, it's another story. In the previous chapter, we learned that trading bots declare war over a few milliseconds. A tiny time advantage in trading on the stock market can lead to mind-boggling gains or losses. As is woven into the plot of the Belgian-Canadian film *The Hummingbird Project,* starring Salma Hayek, in which two cousins in New York plan to beat the global financial system by pulling the straightest possible fibre-optic cable between Kansas City and the New York stock exchange.[34] The stakes: a millisecond gained, and a tidy sum of $500 million a year. The storyline is amusing, and there's an entertaining mix of actors.

But it is not fiction.

We go back to 2010, the year when the US firm Hibernia Atlantic announces its plans to build the Hibernia Express cable.[35] More than the first transatlantic route deployed in 12 years, it will be, say its promoters, a 4,600-kilometre cable linking the London and New York stock exchanges ... in less than 60 milliseconds there and back. It is an important number, for there will be a few milliseconds gained over all the cables connecting both sides of the Atlantic. The investments are colossal—around $300 million—but what does that matter? Hibernia Atlantic has convinced itself that the system will be snapped up by trading companies for whom a click of the fingers is still too long, and the bat of an eyelid (100 milliseconds) is an eternity.

Alasdair Wilkie, a British citizen and an old veteran of the cable industry, found himself heading up operations. When I met him in 2020, he was voluble and spoke openly, with no details spared, about the 'two years of [his] life working at a high level, on such a unique cable'.[36] Even a three-year-old child can understand the challenge faced by Wilkie and the 200 people under him: to determine the straightest, most direct, line there is, and to deviate from it as little as possible. The slightest curve, the tiniest bend, and the distance becomes longer. That means time—and therefore money—lost. This arithmetical quest starts by a rough line drawn, with a ruler, on a nautical chart. That's it. Yet the itinerary is intrepid, perilous even: it goes through shallow waters used extensively by trawlers, and crosses the North Atlantic amid drifting icebergs.[37] So unsafe is the route, in fact, that it hasn't been used in a century![38] Wilkie was unfazed. 'As we all said, we're the ones taking the risk, so we're pocketing the money', he recalled.[39]

The environmental diagnostics showed that the line overlapped the ancestral fishing grounds of the Mi'kmaq, a First Nations people occupying three provinces on Canada's Atlantic coast.[40] But for every problem there is a solution: to get in Ottawa's good graces, Wilkie hires two members of the tribe.[41] Once the plans were approved, the future undersea cable's path had to be clear of the 82 old, abandoned cables; should these come loose from the ocean floor, they could take the Hibernia Express with them. Several ships were dispatched over four months to cut 63 sections of cable.[42] Then came the deployment phase. Over four additional months, two boats unwound the Hibernia Express from the towns of Halifax (Canada) and Brean (in the UK), while a third connected both ends in the middle of the North Atlantic. The weather conditions were not always favourable, and off the coast of Canada, a number of oil platforms and two gas pipelines had to be bypassed.[43] On the European side, Wilkie wanted to steer clear of Ireland's territorial waters around Fastnet Rock and its annual toll of 200,000 euros.[44] That meant having to make a two-kilometre detour. 'It takes one millimetre to travel 100 kilometres, so this detour didn't really increase the travel time', Wilkie explained. Once the cable reached the east coast of Canada, all that remained to be done was to direct the information via a network of antennas, 'because light travels faster in the air than through optical fibre', a specialist from the cable industry explained.[45]

On 15 September 2015, the cable was at last ready to go live. The directors of Hibernia Atlantic patted themselves on the back: their fibre-optic cable connected the two terminals in 58.95 milliseconds—5 milliseconds faster than the competition.[46] (See appendix II.) Wilkie popped a bottle of champagne and said: 'We've killed the market!' All the biggest traders switched to the Hibernia Express. 'No one will beat us,' he said.

That is, unless the cable deteriorates, or the low-orbit satellite constellations, such those deployed by Elon Musk and his company Starlink, one day offer a service that is 30 per cent faster.[47] Technically, it's possible. Until then, clients are moving to Hibernia Atlantic in their droves. Trading companies will do whatever it takes to buy and sell faster than their competitors. 'Accessing Hibernia Atlantic cost 100 times more than the "normal" route', explains an anonymous source who operates the cable. 'But our clients handle billions ... If not connecting means losing business, well, you'll pay anything to connect.'[48]

Of interest is that the internet was meant to eliminate distances; yet never had the developers of the Hibernia been so fixated on kilometres. The web is also meant to erase borders; yet every country that finds itself on the route has asserted its rights over its territory. Far from scoffing at geography, the digital industry has glorified it. None know this better than the architects of the web. But have they considered these impacts of its tentacles on the environment?

The second life of undersea cables

Curious operations are taking place this morning in November 2020 on quay number 2 of the Port of Leixões, north of Porto (Portugal). Moored three days earlier, the *Layla*—a red-and-blue cargo ship measuring 60 metres—regurgitates kilometre after kilometre of fibre-optic cables onto land with the help of a winding machine. The 200 reels of cables from the ship's four cargo bays are already neatly lined up on the tarmac, and around 20 repeaters have been placed in a container nearby.[49] Advancing at a pace of 15 kilometres an hour, amid the cries of seagulls, and intoxicated by the fumes of burnt fuel, the crew of *Layla* will need an extra two days to transfer the sections of the CanBer and TAT-9 systems it has brought up from the bottom of the sea onto the quay. These two names open a window into the history of telecommunications. In 1971, CanBer was deployed between Canada and Bermuda; 20 years later, TAT-9 connected the United States and Spain—in time, inter alia, for North American viewers to catch every moment of the 1992 Olympic Games in Barcelona.

'Because of technological progress, these cables were deactivated eight or nine years ago', explains the ship's captain, Rudi Reinders, a Dutchman in his fifties with an averted gaze. His cargo ship was sent out off the coast of the state of New York (US) and Nova Scotia (Canada) to salvage several sections of cable measuring a total of 1,189 kilometres. I had asked if I could observe the operation, but Mertech Marine, the company that chartered the *Layla*, advised me it would involve a three-month journey at sea. That took the wind out of my sails. Captain Reinders led me to the cargo bays, where I laid my eyes upon the undulations of a 1,300-tonne 'sea serpent'. Despite decades spent underwater, the beast looked new. Suddenly, I was reminded of Swedish Lapland. Just like in the Hydro66 data centre, in the hold of the *Layla* I discovered that the internet has a colour: the yellow of the TAT-9, the pale green of the CanBer, and the black of the repeaters. But it also has the inflexible rigidity of a crowbar, and a salty taste, for the cables are still wet.

Not that Reinders notices any of this anymore, having already hauled 30,000 kilometres of cable from the depths of the Atlantic and the Pacific since 2014. He resists being called an ecologist, but concedes that he is sensitive to the environment. 'Before rolling out a new cable, you should start by removing the old ones! It's good to clean the sea'. Today, there are a million kilometres of out-of-service fibre-optic cables—so-called 'zombie cables'—lurking on the ocean floor. They have a useful lifespan of around 25 years, after which their owners 'don't have the moral courtesy to recycle them. I don't know a single one who listened to their environmental conscience', said an industry insider.[50]

Which raises the question of the cables' environmental impact. Some researchers wonder whether they strongly increase the magnetic field of the seabed, thereby affecting surrounding ecosystems.[51] Their presence could also favour the development of alien plant and animal species in local habitats.[52] In 1957, a researcher discovered that whales had strangled themselves in old telegraphic cables, but there have been virtually no such events since.[53] Some cables can threaten protected marine areas, despite the cable owners being required most of the time to avoid them. Overall, the underwater web is supposedly almost harmless for the environment. The industry is nevertheless on its guard; it wouldn't want debates on the health risks of 5G linked back to its activity. 'It's complicated enough as it is getting permission from authorities, but if we also have to deal with Greenpeace or a marine animal-rights group who wouldn't understand that cables are not toxic, we wouldn't see the end of it', an undersea cable specialist told me in confidence. None of this rules out the question set to become all the more relevant as we colonise every crevice of the ocean: what will we do with all the obsolete cables piling up?

Nine thousand kilometres from the Port of Leixões, in the South African city of Cape Town, Alwyn du Plessis, the head of Mertech Marine, runs a business that generally leaves people agog: recycling the parts of the World Wide Web abandoned at the bottom of the ocean. 'From a carbon footprint point of view, recycling always makes sense comparing to mining', he told me.[54] Since 2008, three Mertech Marine ships have extracted tens of thousands of tonnes of fibre-optic cables.[55] The steel and copper they contain are recycled at a Mertech factory, and used to manufacture anything from fences to electronics, while the repeaters are passed onto the South African Nuclear Energy Corporation (NECSA). Listening to du Plessis, his job is no picnic: buying the cable from the owners can cost as much as two million euros; recovery costs are astronomical; the raw materials market volatile ... all challenging Mertech Marine's economic model.[56]

Then there is the small matter of finding the cables! Some lie 7,000 metres deep in the middle of the Earth's vast waters. At these depths, they are impossible to detect by radar, which means having to use on-board resources as plan B. 'We use maps showing the coordinates of the cables, and snag them by dragging a hook across the seafloor', explains du Plessis. Sometimes two days are enough to fish out a cable, as was the case for TAT-9 pulled out by the *Layla*. But some operations can drag on for two weeks, with currents carrying the entrails several hundred metres off course. The weather sometimes complicates matters, as Rudi Reinders can attest to: his crew had to ride out three hurricanes ('Epsilon, Paulette, and Teddy', he rattles off) during the previous expedition. 'The work is very physical', said du Plessis. Not to mention counterintuitive: what could possibly be the link between super calculators and hyperscale data centres, and a string of sailors handling a miserable grapnel in the middle of the Atlantic? But these seacombers may very well be seen as trailblazers. And with the exponential growth of cables, countries such as Australia—pioneers in marine preservation—could one day require the co-owners of the backbone of the global internet to recover their strands of light from the seafloor.

Heading towards a 'capacity crunch'?

The reality is that the true environmental impact of the web lies in what this optical underworld allows us to do. Just as railways were the first step in conquering the American west, the Dunant's commissioning in January 2021 made virtual reality, IoT, and 'deep learning' possible. 'We can make the analogy with the road network: as it grows, so do the number of cars that use it. Similarly, more capacity begets more appetite for capacity', according to an undersea systems expert.[57] 'The data market is maintained by people—the FAANGs—who build their own highways, and more and more of them', agreed another expert. 'So there's no need for them to set themselves a limit.'[58] The pollution caused directly by undersea cables is insignificant, but they are allowing the digital universe to expand, bringing with it more devices, data centres, and energy infrastructure.

When Covid locked us down for part of 2020, we learned to hold meetings on Zoom, and meet for drinks with friends on WhatsApp. This new digital behaviour caused traffic to explode, and YouTube and Netflix were forced to lower the quality of their streaming services to cool down the networks.[59] 'In ten years' time, we'll spend the next pandemic wearing virtual reality headsets!' predicted a professional from the undersea cable industry.[60] 'Because consumers will want to, but mostly because technological advances in communication will mean they can.'

Yet back in 2015, Andrew Ellis, professor of engineering and applied sciences at the University of Aston in Birmingham in the UK, sounded the alert. He observed that we were producing more data than the network could handle, and that, effectively, we would exceed the system's capacity in eight years' time—that is, in 2023.[61] The term he used was 'capacity crunch'. Echoing these statements, the undersea cable industry recognises that we are approaching what is known as the 'Shannon Limit', which is the maximum quantity of information that optical fibres can send down the line.[62] The industry also admits that bottlenecks exist—in the straits, for instance, where high numbers of strategic cables converge. An incident in any one of these clusters could have continental, if not global, consequences.

This is the case for the Brazilian city of Fortaleza. 'It is a single point of failure for all undersea cables from Brazil to the United States', wrote an academic. 'If Fortaleza were shut down, all data traffic that flows north and south would come to a halt.'[63] This is also true for Alexandria, Egypt, where five of the most important transnational cables intertwine, and for the Luzon and Malacca straits.[64] It is important to note that bottlenecks result not only from a glut of cables, but also from a lack of cables, which renders a country entirely dependent on just a handful of lines. (This is the case in New Zealand, which relies on only three cables.) Ownership of a system by just one entity also increases the threat of denial-of-service, and the risk of regulatory obstructions.[65] In 2011, Indonesia decreed that only boats flying the local flag, and manned by a local crew, could carry out repairs in its territorial waters. Except that there were no boats available then, which led to delays and blockages.[66] A shortage of human resources capable of urgently handling a serious incident could also paralyse the system.[67]

But the world is hardly about to seize up due to a lack of bandwidth. Transmission technologies are constantly improving, and the fibre-pair count of cables is continually increasing. Some believe that over the next two decades, quantum technology might open up the possibility of 'data transmission without transmission', as physical particles will no longer need to travel between the transmitter and the receiver.[68] The network will also be resilient because the architects of the internet will redefine its geography: the multiplication of edge data centres (see chapter six) will allow data to be processed more locally, relieving the burden on transcontinental networks. However, Andrew Ellis retorts that even if all these measures defer the risks of a capacity crunch to beyond 2023, they will not solve the fundamental problem of our data addiction. Moreover, it would mean having to continuously defer a problem that we are tirelessly growing.[69]

This makes perfect sense. Yet what's stopping the fabulously wealthy FAANGs from just reeling out new cables, no thicker than a domestic hosepipe, capable of handling even more terabytes? The planet is big enough to accommodate an infinite number of them. This thought leads to another, even more interesting, thought: does the fact that technology is always one step ahead mean that we will never see the end of this saga? Will we come up against other ceilings yet unimagined? For other factors could hold back this quest for perpetual technological advancement: our own personal limits. The first of these, I believe, could be the protection of our physical health. In 2011, the International Agency for Research on Cancer of the World Health Organisation classified radiofrequency electromagnetic fields as potentially carcinogenic.[70] Could this classification be the first in a long series of warnings for us to use digital technologies with more moderation? The second factor could be the preservation of our mental wellbeing, as demonstrated by the extensive literature addressing the psychological effects of mobile phones and social media on individuals. The third factor is quite simply the protection of our privacy, and ultimately our democracies, which have been weakened by the collection of data, and the violent potential of social networks. And let's not forget the ecological impact of the internet, whose material input per service unit (MIPS) (see chapter three) is only growing as we dig deeper into the ground for resources. We may one day reduce our use of the internet; not because the networks will no longer have the capacity, but for the sake of our species, the environment, and because our values dictate it. Put plainly, the limits of the internet will be less technical than sociopolitical.

But these questions are barely raised while the internet continues to expand. We continue to produce more data, catapulting it at increasing speeds along the information superhighways. And rather than curb this trend, the geopolitics of cables is accelerating it.

CHAPTER TEN

The geopolitics of digital infrastructure

IT IS NOW IRREFUTABLE THAT OUR DIGITAL LIVES ARE duplicated in an infrastructure of metal, concrete, and glass, in which we are all distracted and indifferent cohabitants. When walking along a beach, our phones in our pockets, we leave footprints not only in the sand, but in Scandinavian data centres that store our geopositioning data. When taking a selfie on the terrasse of a café in Paris, we produce pixels that a ribbon of glass will propel as far as—who knows?—Virginia Beach. We are literally mirroring ourselves, all the time. The internet bestows on us this gift of ubiquity, and gives our actions physical consistency both here and thousands of kilometres away. Under the pretext of dematerialising everything, digital technologies materialise twofold what we do. But with the material world comes presence, occupation, power plays, and geopolitics. As we tweet, like, post, swipe, and surf, tightening the mesh of the web as we do so, crucial questions arise. Which regions, some unspoiled, will become new information highway epicentres? Which states or companies will control them? And by what means, including military, will they protect them?

In April 2020, at the headquarters of Telecom Egypt in the Smart Village business park east of Cairo, the news exploded like a thunderclap: Israeli media revealed that Google, together with other telecom operators, planned to lay its Blue-Raman fibre-optic cable between Mumbai and Genoa, bypassing the Suez Canal altogether.[1] A first! The Suez Canal today offers the shortest data-transmission route between Europe and Asia.[2] For decades, the ancient cradle of the Pharaohs has known just how important a route it is. It squeezes millions of US dollars in tolls from operators. Indeed, 'It costs as much money to cross the 200 kilometres of Egypt landline as it does to lay the fibre from Singapore to France', grumbled an expert from the undersea cable industry, probably exaggerating the numbers.[3] But to route the Blue-Raman cable, as Google plans to do, through Israel—a state not recognised by many of its neighbours! (See appendix 12.) So Google has come up with a diplomatic workaround to offend as few Arab capitals as possible: one portion of the Blue-Raman will run from India to Jordan via Saudi Arabia; the other portion will pick up the signal and pass through Israel to Italy. Same content; different packaging. Riyad will be able to save face, and swear that it never had any dealings with the Jewish state.

Other than halving transport costs, and only very slightly increasing latency, going via Israel will also diversify information-highway routing. By doing so, Google is securing the transport of data, which will no longer be at the sole mercy of Egypt. In the same spirit, the future Europe-Persia Express Gateway (EPEG) cable, operated by Vodafone, among others, will pass though Iran, again drawing the ire of Cairo. (See appendix 12.) Thus the redrawn world map of undersea cables exposes new geopolitics, whereby regions and states stand to gain from advantageous positioning: the Suez Canal, but also Great Britain, the Strait of Malacca, Djibouti, and Washington State. But these planetary hotspots also stand to lose out as other countries offer to expand the reach of the web: Australia, France, and Brazil, which recently connected to Portugal without crossing, as is customary, the United States.[4]

It has been observed that with the continuing diversification of the network comes a relative decrease in the US domination of the internet's architecture.[5] The same has happened to the UK — possibly on account of the legal grey areas related to Brexit. 'They haven't had any new projects in four or five years', said one expert.[6] But the same is true for Europe overall, as it faces heightened competition from Asian cables transporting African data.[7] For the sake of influence and economic growth, but also the resilience of the network, it's in every stakeholder's interest not to sit on the sidelines, but to be at the very centre of this fibre-optic web that is growing unstoppably. Could this go as far as ejecting Egypt and the Middle East from their plum position on the routes between Europe and Asia?

One cable, in particular, could be a complete gamechanger; an inconceivable project to lay fibre-optic cable through an extreme route never before taken: the Arctic Ocean.

The new Arctic highways

The North Pole lacerated with 'strands of light'? The project is not new; in the early 2000s, the Russian company Polarnet planned to link London to Tokyo via the Northeast Passage with its ROTACS cable.[8] It was a mammoth undertaking worth nearly $2 billion, and financed by a Russian oligarch, Oleg Kim. (See appendix 13)[9] The cable was due to be commissioned in 2016, but it never was. Some blamed the financial sanctions imposed by the West after Russia's annexation of Crimea in 2014 for this outcome.[10] During the same period, the Canadian company Quintillion decided to undertake the same task with its Arctic Fibre cable to connect Tokyo to London, but via the Northwest passage. (See appendix 13.)[11] The first portion of the cable was laid and put into service in 2017 along Alaska's northern coasts.[12] The resources required for the next phase were mind-blowing: 14 icebreakers, and 275 authorisations and permits. And then a scam was uncovered: to secure additional financing, Quintillion's CEO, Elizabeth Pierce, used forged documents to fool investors that the cable had already found its clientele.[13] The $250 million spent would connect a grand total of 13,000 people living in northern Alaskan villages—almost $20,000 per connected user! At that point, the Arctic Fibre project seemed severely compromised.

It was against this backdrop, in 2019, that a third player entered the scene: the Finnish company Cinia and its cable, Arctic Connect. The path so far would connect the UK to China via Norway, the Kola Peninsula (Russia), the Northeast Passage, and Japan.[14] A five-party consortium agreed on an estimated cost of around one billion euros, with commissioning set for 2023.[15] For Cinia, there are only advantages: the cable will serve, across three continents, 85 per cent of the global population. And perhaps what was said of rail can be said of cables. With Arctic Connect, the Finns are about to open up the fastest and straightest line possible between Europe and Asia. Its total distance will only be 14,000 kilometres—12,000 kilometres shorter than going via the Suez Canal. This would place the two continents 150 milliseconds away from one another, thereby relegating the 'Egyptian route' and its interminable 250 milliseconds to the ranks of the common, longer backroad taken by hard-up drivers. This will be much to the delight of traders in London, Frankfurt, and Tokyo, service providers, and, who knows, 'Japanese gamers who'll want to play online with French gamers', believes the Finnish academic Juha Saunavaara.[16]

However, severe weather conditions will most certainly put a damper on deployment and maintenance operations. 'If it were me heading up the installation of such a cable, I would demand a rock-solid technical work package', said a specialist. On the bright side: the melting of the ice caps makes easier work for the icebreakers. As a consequence, this e-colonisation of the Arctic will put on the radar regions hitherto kept in the margins of the fibre-optic web. Transporting data also means storing data: 'Finnish cities such as Rovaniemi, Kajaani, and Raseborg could become hubs for the data-centre industry', predicts Juha Saunavaara. 'Activity in Luleå, Sweden, could also increase.'[17] Even the 3,500 residents of Kirkenes, a tiny town in Norway's extreme north, are getting top billing. Located on the path of the future cable, Kirkenes may well host data centres, and possibly become a 'hub for global data-communication'.[18]

Arctic Connect might also benefit Russia, which sees itself as a polar power. As a company-financer of the cable, Moscow may want to turn certain Siberian cities, such as Murmansk, soon to be served by fibre, into the queen of data, the new oil. This, of course, would enhance Moscow's digital stature. All told, the cable 'will shift the geographical centre of gravity of the data traffic transiting between Asia and Europe', wrote a Norwegian online newspaper covering the Arctic region.[19] And a specialist adviser foresees that 'it would also mean [the advent of] "different geopolitics"'.[20] These shifting dynamics are hard to follow, but for Cinia it is already a sure bet that Arctic Connect will be respectful of the environment.[21]

The impact of the economic activity stimulated in the middle of the polar landscape by the arrival of the noble fibre is another story altogether ... 'Ethically speaking, I wouldn't feel comfortable contributing to a project like this', a consultant told me in confidence. 'It will just mean more data centres popping up along its path! And none of that's good for the environment.' But enough with the misgivings. While Arctic Connect will increase the exposure of the North Pole, China is using its maritime highways to displace the balance of cable geopolitics towards the Far East and Eurasia.

When China paves its 'digital silk road'

In 2015, the National Development and Reform Commission—China's main economic regulator—published a report that, decades from now, may be remembered for its role in changing the face of the Earth. In it, Chinese bureaucrats outlined a vast transnational fibre-optic cable construction program to 'create an Information Silk Road'.[22] Already two years prior, President Xi Jinping had launched the 'Belt and Road Initiative'—a titanic project to construct road, rail, and port infrastructure from China to west and east Africa, via Central

Asia and the Indian Ocean. By 2027, $1,200 billion will have been invested in around 60 countries to realise this ambition, onto which Beijing has now tacked a digital program.

As stated by the Chinese leader, the aim is to strengthen international cooperation in artificial intelligence, nanotechnologies, quantum computing, and cloud computing.[23] China plans to invest $79 billion to install telephone and surveillance technology equipment, build smart cities, and, of course, lay an ambitious undersea cable network. Beijing is believed to have put into service—or is currently laying—fibre-optic networks in 76 countries, from its nearby neighbours to as far as Latin America. One of the most emblematic of these is without a doubt the PEACE (Pakistan and East Africa Connecting Europe) cable, which, in 2022, connected the cities of Karachi in Pakistan and Marseille in France. (See appendix 14).[24] The fibre-optic network is already equipped with the BeiDou Navigation Satellite System (BDS) for ultra-high-performance geopositioning and navigation services (now referred to as the 'space silk road'). In summary, for Beijing, 'silk roads' are simply inconceivable without information technology—the veritable 'digital glue' of infrastructure built on terra firma.[25]

China has three outcomes in mind:

- The extension of its economic interests. By multiplying its fibre-optic networks, China can extend to the rest of the world the digital services of its own FAANGs, the BATXs: the search engine Baidu; e-commerce site Alibaba; online gaming and mobile app group Tencent; and connected-devices firm Xiaomi.[26] The BATXs have a total commercial value of $1,885 billion. 'With undersea links such as PEACE, and the additional bandwidth, internet users the

world over will be more inclined to use Chinese platforms',
predicts an undersea telecommunications expert.[27]

- The expansion of its political model. Beijing's digital
  silk road already allows it to market its surveillance
  technologies around the world. This was how the Chinese
  company CloudWalk was able to sell its facial-recognition
  software in Zimbabwe, and its competitor Yitu was able
  to sell its software to the Malaysian government. The
  tech giant Huawei recently helped the governments
  of Uganda and Zambia to intercept the encrypted
  communication of their political opponents and to
  monitor their movements.[28] Also for sale: tools developed
  by Alibaba and Tencent to filter internet content and
  moderate social media.[29] To quote a prominent European
  newspaper, 'China is looking to export its authoritarian
  cyber surveillance model.'[30]

- The protection of its security interests. By building its own
  communication infrastructure, China intends to counter
  what it sees as 'an intolerable "network hegemony"' of
  the West over the central architecture of the internet.[31]
  Such a situation is not compatible with the security of
  the Chinese communication networks; in the words of
  Xi Jinping, 'without network security, there would be
  no national security'.[32] The strategists of the Chinese
  Communist Party (CCP) are in fact convinced that 'the
  struggle for information dominance will greatly influence
  the outcome of future wars', according to one researcher.[33]

This analysis of Beijing's strategy indicates to what extent it is laying down, day after day, the milestones of a 'veritable geopolitical road map, while we, in the West, are just doing business', a specialist told me anonymously. The role of fibre-optic cables in the expansion of China's soft power is essential, crucial even, given all infrastructure set up along the new silk roads. 'Transporting raw materials is important; transporting data has become even more so', Jean Devos, a former director of Alcatel Submarcom, said.[34] Of course, there will always be commentators to paint this program with noble intentions. A Chinese academic is quoted by the official press agency of the CCP as saying that the digital silk road, through the collection and analysis of environment data, will promote sustainable development, green growth, and human wellbeing.[35]

You would have to be a complete fool to give an ounce of credit to such obsequious statements. It bears repeating: caring about the environment is not in the internet's DNA—if it were, the internet might not even exist, or at least not in its current form. The reality is far more prosaic. The internet is a new instrument in the quest for power and money. Beijing has clearly recognised that in the twenty-first century, digital entertainment will be only one of many means for continuing the war. We will continue to consume more digital content, not only because cables will have greater capacity, and data centres will be more advanced, but because data is the new fuel of the eternal engines of history. And that is the quest for power, prestige, influence, and prosperity, to which China and its rivals aspire. Consequently, the geopolitics of the internet and the new balance of power crystallised by the network will only enhance the might of the digital industry—and therefore its ecological impact.

Fibre-optic systems versus cable ships: the Global Marine saga

But a whole world stands between dream and reality. For Beijing must first control all fibre-optic cable technologies, from manufacture to deployment. It's a domain where the Chinese had been judged as being too far behind to possibly catch up with the likes of the US, the UK, France, and Japan. Enter Huawei. In the early 2000s, the multinational was already industrialising optical technologies and terminals, but lacked expertise for manufacturing cables. According to an anonymous source, it had only recently acquired via one of its subsidiaries 6,000 kilometres of cable from the French company Nexans ... which it then proceeded to copy. Huawei knew how to manufacture repeaters, but 'acquired' the know-how for connecting and sealing them from Alcatel and SubCom contractors.[36] And then there was the industrial segment that accounts for 20 to 30 per cent of fibre-optic cable installation costs: cable ships.

Well into the 2000s, Huawei approached the UK company Global Marine—one of the biggest undersea cable installers in the world. Huawei pitched its ambitions in internet cable installation, and its expertise in fibre-optic systems. Global Marine had its eye on the Chinese market. It made sense to join forces. And so, in 2008, the joint venture Huawei Marine Networks was born.[37] Several British consultants also weighed in with their expertise. What followed remains unclear. According to numerous sources—who did not, however, substantiate their views—the joint venture facilitated, over a period of ten years, the transfer of Global Marine's technology to Huawei. It didn't stop there. 'The British consultants [also] opened their network to the Chinese: suppliers of aluminium, copper, electronic components, welders, stranding machines, etc. An entire ecosystem that was foreign to Huawei. The Chinese caught up by 10 years in the whole affair', Jean Devos said.[38]

The joint venture prospered until 2019, when Global Marine sold its stake in Huawei Marine Networks—including its fleet of cable ships—to the Chinese company Hengtong Optic-Electric for $285 million.[39] It was whispered that the US investment firm HC2 Holdings, Global Marine's sole shareholder, had been unable to resist the siren song of such a lucrative financial transaction. The acquisition propelled Hengtong to another level entirely, as it become one of the rare companies to control the entire fibre-optic value chain: cables, repeaters, terminals, and fleet. 'They can go up to anyone and offer a turnkey system', Devos said.[40]

In the space of 20 years, Beijing succeeded in executing its strategy to become autonomous in the vastly critical sector of fibre-optic cables. 'They operated in this industry just as they've done in other industries for the last 15 years: by going out looking for expertise abroad to train their own engineers, and work their way up to the level of Western powers', comments according to an expert.[41] The West only has itself to blame. First for accommodating the Chinese with condescendence—if not arrogance—doubting their talent, and even trying to bar them access to a market to which they had a rightful claim. And then 'we are completely naïve', Jean Devos said. 'We didn't think the Chinese could pull it off, and when they did, we couldn't believe it!'[42]

Meanwhile, Huawei Marine Networks (now called HMN Tech) continued to 'Sinicise the situation', as put politely by a professional in the industry.[43] Mike Constable, a New Zealand citizen, quit his job as CEO of Huawei Marine Networks in August

2020. 'What that means is that once they've used the Westerner to help drum up business, they dispense with them', according to a consultant.[44] Faced with the unavoidable Chinese awakening, will Westerners opt for peaceful cooperation or confrontation? Unless, in our frantic quest for speed and power, we don't even bother to think about it ... Will it come down to the intention to have an intention?

By inspecting the depths of the ocean too closely, we are missing the higher ground from which to see where this nascent century is heading. And does China intend to install its own worldwide web, parallel to and independent of the current internet? It only takes a quick glance at a world map to see the fibre-optic loop that Beijing is weaving over the globe, particularly via the southern hemisphere. China's sudden emergence in the cable industry clearly signals a formidable reversal of history. The era of Europeans pulling cables called 'Fraternity' and 'Friendship' to Africa has given way to a new era, in which Beijing prepares to land its PEACE cable in Marseille, causing the French to fret about the risk of espionage that this entails.

When armies guard the web

Things are moving fast. With its digital silk road, China will now need to secure its cable infrastructure—an ideal target in the event of a conflict. The West, preoccupied with the security of its information highways, has already identified this challenge: 'The risk posed to these ... connections that carry everything from military intelligence to global financial data is real and growing', Rishi Sunak, now UK prime minister, highlighted in a report during his time as a British member of parliament.[45] The slightest attack, he continued, would be 'potentially catastrophic', with the ability to cause 'significant economic disruption and damage military communications'.[46]

By Sunak's account, Russia would not Be averse to severing telecommunication cables, as it did when it invaded Crimea, to control the flow of information during a time of war. Or Moscow could use its submarines to tap into cables carrying information. It's not impossible. In fact, Washington, Beijing, and Paris already do just that.[47] The reality of such a threat is a subject of debate. Either way, China's new material interests along the silk road—both physical and digital—are already subject to regular attacks.

This is evident nowhere more so than along the China–Pakistan Economic Corridor (CPEC): 3,000 kilometres of communication networks combining road, rail, and electricity infrastructure between the city of Kashgar, in the Xinjiang region, and the Gwadar Port in Pakistan, on the shores of the Arabian Sea.[48] It traces the overland extension of the PEACE cable. But the CPEC—and therefore the cable—crosses deeply unstable regions, starting with Baluchistan in southern Pakistan. China's interests there come under regular assaults orchestrated by Baloch separatists, who doubt that the silk roads will benefit their communities: an armed attack at a hotel in Gwadar where Chinese expatriates were staying; an ambush of a convoy of oil workers; an attempted attack of the Karachi stock exchange, partially held by Chinese companies ...[49] Beijing must contend with threats such as these that grow as its international positions multiply. What can its army do under such circumstances?

Traditionally, the CCP was hardly inclined to extend the reach of the People's Liberation Army (PLA). In 1998, China had made it clear that it 'does not station troops or set up military bases in any foreign country'.[50] In the past, China swore time and time again that it would not interfere in the domestic affairs of the countries where it was present. But, clearly, this doctrine is changing. The foremost example of this is the installation of Beijing's first permanent military base in Djibouti in 2017. And since 2016, local authorities have given PLA units free reign to patrol parts of Afghanistan and Tajikistan close to China's eastern borders besieged by terrorist threats. This raises the inevitable question: will the Middle Kingdom dispatch its army to its direct or indirect neighbours to protect the infrastructure—ports, railways, fibre-optic cables, satellite ground stations—it builds along the silk roads? For many analysts, the answer is quite clear. Especially since Beijing has quite openly stated that 'where national interests expand, the support of the military force has to follow'.[51]

When can we expect to see this realised? No one knows, but it seems logical that China's military presence will expand so long as the crises—namely, terrorist attacks—justify it. In what form? It's a difficult question. The Chinese army lacks qualified personnel, as well as skills in the operational command of armed forces.[52] Then there's the matter of the country's reputation, at a time when the Covid-19 crisis cast China in a poor light internationally. On the other hand, Beijing has access to a pool of three million professionals employed in 5,000 private security companies. A handful of them currently have agency outside China's borders: the China Cityguard Security Service, active in Pakistan; the China Overseas Security Group; and, most notably, the Frontier Services Group. Founded in 2014 by Erik Prince, former director of the US firm Blackwater Security, Frontier

Services Group's primary shareholder is the Chinese financial conglomerate CITIC (China International Trust and Investment Corporation).[33] These private security companies could discreetly protect China's infrastructure. But would that be enough to take on such a colossal task?

To stealthily develop its international presence, Beijing's strategists apparently decided to turn commercial ports, today controlled by the Chinese private sector, into naval bases. This was the case for Gwadar, the PEACE cable landing point. Proof of the importance of this logistics node? In 2015, Gwadar was taken over by the company Chinese Overseas Ports. But according to Jonathan Hillman, researcher and author of a book on the new silk road, the Pakistanis invited the Chinese to dock their warships there, probably in 2014. 'I don't know how enthusiastic the Chinese were about it', he points out. 'In the short term, it is unlikely that Beijing will set up a military base in Gwadar like the one it has in Djibouti. But it wouldn't surprise anyone if such a scenario one day came to be.'[34] The possibility has nevertheless 'generated considerable concerns [particularly among US forces] about the potential for Chinese military expansion', according to one academic, and could raise tensions with the US, and with China's neighbouring countries.[35]

Is China merely seeking, in all sincerity, to protect its material interests, always choosing the diplomatic route from the outset? Or are the silk roads just a 'advanced pretext to deploy its military presence abroad', as Hillman thinks?[36] Answering these questions would mean unlocking the persistently opaque intentions of the CCP. And here is where ignorance gives way to blindness: we fail to comprehend that we are engendering a world where satisfying the hunger for entertainment will be a source of tension—if not conflict—because it will come at the cost of spatial and material impacts from which we can never escape. In the twenty-first century, states will be prepared to go to war so that we can amuse ourselves. Regardless of what the proponents of dematerialisation say, we will continue to be governed by the fundamental particles of matter, just as much as by time's arrow, the force of gravity, and the laws of thermodynamics.

Europe's quest for digital sovereignty

In the shorter term, China's ascension in the cable industry doesn't necessarily entail Western reliance on infrastructure 'made in China', the operation of which could be hampered by the CCP. There is substance to such concerns, the Trump administration having barred in 2020 the PLCN cable that should have connected Hong Kong to Los Angeles.[57] The problem was that one of the investors in the cable, alongside Facebook and Google, was Hong Kong investor Pacific Light Data Communication. This stoked fears in the US that the cable would be used by the Chinese to collect data on US citizens.[58]

And will the economic model of the Western cable industry continue to be viable? The question seems absurd on the surface, given just how much in demand the plumbers of the net are. But despite the sector's undeniably strategic size, it is almost entirely privatised, leaving it particularly exposed to economic cycles, which go through constant disruptions (as with the dotcom bubble in 2001, and the subprime crisis in 2008). On top of this, the FAANGs wield enormous power and pressure on prices, squeezing the profit margins of their business partners, with the result that 'few people are willing to take a gamble by investing in [them]', according to an expert.[59] On a global scale, the industry therefore works with no more than some 30 transoceanic cable-laying ships, divided primarily between three key players: the French company Alcatel Submarine Networks (ASN); the US company SubCom; and the Japanese company NEC.[60] Added to this are the difficulties in recruiting young talent to the sector (the words 'big data' not featuring on the job description, laments a specialist), leaving it to shipowners who may struggle to stay afloat ...

'The global infrastructure relies on suppliers who are not particularly resilient', according to the French consultant Bertrand Clesca.[61] What would happen if they were to fall on hard times, lasting years, rendering them unable to honour their commitments? One could think of the FAANGs putting their price war on hold to avoid 'sinking' their strategic partners. 'Perhaps they've even considered, in the worst-case scenario, buying up one of them ...', our consultant would like to believe.[62] The risk emerging from that would be states finding themselves subordinate to powerful private conglomerates whose financial needs do not necessarily coincide with national security imperatives. 'Barely a single cable today involves Facebook or Google chipping in', according to a fibre-optic-cable expert I consulted. How far will their control of the framework of the internet go? And what kind of situations created by reliance on the most powerful companies in the world will Westerners find themselves in? 'We are currently witnessing the privatisation of a part of the internet by a clutch of players, and nobody is batting an eyelid', according to a subsea telecommunications expert.[63]

A first political test was resolved around the destiny of Alcatel

Submarine Networks. The French industrial company has been the property of Nokia since 2016. However, the Finnish group delivered a mixed performance, and rumours of Nokia selling ASN had, until 2019, been circulating in the industry. Yet Alcatel Submarine Networks is seen as a key to Europe's digital sovereignty, allowing it to hold onto a technology that, today, only benefits a handful of countries. That is why 'ensuring ASN remains a European asset is a decisive factor for not depending on a non-European cable ship that could impose its own law', a director of an undersea cable company warned. Paris is nevertheless aware of what's at stake. 'Quite clearly, the company is being monitored', a specialist told me. As for France controlling the cable—and the data it carries—in its entirety, 'it is already too late', a consultant observed. 'There would need to be a Europe-wide strategy.'64 And entertained internet users would need to realise that behind all the fun and games is a pursuit of power that is accelerating at a mind-boggling speed.

Conclusion

PARIS, 15 APRIL 1900. IT'S EIGHT O'CLOCK IN THE MORNING, and the City of Lights is about to open the fifth universal exhibition to the public. These world fairs, celebrating technical, economic, and social progress in the service of humanity, have been taking place, one after the other, since 1851 in the United States, Europe, and Australia. Now, at the dawn of the twentieth century, France intends to host the most grandiose *exposition universelle* of them all. Forty countries have set up their sumptuous pavilions on a 112-hectare site encircling the Eiffel Tower. Train stations have been renovated, bridges laced from one side of the Seine to the other, and the first line of the Paris metro has gone into service to transport the exposition's 50 million visitors.

The fair's 83,000 exhibitors are showcasing extraordinary inventions: a big wheel, night-time lighting, the biggest refracting telescope ever built, big-screen projections of films by the Lumière brothers, and a mechanical footpath forming a loop of several kilometres around the site of the expo. This moving footpath will prove immensely popular, for some six million people will use it. And because people believe that the footpaths of tomorrow will all work this way, the invention is named the 'Street of the Future'—evidence of just how much faith there is at the time in the benefits of technology.

In the twenty-first century, a great many technical utopias have become a reality. We live by the beat of the light pulses of the internet, the power of algorithms, and the data-transmission rate of 5G antennas. We are dazzled by these tools, yet we are also concerned about the threats they pose to our mental health, to democracies, and to the climate. So which information technologies do we want to take with us into the future? And made out of what processes and materials? Do we want a centralised network composed of heavy infrastructure to allow energy savings at scale, or one that is dispersed in order to localise the hugely electricity-intensive transmission of data? Do we want it to be neutral and deregulated, or partial and hostile to unbridled freedom by only allowing data deemed to be 'essential'? Should it be free of charge, or should users have to pay? Will we put 'sobriety' in our consumption of energy and digital technologies above innovations that enhance digital performance, or the opposite?

'The internet has only been open to all for 23 years—it's very young! We're still at the age of *Homo habilis*, the prehistory of digital', the entrepreneur Inès Leonarduzzi says. 'But now we're moving into the digital Age of Enlightenment.' These are fine words, but if we all agreed on this admirable goal, it would mean having to choose from a profusion of possible—and often indiscernible—actions. Over the two years spent writing this book, I discovered that the 'streets of the future', these paths bringing to life the digital Age of Enlightenment, are as numerous as they are contradictory.

I debated this at length with Anwar Osseyran at an elegant restaurant on the Amstel in Amsterdam. Osseyran, the professor of business analytics and computer science at the University of Amsterdam, maintained that digital technologies should be deployed to balance the objectives of human development, environmental protection, and economic growth—the fulfilment of what he refers to as a 'people, planet, profit State'. 'Our actions must be ecological, but also socially, economically, and politically sustainable', he argued. Yet, Anwar adds, humanity will only be more prosperous if digital technologies are improved to make the processing capacity of our current information tools even more powerful. Here, professor Osseyran referred to the advent of quantum computing, and—citing American futurist Raymond Kurzweil—free and unlimited solar energy for the entire planet by 2030. As for the environmental cost of data, 'it is enormous, but it is outweighed by the potential benefits'. On the condition, he added, that this data is easy to access, open, and can be combined with other data.[2] Moreover, this technologist approach will need to be counterbalanced by dissuasive carbon taxes, an efficient carbon market, and companies factoring environmental, social, and ethical consideration into their operations.[3]

I also interviewed James Warren and Carelyn Campbell, researchers at the National Institute of Standards and Technology, based in northern Washington, DC. They strongly believe in the prodigious potential of materials science, as exemplified by the new 5-cent pieces in circulation in the US, which are made from a new alloy of copper, nickel, and zinc that is 40 per cent cheaper than the previous alloy.[4] This was the outcome, obtained in 2018, of just 19 months of research using digital technologies 'to model and predict the evolution of alloys', they explained. Following this discovery, some say that 'new materials are tomorrow's oil, and that next to their activities, the FAANGs are already part of the old world. The future is in materials.'[5]

Taking their cue from scientists, a network of multinationals and start-ups—we'll call them 'techblazers'—are refining a narrative in which the protection of the planet is conditional on the unlimited development of technologies, and, in particular, digital technologies. They propose, for example, less energy-intensive 'smart mines', robots used for recycling (such as Apple's robot Daisy), and tools such as blockchain to trace the source of raw materials (such as the company Circulor).[6] The techblazers will thrive in the 'people, planet, profit State' and the actions it champions. Some of them will become so powerful that they could one day contest the authority of nations in the fight to protect the environment.

Another philosophy, another set of pioneers: a few months earlier, in Amsterdam, I looked into the Waag Society.[7] It formed around a radically different vision of the goals of digital technology, and advocates the use of digital technologies for social good. Engineer Henk Buursen teaches his students, who come from all around the world, how mobile phones and software work, so that they can take back real ownership of them. 'Robots, artificial intelligence [AI] are made by humans. My students must not forget that these technologies only work thanks to them, and not separately from them', he explained. Like the Waag Society, communities of men and women—we'll call them 'resilient frugalists'—are multiplying worldwide. Like the coordinators of the LibrePlanet and Framasoft networks, they believe in the virtues of free-access software (such as Linux).[8] They often swear by the low tech of simplified manufacturing, which is easier to repair and recycle. They see a future in which the use of digital technologies will decline, even to the point of the 'de-digitalisation' of our societies. Also central to their cause are localised internet networks: the first of these has been installed with the Mesh and Guifi communication networks, already in operation at a local scale in Catalonia, India, and South Africa.[9]

Could this ethic inspire our governments? A fascinating report by the think tank The Shift Project states that, faced with the increasingly deleterious impact of online videos on the environment, 'the role of the public authorities ... is to prioritise certain uses in relation to others, on the basis of their pertinence and their essential nature'.[10] Such prioritisation is tantamount to revoking the sacrosanct principle of internet neutrality, according to which everyone and anyone and for whatever reason can access absolutely any content online. What we see here are the first constituent elements of a political entity we could call a 'dark-green government': a strong regime advocated by researchers that would work to limit digital pollution through policies that curtail certain civil liberties. The consumption of digital services could be managed using connection quotas and technical constraints, such as a limit on the capacity of infrastructure. Only data considered 'essential to the common good' (medical, military, financial) by an entrusted public body would be prioritised. By reducing data to its meanest share, users would need to pay to access some of the internet. We could imagine a dark-green government pushing this logic further by choosing not to cross certain technological frontiers, such as strong AI or quantum computing, as the negative effects would be considered to outweigh the expected benefits.

Our street of the future will probably be a hybridisation of all these solutions applied across the four corners of the globe.

Let's bargain on the wisdom of the men and women championing the best of these solutions to find common ground around solid, shared goals, and beyond their divergent views. This, hopefully, would start with the goal of delivering an ecosystem not bent on outdoing itself; delivering a world where we care about bettering the real and lived present, before promising a future that is as glorified as it is hypothetical; and developing a tool that helps us to understand this era of our making. In the words of the German essayist and philosopher Byung-Chul Han, '[T]his new medium is reprogramming us, yet we fail to grasp the radical paradigm shift that is underway.'[11]

Perhaps the most difficult consensus to draw out will be how humans should best position themselves in the future in relation to technologies. We are used to seeing digital technologies as a Messiah among men, come to save us. Yet we must recognise, collectively, that the reality is far more prosaic: they are nothing more than a tool created in our image. They are—and will be—no more and no less environmental than we are. If we happily waste food and energy resources, digital technologies will serve to accentuate that inclination. If, however, we wish to awaken a powerful movement of generosity, we will mobilise legions of volunteers in a heartbeat. These technologies work as a catalyst for our daily undertakings, from the least honourable to the most noble. They elevate our legacy for future generations. To the demigods we have become, largely unaware of the incommensurable powers that are now in our hands, digital technology is ultimately an invitation to realise the powerful words of Mahatma Gandhi: 'Be the change you want to see in the world.'

Acknowledgements

AS PROOF OF HOW VERY MATERIAL A 'LIKE' REALLY IS, THIS investigation required extensive international travel. Shoe-leather journalism is expensive, and this book would not have been possible without the constant support of my French editors, Henri Trubert and Sophie Marinopoulos. I am grateful to them for putting their faith in me; this book is in large part thanks to them.

Each page required on average 10 pages of notes, research, and interviews. For that, I could count on the remarkable professionalism of several investigators and analysts from Sciences Po, HEC Business School, and the CJF school of journalism. Without their passion for the issues evidenced in this work, their close and constant attention to checking the facts, and their indulgence towards my requests, which (I admit) were often excessive, this book would not be the one you have in your hands today. My special thanks to:

Rime Abdallah, who researched digital pollution, and helped to build a project on the issue.

Isha Badoniya, for her research on Bangalore to which she dedicated herself selflessly to meet my expectations for this work.

Alice Bello, for her work on (but not only on) the aesthetics of the immaterial, green artificial intelligence (AI), Bluffdale, the environmental cost of state surveillance, the material input per service (MIPS) unit, Masdar City, Encana, the colours red and blue, Dominion Energy, the coal of the Appalachian mountains, the history of media critique, etc., to which she applied her impressive analytical and summarising skills.

Gwendoline Créno, for her research on (but not only on) F-gases and Honeywell, the connection between mathematics and nature, the geography of a 'like', the paradoxes of the Greta generation, the lobbying by Dominion Energy, fibre-optic cables, the aesthetics of smartphones, green energy certificates, the connection between smartphones and Zen Buddhism, which she carried out with admirable commitment to the investigation, and unwavering motivation.

Marie-Astrid Guégan, for her research on (but not only on), the Dunant cable, the coal of the Appalachian mountains, Ashburn, the translation of data in volumes of water, Kolos, green energy certificates, for her preparation of investigations in the Netherlands, the UK, the US, Sweden, and Norway ... all at the price of tremendous endurance, and a good measure of humility.

Camille Richir, for her investigation on (but not only on) the establishment of Facebook in Luleå, the impact of hydroelectric dams on the river Luleälven, e-scooters, electronic purges, the Dunant cable, passive finance, integrated circuits, 5G, connected and driverless vehicles. Her work is powerful; her passion for investigation, rare.

Caroline Robin, for her research on connected and driverless vehicles with consistency and persistence.

Sandrine Tran, for her perseverance in the face of the enormity of the work on integrated circuits and the Smarter2030 report, as well as for the preparation of the investigation in Tallinn.

Jeanne Vincent, for her research on the responsible sourcing of minerals, pollution generated by robots, obstacles to the right to repair one's own electronic equipment, served by great care for factual accuracy and fine analytical skills.

I would also like to thank Cédric Molle-Laurençon, academic co-director at the CFJ, and his teams, for their confidence by relaying my offers of collaboration to their students.

This book then passed into the hands of numerous proof-readers, all French and international specialists in their fields. I am infinitely in their debt for the time they dedicated to rereading and revising certain passages. (Of course, I take sole responsibility for any errors that may remain.) They are Paul Benoit, co-founder and director of Qarnot Computing, and Philippe Luce, director of Institut Datacenter, founder of the consultancy Plus Conseil, and co-founder of the think tank 'Datacenter en transition', for chapters four, five, and six on data centres.

Jean-Pierre Colinge, former director in the chief technology office of Taiwan Semiconductor Manufacturing Company Limited, for the passage on integrated circuits.

John Devos, former managing director of Alcatel Submarcom/ASN and former marketing director of Tyco/SubCom, and Laurent Campagne, senior consultant at AQEST, for chapters nine and ten dealing with fibre-optic cables.

Jérémy Désir, former quantitative analyst at HSBC and co-founder of the non-profit Vous n'êtes pas seuls (You Are Not Alone), for the passage on quantitative funds.

Klorydryk, member of the non-profit Quadrature du Net, for the passage on e-scooters and data capture.

Ivy Main, lawyer and advocate with the Sierra Club, for the developments on Dominion Energy.

The entire book was also read by Agnès Crépet, head of software longevity and IT at Fairphone, the gracious Éric Rousseau (Université populaire d'Albertville), and the meticulous Axel Robine. Thank you for your demanding and constructive reads.

I confidently put my trust in Monique Devauton, for her scrupulous fact-checking.

Lastly, this editorial adventure was carried through at a time of restrictions that, between investigations, allowed for calm and regular enquiry and writing. From the ponds of Brenne Regional Nature Park to the vineyards of the Bordeaux hinterland, I could rely on the company of old stones, trees, and animals, and the kind support of my family and those dear to me.

Appendixes

APPENDIX 1

The seven 'layers' of how the internet works

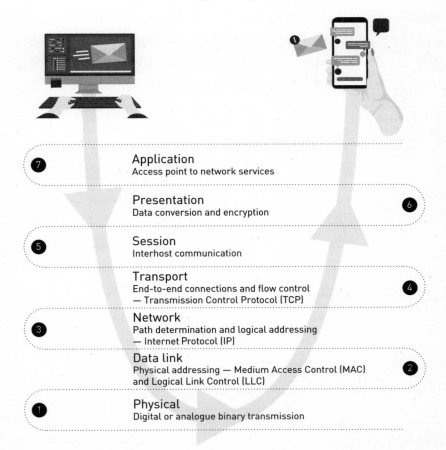

Application
Access point to network services

Presentation
Data conversion and encryption

Session
Interhost communication

Transport
End-to-end connections and flow control
— Transmission Control Protocol (TCP)

Network
Path determination and logical addressing
— Internet Protocol (IP)

Data link
Physical addressing — Medium Access Control (MAC)
and Logical Link Control (LLC)

Physical
Digital or analogue binary transmission

APPENDIX 2

Number of raw materials in a telephone

1960

1990

2021

10 elements

24 elements

54 elements

10 elements
Aluminium
Carbon
Chromium
Copper
Hydrogen
Nickel
Nitrogen
Oxygen
Lead
Zinc

24 elements	
Aluminium	Manganese
Antimony	Molybdenum
Barium	Nickel
Beryllium	Nitrogen
Boron	Oxygen
Bromine	Phosphorus
Cadmium	Lead
Carbon	Silicium
Chromium	Tantalum
Copper	Titanium
Cobalt	Tungsten
Tin	
Fluorine	
Hydrogen	
Helium	

54 elements		
Aluminium	Germanium	Platinum
Americium	Gold	Potassium
Antimony	Hafnium	Rubidium
Barium	Hydrogen	Scandium
Beryllium	Indium	Silicium
Bismuth	Iodine	Silver
Bromine	Iridium	Sodium
Calcium	Lead	Strontium
Carbon	Lithium	Sulphur
Chlorine	Magnesium	Tellurium
Chromium	Manganese	Thallium
Cobalt	Neodymium	Thulium
Copper	Neon	Titanium
Erbium	Nickel	Tungsten
Iron	Nitrogen	Vanadium
Fluorine	Oxygen	Yttrium
Gadolinium	Palladium	Zinc
Gallium	Phosphorus	Zirconium

Source: Prof. Mike Ashby, Cambridge University; Prof. Jean-Pierre Raskin, Université catholique de Louvain.

APPENDIX 3

Share of global metals production
for digital technologies

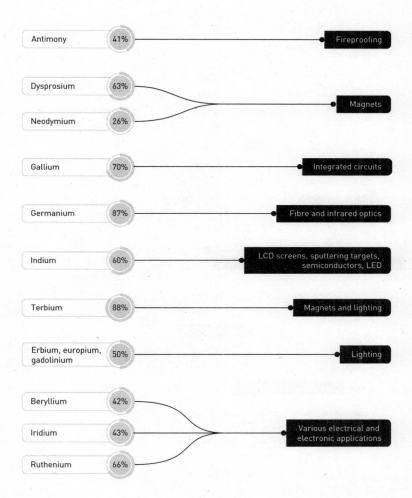

Metal	Share	Application
Antimony	41%	Fireproofing
Dysprosium	63%	Magnets
Neodymium	26%	
Gallium	70%	Integrated circuits
Germanium	87%	Fibre and infrared optics
Indium	60%	LCD screens, sputtering targets, semiconductors, LED
Terbium	88%	Magnets and lighting
Erbium, europium, gadolinium	50%	Lighting
Beryllium	42%	Various electrical and electronic applications
Iridium	43%	
Ruthenium	66%	

Source: Joint Research Centre (JRC), European Union

APPENDIX 4

World map of data centres

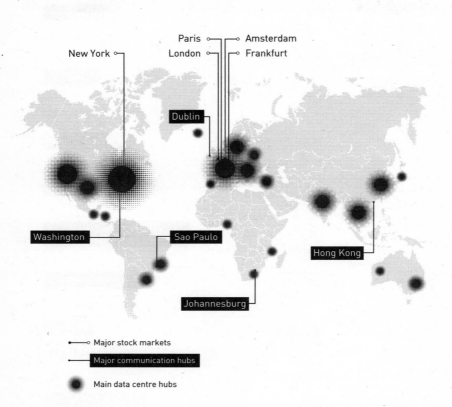

Source: Data Center Map

APPENDIX 5

If a byte were a drop of water...

UNIT OF MEASURE	APPLICATION	VOLUME OF WATER	EQUIVALENCE
1 kilobyte ↓ 1,000 bytes	1 short email	100 millilitres	½ a glass of water
1 megabyte ↓ 1,000 kilobytes	1 minute MP3 audio file	100 litres	1 footbath
1 gigabyte ↓ 1,000 megabytes	1 two-hour film	100,000 litres	1 large rainwater tank
1 terabyte ↓ 1,000 gigabytes	6 million books Almost half of the catalogue of the national library of France	100 million litres	Almost 27 Olympic-size swimming pools
1 petabyte ↓ 1,000 terabytes	2 billion medium-resolution digital photographs	100 billion litres = 100 million cubic metres = 0.1 cubic kilometre	58 times the volume of the Grand Canal of Venice
1 exabyte ↓ 1,000 petabytes	5 exabytes All information produced until 2003	100 cubic kilometres	More than Lake Geneva (89 km³)
1 zettabyte ↓ 1,000 exabytes	1 thousand billion books	100,000 cubic kilometres	The Gulf of California
1 yottabyte ↓ 1,000 zettabytes	1 million data centres each the size of a city block	100 million cubic kilometres	1/3 of the Indian Ocean

Source: Stanford University, High Scalability, *Libération*

APPENDIX 6

Annual volume of world data
produced since 2010 (in zettabytes)*

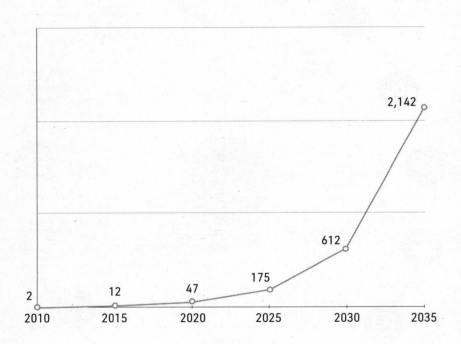

* One zettabyte equals a thousand billion gigabytes

Source: Statista, Digital Economy Compass 2019.

APPENDIX 7

One minute on the internet around the world

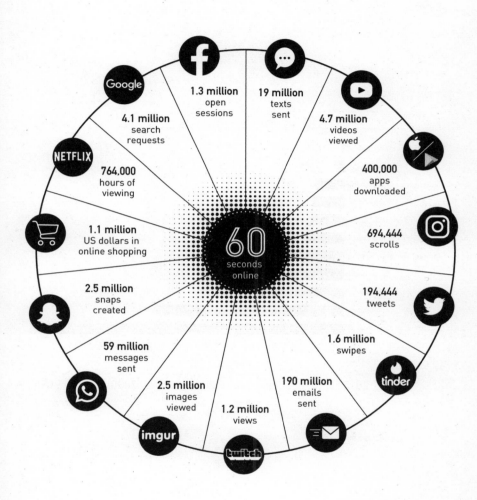

Infographic by @LoriLewis and @officiallyChadd, 2020.

APPENDIX 8

Lines of programming code by digital technology

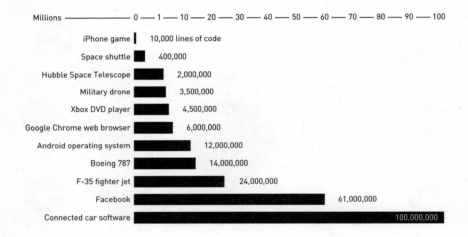

Source: David McCandless, based on data from NASA, and the websites Quora, Ohloh, *Wired* & press report, 2020.

APPENDIX 9

Cross-section of a fibre-optic cable

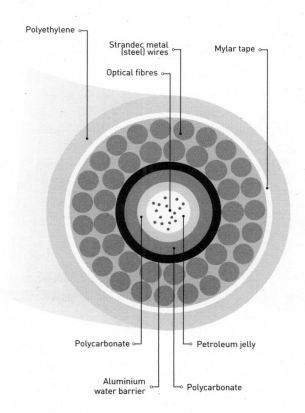

Polyethylene

Strandec metal
(steel) wires

Optical fibres

Mylar tape

Polycarbonate

Petroleum jelly

Aluminium
water barrier

Polycarbonate

Source: SciencePost

APPENDIX 10

World map of undersea cables

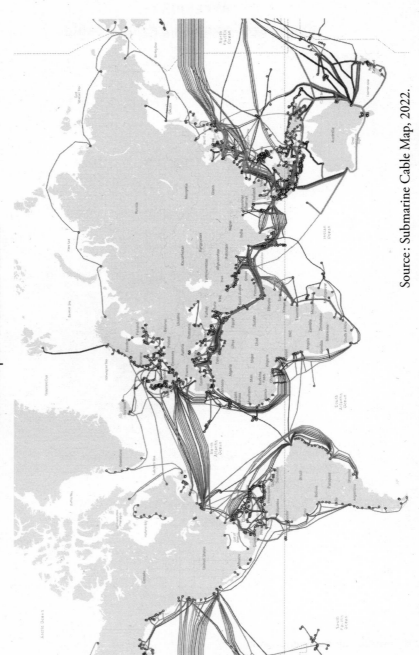

Source: Submarine Cable Map, 2022.

APPENDIX 11

Route of the Hibernia Express cable

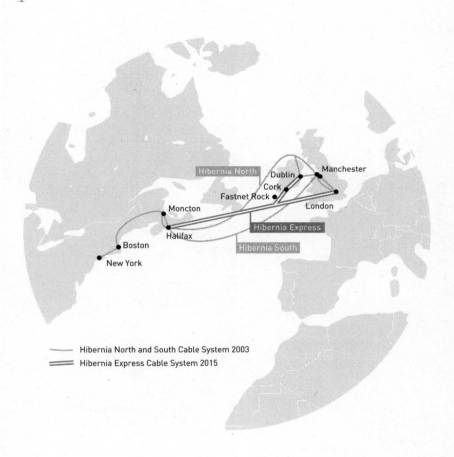

Hibernia North and South Cable System 2003
Hibernia Express Cable System 2015

Source: submarinenetworks.com

APPENDIX 12

Route of future cables
Europe-Persia Express Gateway (EPEG) and Blue-Raman

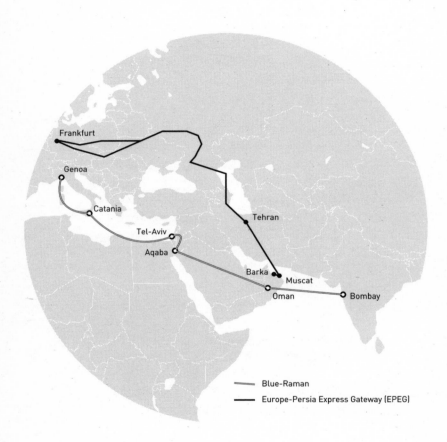

Source : submarinenetworks.com

APPENDIX 13
Provisional route of the ROTACS and Arctic Fibre cables

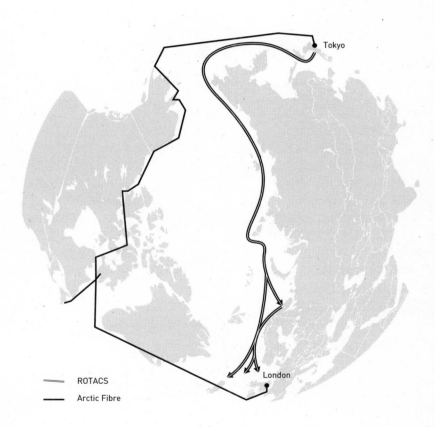

Source: Polarnet Project photo, 2017.

APPENDIX 14
Route of the Pakistan and East Africa Connecting Europe (PEACE) cable

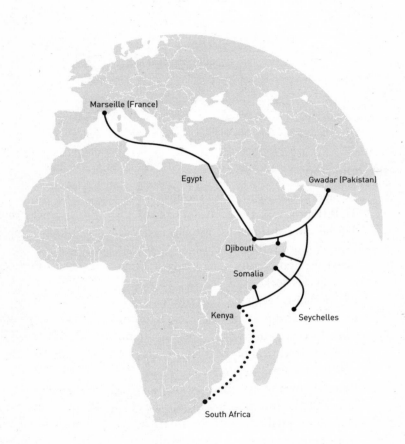

Source: PEACE Cable, 2021.

Notes

Introduction

1   Advanced Research Projects Agency Network.
2   TCP/IP protocol: Transmission Control Protocol/Internet Protocol.
3   'US heading anti-jihadist intelligence sharing operation – report', *The Times of Israel*, 25 March 2021.
4   'YouTube and Netflix are cutting streaming quality in Europe due to coronavirus lockdowns', *CNBC*, 20 March 2020. Several experts, like IT specialist Stéphane Bortzmeyer, believe that the networks were in fact far from saturation. See 'L'Internet pendant le confinement' [the Internet during lockdown], framablog.org, 21 March 2020. 'Why the world is short of computer chips, and why it matters', *Bloomberg*, 17 February 2021.
5   Better known by its abbreviation 'www'. The term was coined by the father of the Internet, British physician Tim Berners-Lee. For further reading on predictions of the Internet's expansion to all of humanity, read 'Humans on the Internet will triple from 2015 to 2022 and hit 6 billion', *Cybercrime Magazine*, 18 July 2019.
6   '10 hot summer trends 2030', *Ericsson ConsumerLab*, December 2019.
7   'Giant cell blob can learn and teach, study shows', *Science News*, 21 December 2016.
8   Interview with Inès Leonarduzzi, director of Digital For The Planet, 2019.
9   Interviews with Françoise Berthoud, IT research engineer, 2019 and 2020.

10   'Lean ICT: Towards Digital Sobriety', report of the working group directed by Hugues Ferreboeuf for the think tank The Shift Project, March 2019.

11   Interview with Jaan Tallinn, founder of Skype and the Future of Life Institute, 2020.

12   Google, Apple, Facebook, Amazon and Microsoft: the five most powerful US companies of the digital economy.

13   To borrow the term used by Agnès Crepet, Head of Software Longevity & IT at Fairphone.

14   fridaysforfuture.org

15   The start-up in question is We Don't Have Time: wedonthavetime.org

16   'What's Behind Climate Change Activist Greta Thunberg's Remarkable Rise to Fame?', *The Spectator*, 13 February 2019.

17   Victoria Rideout, Michael B. Ross, 'The common sense census: media used by tweens and teens', *Common Sense Media*, 2019.

18   'La face cachée du numérique – Réduire les impacts du numérique sur l'environnement' ['The dark side of digital – reducing the impacts of digital on the environment'], *ADEME*, January 2021.

19   Simon Kessler and Johan Boulanger, *Generation Greta,* 53-minute documentary, AFP and Galaxie Presse, 2020.

20   'J'ai trois Greta Thunberg à la maison... Ces ados écolos qui prennent en main le bilan carbone de la famille' ['I have three Greta Thunbergs at home... Green teens taking control of the family carbon footprint'], *Le Monde,* 16 November 2019.

21   'Today's youth, tomorrow's Internet: A Nominet Digital Futures Report', *Nominet*, 2019.

22   'Being young in Europe today—digital world', Eurostat, July 2020.

23   'The Perils of Progress', *The New Republic*, New York, 29 June 2010.

24   Trine Syversten, *Media Resistance: Protest, Dislike, Abstention,* Palgrave Macmillan, 2018.

Chapter One: The digital world's environmental benefits

1   Turkish researcher Gökçe Günel describes Masdar City in her book, *Spaceship in the Desert: energy, climate change and urban design in Abu Dhabi,* Duke University Press, 2019. The pandemic made it impossible to travel to Masdar, and so I base my descriptions on official promotional material.

2   Federico Cugurullo, *Exposing smart cities and eco-cities: Frankenstein urbanism and the sustainability challenges of the experimental city,* Environment and Planning A: Economy and Space, 16 November 2017.

3   Op. cit.

4   See 'Welcome to Masdar City' on YouTube. More promotional material available at masdarcity.ae/en.

5   Interview with Federico Cugurullo, Assistant Professor in Smart and Sustainable Urbanism at Trinity College Dublin, 2020.

6   fosterandpartners.com/projects/masdar-city/

7   For example, if a bird flies in front of a self-driving car it would grind to a halt to avoid hitting it. The PRT also needed to be able to operate in a tunnel—a proposal/feature that was never applied.

8   The numerous anomalies in the measurement of water and air conditioning consumption have not been resolved, 'and no one seems to understand why these features do not work', Gökçe Günel reports in her book *Spaceship in the Desert, op.cit.*

9   'Masdar's zero-carbon dream could become world's first green ghost town', *The Guardian*, 16 February 2016.

10 'Mapping Smart Cities in the EU', *Directorate General for Internal Policies, Policy Department, Economic and Scientific Policy*, January 2014.

11 'Navigant Research's smart city tacker 2Q19 highlights 443 projects spanning 286 cities around the world', *Business Wire*, 20 June 2019. According to the market intelligence firm Navigant Research, the annual global technology market for smart cities, which stood at US$97.4 billion in 2019, is expected to total $263 billion by 2028.

12 Interview with Gökçe Günel, lecturer in anthropology at Rice University in Houston, Texas, 2020.

13 From 1994, in his paper *Green Signals: the environmental role of telecommunications in cities*, the UK researcher Simon J. Marvin challenges the conventional thinking that telecommunications could actively contribute to the development of more sustainable cities. And in an article published in 2014 entitled *'Smart cities and green growth: outsourcing democratic and environmental resilience to the global technology sector'*, UK researchers Jenni Viitanen and Richard Kingston reference and follow on from Simon J. Marvin's research, making tentative assumptions on the environmental impact of smart cities: 'It is likely that the smarter a city gets the more e-waste it will create'. They conclude by calling on policy makers to 'take a less naïve view about the risks and benefits' of smart cities, without making any clear calculations. Finally, in 2016, the report by the Environmental Industries Commission, *Getting the Green Light: will smart technology clean up city environments?* concludes that 'there is a lack of definitive evidence that smart technologies and applications have a major role in improving environmental outcomes in cities'.

14 Kikki Lambrecht Ipsen, Regitze Kjær Zimmermann, Per Sieverts Nielsen, Morten Birkved, 'Environmental assessment of Smart City Solutions using a coupled urban metabolism – life cycle impact assessment approach', *The International Journal of Life Cycle Assessment*, 2019.

15 Two methods were applied. One examined the inflows and outflows of equipment of a city (its urban metabolism); the other, a life-cycle assessment (LCA), examined these material flows at every stage of the city's life cycle, that is, from the extraction of resources to the manufacture of goods, their use, and end of life.

16 Kikki Lambrecht Ipsen, Regitze Kjær Zimmermann, Per Sieverts Nielsen, Morten Birkved, op. cit.

17 Interview with Kikki Lambrecht Ipsen, researcher at the Civil and Building Engineering Department at the University of Sherbrooke in Quebec, Canada, 2020.

18 Mickaël Launay, Stephen S. Wilson (translator), *It All Adds Up: the story of people and mathematics*, William Collins, 2018.

19 The theory of maximum sustainable yield (MSY) was a formulated in 1935 by the British biologist Michael Graham.

20 Interview with Alexandre Gaudin, professor at the AgroParisTech institution, 2020.

21 Trichlorofluoromethane. Stephen A. Montzka, Geoff S. Dutton, Pengfei Yu et al., 'An unexpected and persistent increase in global emissions of ozone-depleting CFC-11', *Nature*, 557, 16 May 2018.

22 Also known as 'space data'. Refer to Andrew Wooden, 'Space data: the final analytics frontier', *Intel*, 2022. Matt Rigby, Sangho Park, Takuya Saito et al., 'Increase in CFC-11 emissions from eastern China based on atmospheric observations', *Nature*, 569, 22 May 2019. See also 'Ozone layer: Banned CFCs traced to China say scientists', BBC, 22 May 2019.

23 George Orwell, *1984*, Secker & Warburg, 1949.

24 Frédéric Bordage, Marine Braud, Damien Demailly et al., 'White Paper on the Digital Economy and the Environment', Institute for Sustainable Development and International Relations (IDDRI), March 2018.

25 Located 200 kilometres south of Shanghai, Hangzhou is the capital of the Zhejiang province.

26 'In China, Alibaba's data-hungry AI is controlling (and watching) cities', *Wired*, 30 May 2018.

27 'Évaluation des systèmes de GTB [gestion technique du bâtiment] dans le tertiaire' ['Evaluation of BEMS (building energy management systems) in the service industry'], report by the French Environment and Energy Management Agency (*ADEME*), December 2015.

28 See cropswap.com and farmmatch.com.

29   See toogoodtogo.org/en.

30   'White Paper on the Digital Economy and the Environment', *op. cit.*

31   Hubert Tardieu, 'La troisième révolution digitale. Agilité et fragilité' ['The third digital revolution: agility and fragility'], *Études*, October 2016.

32   'Lean ICT: towards digital sobriety', report of the working group directed by Hugues Ferreboeuf for the think tank The Shift Project, March 2019.

33   For a deep dive into the history of research on the environmental impact of digital technologies, I recommend the report 'Estimating the enabling potential of ICT – a challenging research task', published by the company Ericsson in 2019. The summary also references an older, more comprehensive study: Jens Malmodin, Pernilla Bergmark, Nina Lövehagen, Mine Ercan, Anna Bondesson, 'Considerations for macro-level studies of ICT's enabling potential', *ICT for Sustainability*, 2014.

34   Billions of tonnes of global annual CO2 equivalent emissions. 'Lean ICT: towards digital sobriety', op. cit.

35   Ibid.

36   'GeSI SMARTer 2020: The role of ICT in driving a sustainable future', *Global e-Sustainability Initiative* and *The Boston Consulting Group, Inc*, December 2012.

37   '#SMARTer2030: ICT Solutions for 21st Century Challenges', *GeSI* and *Accenture Strategy*, 2015.

38   unfcc.int

39   'ICT at COP21: Enormous potential to mitigate emissions', *World Bank Group*, December 2015.

40   'Potentiel de contribution du numérique à la réduction des impacts environnementaux: état des lieux et enjeux pour la prospective' ['Potential of digital's contribution to reducing environmental impacts: status and challenges for the future'], a report by the French Environment and Energy Management Agency (*ADEME*), December 2016.

41   Interview with Françoise Berthoud, research engineer in information technology at the CNRS, 2019 and 2020. Berthoud had to carry out an even more in-depth critical analysis of GeSI reports in the ADEME report referenced earlier: 'On the whole, the [...] reports come across as a communication exercise for industrial groups wanting to promote their technological solutions [...]. Looking at the figures on avoidable emissions by sector and by country, it is hard not to see the pro-industrial bias of both reports, and therefore trust their results and recommendations. [...] A critical review by an independent panel would dispel any doubts as to the partiality of the research.'

42   Including BT Group, Deutsche Telekom, Huawei, Microsoft, and Verizon.

43   According to my sources, the report cost a total of between 500,000 and 2 million euros.

44   Interview with Françoise Berthoud, 2019 and 2020.

45   Ibid.

46   Frédéric Bordage, 'Empreinte environnementale du numérique mondial' ['Environmental footprint of global digital technologies'], *GreenIT.fr*, September 2019.

47   Ibid.

48   Françoise Berthoud, 'Numérique et écologie' ['Digital technologies and the environment'], *Annales des Mines – Responsabilité et environnement*, no. 87, 2017/3. 'Journée du dépassement: Internet est le 3e 'pays' le plus énergivore' ['Overshoot Day: the third most energy-intensive 'country' is the Internet'], *RFI*, 1 August 2018.

49   'Global electricity generation mix, 2010-2020', *International Atomic Energy Agency (IAEA)*, 1 March 2021.

50   'Lean ICT: towards digital sobriety', ibid.

51   'Numérique: le grand gâchis énergétique' ['Digital: the great energy waster'], *CNRS Le journal*, 16 May 2018. According to Bruno Lafage, head of the Geomatics and National Parks division at the French Biodiversity Agency, speaking at the National Biodiversity Conference 2019—Digital Cities and Biodiversity.

52   'Lean ICT: towards digital sobriety', ibid.

53   Interview with Frédéric Bordage, founder of GreenIT, 2018.

54   Interview with Inès Leonarduzzi, director of Digital For The Planet, 2019

55   My thanks to Henri Sabatié-Gravat, general delegate of the French green purchasing association Cap'Oise Hauts-de-France, whose interview in 2020 inspired me to write these lines.

56   'Clicking clean – Who is winning the race to build a green internet?', *Greenpeace International*, 2017.

57   'Lean ICT: Towards Digital Sobriety: our new report on the environmental impact of ICT', *The Shift Project*, 2019.

58   Ibid.

59   Interview with Anne-Cécile Orgerie, researcher at the CNRS (French National Scientific Research Council), IRISA (French Laboratory for Research and Innovation in Digital Science and Technology), 2020.

60   Interview with Mark Acton, head of Data Centre Technical Consulting at CBRE Data Center Solutions, 2020.

61   'White Paper on the Digital Economy and the Environment', *op. cit.*

62   Total Cost of Ownership. tcocertified.com

63 Ruediger Kuehr and Eric Williams, *Computers and the Environment: Understanding and Managing their Impacts*, Springer Netherlands, 2003.

64 Interview with Eric Williams, professor at Rochester Institute of Technology, New York, 2020.

65 Interview with Asta Vonderau, executive director, Centre for interdisciplinary Regional Studies (ZIRS), Martin-Luther de Halle-Wittenberg University (Germany), 2020.

66 Interview with Sophie Rauszer, parliamentary attaché of The Left in the European Parliament (GUE/NGL), 2020.

67 For a more comprehensive overview of the digital footprint of one employee, read Club Green IT & WWF France's 2018 'WeGreenIT' report [available in French only].

68 'Google workers double down on climate demands in new letter', *The Verge*, 4 November 2019.

69 Interview with Inès Leonarduzzi, 2019. See also 'Ces étudiants des grandes écoles qui ne veulent pas travailler dans des entreprises polluantes' ['Students from the *grandes écoles* do not want to work in polluting companies'], francetvinfo.fr, 15 October 2018.

Chapter Two: Smartphones and the art of Zen

1 Not her real name.

2 This trip was for my documentary *The Dark Side of Green Energies,* company-directed with Jean-Louis Perez and produced by Grand Angle, 2020.

3 Chernozem is a humus-rich soil.

4 For more information on the graphite refining process, read the article by Allah D. Jara, Amha Betemariam, Girma Woldetinsae, Jung Yong Kim, 'Purification, application and current market trend of natural graphite: a review', *International Journal of Mining Science and Technology*, vol. 29, no. 5, September 2019.

5 Not his real name.

6 'Heilongjiang promotes investment in graphite industry', *Harbin Today*, 20 December 2019.

7 'Data age 2025. The digitization of the world', *Seagate*, November 2018.

8 A magnetometer is a device that is used to measure the intensity and direction of a magnetic field.

9 'The world of aluminium extrusions – an industry analysis with forecasts to 2025', *AlCircle*, 22 August 2018.

10 'La face cachée du numérique – Réduire les impacts du numérique sur l'environnement' ['The dark side of digital – Reducing the impact of

digital on the environment'], *ADEME*, January 2021. Frédéric Bordage, *Sobriété numérique, les clés pour agir* ['Digital sobriety, the keys for action'], Buchet-Chastel, 2019: 'Eighty per cent of the energy expenditure [of a smartphone] occurs during the manufacturing process.' This figure goes as high as 86 per cent for Apple's iPhone 12 Pro. Read 'The carbon footprint of your phone – and how you can reduce it', *reboxed.co*, 26 February 2021.

11   Interview with Paul Benoit, Qarnot Computing, 2019 and 2020.

12   Jared Diamond is better known for his bestseller *Collapse: how societies choose to fail or succeed*, Penguin Books, 2005 and 2011). 'What's your consumption factor?', *The New York Times*, 2 January 2008.

13   'Global material resources. Outlook to 2060: economic drivers and environmental consequences', *OCDE*, 12 February 2019.

14   Andrew McAfee, *More from Less: the surprising story of how we learned to prosper using fewer resources—and what happens next*, Scribner, 2019. Also listen to McAfee on HBR IdeaCast, Episode 700, *Dematerialisation and What It Means for the Economy—and Climate Change*, 17 September 2019.

15   'An eco-modernist manifesto', *ecomodernism.org*, April 2015. It could also be argued that 'smart farming' will increase yields even more.

16   Interview with Siim Sikkut, the then government chief information officer of Estonia, 2020.

17   It is also considered the Silicon Valley of Europe and has the highest number of unicorns (companies valued at over $1 billion) per inhabitant in the world: Skype, TransferWise, Playtech, and Bolt.

18   Interview with Ott Vatter, the managing director of e-Residence at the time of this interview in 2020.

19   Interview with Robert Krimmer, ERA-chair professor of e-governance in the Ragnar-Nurkse department of innovation and governance at Tallinn University of Technology, 2020.

20   Interview with Toomas Hendrik Ilves, former President of the Republic of Estonia (2006-2016), 2020.

21   This is a debate, taking place centuries apart, between the aesthetician G.W.F. Hegel, for whom the spirituality of art increases as it separates from matter, and the French art historian Henri Focillon, for whom 'there is no abstraction that is not yet matter, in all its volatility, and that is not subject to the structural forces of matter, gravity, inertia, rhythm, etc.' For further reading, Arnaud Macé presents select texts on the debate in his book *La Matière* ['Matter'] (Flammarion, 2013).

22   John Perry Barlow, *A Declaration of the Independence of Cyberspace*, 8 February 1996.

23   Fritz Machlup, *The Production and Distribution of Knowledge in the United States*, Princeton University Press, 1972.

24   If indeed 'our growth is based on raw materials, it cannot be infinite. If it is based on knowledge, however, infinite growth is very easily to achieve', postulates the French researcher Idriss Aberkane in a HuffPost blog in 2014. See 'L'économie de la connaissance est notre nouvelle renaissance' ['The knowledge economy is our new renaissance'], *The Huffington Post*, 4 June 2014.

25   Seth Godin, *Unleashing the Ideavirus: Stop Marketing AT People! Turn Your Ideas into Epidemics by Helping Your Customers Do the Marketing thing for You*, Hachette Books, 2001.

26   Chris Anderson, *Free: The Future of a Radical Price*, Hyperion, 2009.

27   Read Keith D. Foote, 'A Brief History of Cloud Computing', *Dataversity*, 17 December 2021, and Nilesh Shinde, 'Decoding the Cloud Computing timeline', *Atos*, 2 November 2021.

28   Keynote by Bela Loto, Director of Maison de l'informatique responsable, at the Good Planet Foundation conference on the role of digital in environmental damage and climate change ('Dégâts environnementaux, dérèglement climatique: la face cachée du numérique'), Paris, 29 February 2020.

29   Interview with Frédéric Bordage, Founder of GreenIT.fr, 2018. Apple's market cap in 2020 was $2 trillion. In 2015, it spent $1.8 billion on advertising. Apple no longer realises this information. See 'Apple mysteriously stopped disclosing how much it spends on ads', *Business Insider*, 25 November 2016.

30   View the talk by the researcher James Auger, 'Means and Ends', on 'superlative objects' at the 2021 #MiXiT21 conference.

31   Interview with Erick Rinner, managing partner of Milestone Investisseurs and non-executive director of Potential Project, 2020.

32   'How Steve Jobs' love of simplicity fueled a design revolution', *Smithsonian Magazine*, September 2012.

33   Interview with Erick Rinner, 2020.

34   To this trio of professionals we can add engineers, who have improved the internet network. 'In the 1990s, when you dialled up to the internet you really got a sense of the hardware; you could hear the screeching of the network, and it took a while to connect. Then the network became smoother, giving the impression of virtuality', explains the academic Dominique Boullier in 'Les infrastructures d'Internet: quelle géopolitique?' ['The infrastructure of the internet: what are the geopolitics?'] on the radio station *France Culture*, 9 April 2014. For further reading: Lynne Peskoe-Yang, 'Analysing Every Second of the Classic Dial-Up Modem Sound', *Popular Mechanics*, 2 March 2022.

35   Gilles de Chezelles, *La Dématérialisation des échanges* ['The dematerialisation of exchanges'], Lavoisier, 2006.

36 Ibid.

37 Ibid.

38 Ibid.

39 Keynote by Bela Loto, op cit. We should rather talk about 'scaling up matter'—moving from matter to 'multi-matter', instead of 'dematerialisation' given this 'multi-materialisation' we observe. See Florence Rodhain's *La Nouvelle Religion du numérique* ['The new digital religion'], Libre & Solidaire, 2019.

40 'Beijing orders state offices to replace foreign PCs and software', *Financial Times*, 8 December 2019. In 2014, for 'financial security' reasons, Chinese authorities had already asked banks in the country to replace their IBM servers with locally manufactured products. See 'China said to study IBM servers for bank security risks', *Bloomberg*, 28 May 2014.

41 'US telcos ordered to "rip and replace" Huawei components', *bbc.com*, 11 December 2020.

42 'Bouygues to remove 3,000 Huawei mobile antennas in France by 2028', *Reuters*, 27 August 2020.

43 'The data center is dead', *Gartner*, 26 July 2018.

44 'Sonos will stop providing software updates for its oldest products in May', *The Verge*, 21 January 2020.

45 Interview with Adèle Chasson, corporate campaigner of the HOP (Stop Planned Obsolescence) association in 2020. According to research conducted in 2021 by the German institute Fraunhofer, 20 per cent of smartphones are no longer used because of software issues. Read 'Ecodesign preparatory study on mobile phones, smartphones and tablets', Fraunhofer for the European Commission, February 2021.

46 Frédéric Bordage, *Sobriété numérique, les clés pour agir* ['Digital sobriety, the keys for action'], op. cit.

47 Frédéric Bordage, 'Logiciel : la clé de l'obsolescence programmée du matériel informatique' ['Software: the key to planned obsolescence of IT equipment'], *GreenIT.fr*, 24 May 2010.

48 'White Paper on the Digital Economy and the Environment', op. cit.

49 'Working with microbes to clean up electronic waste', *Next Nature Network*, 8 March 2021.

50 Robert M. Hazen et al., 'On the mineralogy of the "Anthropocene Epoch"', *American Mineralogist*, vol. 102, no. 3, March 2017.

51 'John Deere just swindled farmers out of their right to repair', *Wired*, 19 September 2018.

52 Charlie Sorrel, 'Why Apple Doesn't Want You to Fix Your iPhone Camera', *Lifewire*, 1 February 2021.

53 Interview with Kyle Wiens, founder of iFixit, 2020. Visit ifixit.com.

54 Read the fascinating book by Aaron Perzanowski and Jason Schultz, *The End of Ownership: personal property in the digital economy*, MIT Press, 2016. Also visit theendofownership.com.

55 Short for fabrication laboratory.

56 Interview with Martine Postma, founder of the Repair Cafés movement, 2020.

57 For example, 'The environmental footprint of the digital world', *GreenIT*, September 2019.

58 'White Paper on the Digital Economy and the Environment', *op. cit.*

59 The Repairability Index was promulgated under Law no. 2020-105 of 10 February 2020 on anti-waste and the circular economy.

60 'Global e-waste surging: up 21% in 5 years', *United Nations University*, 2 July 2020.

61 closingtheloop.eu

62 A similar initiative, Recy-Call, was launched in 2018 by Belgian entrepreneur Domien Declercq. It ceased its activities in 2019 as it did not have a viable business model.

63 Interview with Agnès Crepet, Head of Software Longevity and IT at Fairphone, 2020.

64 As an example, Fairphone managed to maintain the compatibility of its Fairphone 2 range, manufactured in 2015, with Android 9. Read 'Redefining longevity: Android 9 now available for Fairphone 2', *fairphone. com*, 25 March 2021.

Chapter Three: The dark matter of a digital world

1 *wupperinst.org*.

2 Interview with Jens Teubler, research at the Wuppertal Institute for Climate, Environment and Energy, 2020.

3 See the report 'Calculating MIPS: Resource productivity of products and services', by Michael Ritthof, Holger Rohn and Christa Liedtke, in cooperation with Thomas Merten, *Wuppertal Spezial 27e*, Wuppertal Institute for Climate, Environment and Energy, 2002.

4 Interview with Karine Samuel, professor and researcher at Université Grenoble Alpes, and part of the team 'anticipating and managing risks', 2019.

5 According to the same Wuppertal Institute report, '...all technically caused movements of materials in the ecosphere are examined', Calculating MIPS: Resource productivity of products and services', op. cit.

6   Frans Berkhout, Joyeeta Gupta, Pier Vellinga, *Managing a Material World: Perspectives in Industrial Ecology*, Springer, 2008.

7   'La stratégie du 'facteur 10' et du 'sac à dos écologique', Les Cahiers du développement durable, Cahier 4: outils ['The 'factor 10' and 'ecological rucksack' strategy, the Sustainable Development Books, Book 4: Tools'], *Institut Robert-Schuman Eupen* (Belgium).

8   'La stratégie du 'facteur 10' et du 'sac à dos écologique', op cit.

9   For example, ressourcen-rechner.de/calculator.php?lang=en

10   The overall user average is 40 tonnes.

11   Frédéric Bordage, Aurélie Pontal, Ornella Trudu, 'Quelle démarche Green IT pour les grandes entreprises françaises' ['What steps can French corporations take for green IT?'], *WeGreen IT and WWF*, 2018.

12   Frédéric Bordage, *Sobriété numérique, les clés pour agir* ['Digital sobriety, the keys for action'], Buchet-Chastel, 2019.

13   Ibid.

14   There is, however, the MFCA (Material Flow Cost Accounting) method which, according to the French Environment and Energy Agency (ADEME), is used 'to identify and quantify the flow and stock of materials as well as the costs involved. It targets all flows that do not contribute to the realisation of the final product.' It is especially prevalent in Japan and led to the creation of ISO 14051:2011. See 'Environment management—Material flow cost accounting—General framework', *ISO*, 2018.

15   The expression comes from Corinne Lepage, minister of the environment under the presidency of Jacques Chirac (1995 to 1997), and founding partner of the law firm Huglo Lepage Avocats.

16   See Ernst Ulrich von Weizsäcker, Levin Hunter Lovins, Amory Bloch Lovins, *Factor four: doubling wealth-halving resource use: a new report to the Club of Rome*, St Leonards, N.S.W.: Allen & Unwin, 1997.

17   Interview with Agnès Crepet, head of Software Longevity & IT at Fairphone, 2020.

18   Anti-static suits are worn to prevent an accumulation of static electricity.

19   The French Alternative Energies and Atomic Energy Commission. See leti-cea.com.

20   An invention which earned Jack Kilby (1923–2005) the Nobel Prize in Physics in 2000.

21   TSMC: Taiwan Semiconductor Manufacturing Company.

22   'The chip industry can proclaim 1 trillion served', *Market Watch*, 4 February 2019.

23   Just as the surface of the chips hasn't increased, their prices have not budged, which is a real feat. 'If the car industry did the same today, it

could sell a Rolls Royce for the price of a Citroën 2CV', says François Martin.

24   Interview with Jean-Pierre Colinge, director from 2012 to 2017 at the chief technology office of TSMC, 2020.

25   Ibid.

26   The package enables electric contacts between the chip and the printed circuit board.

27   Ibid.

28   Interview with Karine Samuel, 2019.

29   Extreme ultraviolet lithography is used for carving transistors with unparalleled precision.

30   Interview with Jean-Pierre Colinge, 2020.

31   Interview with Agnès Crepet, 2020.

32   Interview with Jean-Pierre Colinge, 2020.

33   'Short on space, Taiwan embraces a boom in recycling', *The New York Times*, 29 November 2013. The Taiwanese ICT industry makes up 40% of the island nation's exports and 20% of its GDP.

34   Interview with Yongchien Ling, Professor in the Chemistry Department of National Tsing Hua University, 2020.

35   Williams, Eric D., Ayres, Robert U., Heller, Miriam, 'The 1.7 Kilogram Microchip: Energy and Material Use in the Production of Semiconductor Devices', *Environmental Science & Technology, vol. 36, issue 24, pp. 5504–5510*, December 2002.

36   See 'Taiwan's ASE ordered to shut factory for polluting river', *Phys.org*, 20 December 2013. For more on Nerca, refer to 'High tech waste out of control', *CommonWealth Magazine*, vol. 568, 18 March 2015.

37   Interview with Jean-Pierre Colinge, 2020.

38   When another drought hit the country in 2021, TSMC sent water tankers back to the river. Read 'Taiwan's chip industry under threat as drought turns critical', Nikkei Asia, 25 February 2021.

39   'The conundrums of sustainability: carbon emissions and electricity consumption in the electronics and petrochemical industries in Taiwan', MDPI, *Sustainability*, vol. 11, October 2019.

40   Interview with Jean-Pierre Colinge, 2020.

41   'What will it take to improve Taiwan's air?', *The News Lens*, 19 February 2018.

42   'Interview with Han-Lin Li, activist with the NGO Citizen of the Earth, Taiwan, 2020.

43   Ibid.

44   Such as methane and nitrous oxide.

45   In order: hydrofluorocarbons, sulphur hexafluoride, perfluorocarbons, nitrogen trifluoride, and carbon tetrafluoride. According to Guus Velders, a senior scientist in air quality and climate change at the National Institute for Public Health and the Environment (RIVM) in the Netherlands, around 10 per cent of HFCs in the world are used for cooling data centres. At present, little is known about countries like China's ability to deal with data centres at the end of their lifespan, as well as the fluorinated greenhouse gases contained in their air conditioning systems.

46   These gases are stable and electronegative. Also, 80 per cent of SF6 is used to prevent the risk of short-circuits in electrical power systems, and 8 per cent is used by the electronics industry (read Matthew Rigby, Ray F. Weiss, Tim Arnold et al., The increasing atmospheric burden of the greenhouse gas sulphur hexafluoride (SF6), *Atmospheric Chemistry and Physics*, 2020). The semiconductor industry accounts for 45.9 per cent of NF3 consumption. (Read 'NF3 & F2 trend analysis report', *Grand View Research*, September 2015.)

47   Interview in 2020 with BBC journalist Matt McGrath. Read his article 'Climate change: Electrical industry's 'dirty secret' boosts warming', *BBC*, 13 September 2019. He writes that the SF6 leaks in the UK and the European Union in 2017 was equal to the greenhouse-gas emissions of 1.3 million cars over the same year.

48   Already in 2009, Guus Velders co-authored a study in which he warned that this figure could be as high as 20 per cent of total greenhouse-gas emissions: 'The large contribution of projected HFC emissions to future climate forcing', *PNAS (Proceedings of the National Academy of Sciences of the United States of America)*, July 2009. This estimate has since been revised downwards.

49   Tim Arnold et. al., 'Inverse modelling of CF4 and NF3 emissions in East Asia', *Atmospheric Chemistry and Physics*, articles, vol. 18, no. 18, 2018.

50   And since the effects of SF6 and NF3 are far greater than those of CO2 which subside after a century, ultimately there could be more of these gases in the atmosphere than CO2', highlights Tim Arnold, a senior lecturer at the University of Edinburgh (interviewed in 2020). These forecasts are more than likely modest given the unchecked leaks of fluorinated gases which, according to my different sources, are hard to calculate.

51   'HFCs and other F-gases: The worst greenhouse gases you've never heard of', *Greenpeace*, 2009.

52   Veerabhadran Ramanathan, 'Greenhouse effect due to chlorofluorocarbons: climatic implications', *Science*, vol. 190, no. 4209, 3 October 1975.

53   Interview with Durwood Zaelke, president of the Institute for Governance & Sustainable Development (IGSD), 2020.

54   'HFOs come on the scene in refrigeration and air conditioning systems', *Climalife*, 3 January 2013.

55   HFO-1234ze, for example, is starting to be used for data centre cooling systems, as explained to me by Stéphanie Barrault during an interview in 2020. Barrault is in charge of communication and innovation support at CITEPA—the French Technical Reference Centre for Air Pollution and Climate Change.

56   'Honeywell invests $300m in green refrigerant', *Chemistry World*, December 2013.

57   'Position paper on HFO', *Greenpeace*, November 2012.

58   Interview with Durwood Zaelke, 2020.

59   Interview with Paula Tejon, campaign strategist at Greenpeace, 2020.

60   These natural refrigerants comprise water, ammoniac, propane and butane. Read the report by Greenpeace (undated), 'Natural refrigerants: the solutions'.

61   'Courts strike down US restrictions on HFCs', *Chemical & Engineering News*, August 2017.

62   Regulation (EC) No 842/2006 of the European Parliament and of the Council of 17 May 2006 on certain fluorinated greenhouse gases, replaced by Regulation (EU) No 517/2014 of the European Parliament and of the Council of 16 April 2014 on fluorinated greenhouse gases.

63   Interview with Guus Velders, 2020.

64   Interview with Kristen Taddonio, senior climate and energy adviser at the Institute for Governance & Sustainable Development (IGSD), Washington, 2020.

Chapter Four: Investigating a cloud

1   Interview with Fredrik Kallioniemi, commercial director of Hydro66, 2020.

2   Interview with Yves Grandmontagne, editor-in-chief of *Datacenter Magazine*, 2020.

3   Interview with Paul Benoit, co-founder and director of Qarnot Computing, 2020.

4   Such as that of the French manufacturer Delage in Courbevoie near Paris. Read the fascinating report written under the supervision of Cécile Diguet and Fanny Lopez, 'The spatial and energy impact of data centres on the territories', *French Environment and Energy Management Agency (ADEME)*, 2019.

5   'The spatial and energy impact of data centres on the territories', op cit.

6   'The "World's most beautiful data center" is a supercomputer housed in a church', *Vice*, 15 January 2019.

7   Refer to the ADEME report 'The spatial and energy impact of data centres on the territories' (op cit.), which cites the findings of Séverine Hanauer, an expert at the data centre company Vertiv.

8   For more information, the website cloudinfrastructuremap.com maps where the 'cloud' is located around the world. Interview with Paul Benoit, 2019.

9   'The web is much bigger (and smaller) than you think', *Forbes*, 24 April 2012. An exabyte is the equivalent of one billion billion—or one quintillion—bytes.

10   Interview with Fredrik Kallioniemi, 2020.

11   The Australian think tank Consumer Policy Research Centre identifies nine categories of consumer-created data: those related to the device being used, the location of the device, and the consumers' habits and their search history. Added to that are communication content, connections with other consumers, biometric indicators, transactions, and the type of purchase of interest to an individual.

12   Daniel Schellong, Philipp Sadek, Carsten Schaetzberger, and Tyler Barrack, *The promise and pitfalls of e-scooter sharing*, Boston Consulting Group, 16 May 2019.

13   Interview with Mohammad Tasjar, staff attorney at the American Civil Liberties Union (ACLU), 2020.

14   Refer to the privacy policy of the operator Bird: https://www.bird.co/privacy/

15   Ibid.

16   Interview with Klorydryk (pseudonym) of French digital rights advocacy group La Quadrature du Net, 2020. Other mobility companies like Tesla take an even longer view, and want as much data as possible produced by their connected vehicles for their future fleet of self-driving taxis. Given the competition, 'the more data you will have collected, the stronger you are to build and defeat the competition', explained Mohammad Tasjar in 2020. La Quadrature du Net is an advocacy group that 'promotes and defends fundamental freedoms in the digital world'. See laquadrature.net/en.

17   Interview with Raphaël Rollier, innovation and product director, Swisstopo, and author of the blog *Vers une économie numérique* ['Towards a digital economy'] (blogs.letemps.ch/raphael-rollier), 2020.

18   See li.me/en-po/legal/privacy-policy.

19   Interview with Mohammad Tasjar, 2020.

20   The word 'hacktivist' is a contraction of 'hacker' and 'activist'. Hacktivists
      use their computer and information system hacking skills not for
      financial gain, but to bring about more political and social justice in
      society.

21   Interview with MeTaL_PoU (pseudonym), Exodus Privacy, 2020.

22   A list of trackers are available on the Exodus Privacy website: reports.
      exodus-privacy.eu.org/en/trackers/

23   Interview with Raphaël Rollier, 2020.

24   Interview with Mohammad Tasjar, 2020.

25   'NYC taxi data blunder reveals which celebs don't tip—and who
      frequents strip clubs', Fast Company, 2 October 2014.

26   Yves-Alexandre de Montjoye, César A. Hidalgo, Michel Verleysen, and
      Vincent D. Blondel, 'Unique in the crowd: the privacy bounds of human
      mobility', *Scientific Reports*, vol. 3, 2013.

27   Interview with Liam Newcombe, co-author of 'The EU Code of Conduct
      on Data Centres', published in 2015 by the Renewable Energies section of
      the European Commission.

28   Interview with Thorsten Strufe, professor of privacy and IT security at
      the Karlsruhe Institute of Technology, 2020.

29   'Electric scooters are racing to collect your data', ACLU Northern
      California, 25 July 2018.

30   'Federal agencies use cellphone location data for immigration
      enforcement', *The Wall Street Journal*, 7 February 2020. Read also 'Trump
      administration orders Facebook to hand over private information on
      "antiadministration activists"', *The Independent*, 30 September 2017.

31   'Electric scooters are racing to collect your data', op. cit.

32   Currently developed by the Chinese state apparatus on its territory, the
      social-credit system attributes positive or negative ratings to all people
      for their every action in their daily lives. Based on their overall score,
      each person will either receive a reward or, opposite to that, restrictions
      on their freedom.

33   'E-Scooter—the data travel with you', *The Hamburg Commissioner for Data
      Protection and Freedom of Information*, 13 September 2019.

34   'Datenschutzexperten warnen vor E-Scooter-Verleihern', *Fuldainfo.de*, 26
      November 2019.

35   Regulation (EU) 2016/679 of the European Parliament and of the
      Council of 27 April 2016 on the protection of natural persons with
      regard to the processing of personal data and on the free movement of
      such data.

36   torproject.org. Interview with Thorsten Strufe, 2020.

37 A trend that is very clearly explained in *Géopolitique d'Internet. Qui gouverne le monde?* ['The geopolitics of the internet. Who governs the world?'] by David Fayon, Economica, 2013.

38 I recommend Chris Anderson's fascinating analysis of the free economy in his book *Free: The Future of a Radical Price*, op cit.: 'Free does not mean non-profit but means that the product has to go on an indirect route to the market.' This economy exists thanks to advertising, starting with American radio stations in the 1920s, then television, then the internet (the first ad banner appeared in 1994), much to the ire of the pioneers of the Web who conceived the internet as a space rid of the rationale of profit. Today 'the Web represents the extension of the media business model to industries of all.'

39 Julien Le Bot, *Dans la tête de Marc Zuckerberg* ['In the head of Mark Zuckerberg'], Actes Sud, 2019.

40 Interview with Douwe Schmidt, Smart Citizens Lab, Waag Society, 2020.

41 Watch the forty-eight-minute documentary by Sandy Smolan, *The Human Face of Big Data*, Against All Odds Production, 2014. The holy grail is the advent of strong artificial intelligence—a prospect many experts are dubious about, which I address in chapter 8. In his book, the Taiwanese writer Kai-Fu Lee maintains that China will be the master of artificial intelligence, not because its engineers and algorithms will be better than their American counterparts, but because their machines will be rendered more intelligent from the sheer volume of data collected by the Chinese digital giants, the BATX (Baidu, Alibaba, Tencent and Xiaomi). *AI Superpowers: China, Silicon Valley, and the New World Order*, Houghton Mifflin Harcourt Publishing Company, 2018.

42 Interview with Karl Andersson, researcher at Luleå University of Technology, Sweden, 2020.

43 Interview with Hugues Ferreboeuf, associate director of Virtus Management and member of the think tank The Shift Project, 2019.

44 According to the document *Data never sleeps 6.0*, published in 2018 by the US software company Domo, each internet user had, by 2020, consumed an estimated 1.7 megabytes per second—or 146.88 gigabytes per day—of data. Although not updated, this figure has probably been exceeded since.

45 One zettabyte equals 1,000 exabytes.

46 Interview with Fredrik Kallioniemi, 2020.

47 The company Uber (whose e-scooters represent only a minor part of its business) claims to have collected 100 petabytes of data to date, or the equivalent of 660 billion photos posted on Facebook. Read 'Uber's big

data platform: 100+ petabytes with minute latency', *Uber Engineering*, 17 October 2018.

48   'Interxion construit le plus gros datacenter de France, près de Paris' ['Interxion builds the biggest data centre in France, near Paris'], *L'Usine nouvelle*, 6 May 2020.

49   'And the title of the largest data center in the world and largest data center in US goes to ...', *Datacenters.com*, 15 June 2018.

50   An internet exchange point is the infrastructure which providers can access to exchange data among their respective networks. 'Why is Ashburn known as data center alley?', *Upstack*, undated.

51   'Why is Ashburn the data center capital of the world?', *Datacenter.com*, 29 August 2019.

52   'Why is Ashburn known as data center alley?', op. cit.

53   'In Loudoun, neighbors want better looking data centers', *Data Center Frontier*, 9 September 2019.

54   Interview with Brian Carr, Ashburn resident, 2020.

55   'Farmland to data centers switch worries neighbors', *Loudoun Now*, 21 February 2019.

56   Ibid.

57   'Loudoun county's data centers: computing the costs', *Patch*, 2 February 2020.

58   Interview with Brian Carr, 2020.

59   'The NIMBY challenge: A way forward for the data center industry', Data Center Frontier, 21 October 2015.

60   'The NSA is building the country's biggest spy center (Watch what you say)', *Wired*, 15 March 2012.

61   'What happens when the NSA comes to town', *Esquire*, 11 March 2014.

62   'Malls fill vacant stores with server rooms', *The Wall Street Journal*, 3 November 2014.

63   'National Security Agency response to Salt Lake Tribune request for Utah data center water records', *Scribd.com*, uploaded by The Salt Lake Tribune, 2014.

64   'Bluffdale releases water bill for NSA data center', *Fox 13*, 25 April 2014.

65   'A constitutional strategy to stop NSA spying', *American Thinker*, 16 November 2013.

66   Interview with Michael Maharrey, Tenth Amendment Center, 2020.

67   'Nevada beats feds by turning off their water', Tenth Amendment Center, 30 August 2014.

68   Interview with Michael Maharrey, 2020.

69   For a more detailed analysis of Marc Roberts' various positions, enter his name into the website ballotpedia.org. See also his website

robertsmarc.com. Marc Roberts did not respond to my requests for an interview.

70 'Utah lawmaker floats bill to cut off NSA data centre's water supply', *The Guardian*, 12 February 2014.

71 House Bill: H.B 161, Prohibition on electronic data collection assistance, 2014 General Session, State of Utah. Chief Sponsor: Marc K. Roberts.

72 'Utah lawmaker floats bill to cut off NSA data centre's water supply', op. cit.

73 House Bill: H.B 150, Prohibition on electronic data collection assistance, 2015 General Session, State of Utah. Chief Sponsor: Marc K. Roberts.

74 'Rep. Marc Roberts of Utah visits The Jason Stapleton Program to discuss NSA Reform Bill', The Jason Stapleton Program, *The Live Show*, 2 December 2014.

75 Interview with Michael Maharrey, 2020.

76 Ibid.

77 'New pictures show Facebook's massive new data center taking shape in Utah as tech giant plans 900,000 sq. ft expansion to house its servers', *The Daily Mail*, 2 March 2021.

78 I refer you to Mél Hogan's excellent research, 'Data flows and water woes: The Utah Data Center', *Big Data & Society*, 13 July 2015.

79 An opinion already expressed by Ben Tarnoff, a journalist at *The Guardian*. In the article 'To decarbonize we must decomputerize: why we need a Luddite revolution', published in *The Guardian* on 18 September 2019, he writes: '[p]reventing a local police department from constructing an ML-powered panopticon is a matter of [...] climate justice'.

80 The inspiration for this hybridisation of causes goes back to 'environmental racism' which emerged in US in the 1980s. The concept drew parallels between racial equality and ecological questions, as people seen as 'racialised' are more likely to live close to a polluted river, and 'first nations' reserves have a higher prevalence of oil pipelines. Today, a much more general ecological movement is gaining ground, with the environment at the core of every fight. According to its architects, the slightest social or political problem is inevitably linked to a bigger climate issue. To quote Alyssa Battistoni, 'every issue is a climate issue' from her article 'Within and against capitalism', *Jacobin Magazine*, 15 August 2017.

81 Interview with Ben Tarnoff, journalist at *The Guardian*, 2020.

82 'CC1 renewable energy showcase project ribbon cutting ceremony', *NSA*, undated. I also recommend reading 'NSA goes green', a masterpiece in greenwashing: nsa.gov/news-features/initiatives/nsa-goes-green/green-roofs.

83 'The energy secrets of MI6 headquarters', *BBC*, 14 May 2014.

Chapter Five: An appalling waste of electricity

1 '2020—*This is what happens in an Internet minute*', Infographics by Lori Lewis and Chadd Callahan, US digital specialists (@LoriLewis et @ OfficiallyChadd).

2 'A summer storm's disruption is felt in the technology cloud', *The New York Times*, 1 July 2012.

3 'Google goes down for a few minutes, web traffic drops 40 percent', *Wired*, 17 August 2013.

4 'Google's Gmail and Drive suffer global outages', *The Guardian*, 13 March 2019.

5 'Annual data center survey results, *Uptime Institute*, Seattle, Washington, 2019.

6 Interview with Mark Acton, head of the data centre technical advisory division, CBRE Data Center Solutions, 2020.

7 OVH, short for *On vous héberge* ('we host you'), was founded in France in 1999.

8 Companies using OVH include Michelin, Danone, and French government entities including the Centre Pompidou Museum and the Élysée Palace, the residence of the French president.

9 'Numérique: le grand gâchis énergétique' [Digital: the great energy waster'], *CNRS Le journal*, 16 May 2018.

10 Interview with Philippe Luce, director of Institut Datacenter, founder of the consultancy Plus Conseil, and co-founder of the think tank 'Datacenter en transition', 2020.

11 On this, read Elsa Godart's interview 'Le virtuel pose la question de l'effacement des limites' ['The virtual raises the question of erasing boundaries'], *Le Monde*, 2 September 2019. A clear example of this dictate for more immediacy is that a lot of internet boxes don't come with an on/off button, since users no longer have the patience to wait 90 seconds to get a WiFi signal.

12 Interview with Philippe Luce, 2020.

13 Ibid.

14 Despite this, the group did not answer my request for an interview.

15 And more recently, in March 2021, one of the OVH data centres in Strasbourg was, this time, destroyed by a fire. Thousands of clients were affected, and huge amounts of data were lost. For more, read 'French Cloud Computing Firm Catches Fire; websites, companies' services disrupted [VIDEO], *Tech Times*, 11 March 2021.

16 Interview with Paul Benoit, co-founder of Qarnot Computing, 2019.

17 Cécile Diguet and Fanny Lopez, *The spatial and energy impact of data centers on the territories*, ADEME Report, 2019.

18 Interview with Philippe Luce, 2020.

19 Ibid.

20 Interview with Mark Acton, 2020.

21 'Numérique: le grand gâchis énergétique' [Digital: the great energy waster'], op. cit.

22 'Power, pollution and the Internet', *The New York Times*, 22 September 2012. While these findings should be taken with a pinch of salt, they do give a good idea of the extent of wasted electricity.

23 Interview with Philippe Luce, 2020. TikTok is a video-sharing application that is particularly popular with teenagers.

24 Interview with Paul Benoit, 2019.

25 Interview with Thomas Ernst, Scientific Director at the research institute for electronics and information technologies (CEA-Leti), 2019.

26 Keynote by José Guignard, GrDF (Gaz réseau distribution France—the country's distributor of natural gas), Data Centre World, November 2019.

27 As usual, observers clash over how much of the world's electricity data centres actually consume. The most optimistic—and vehemently contested—estimates put the figure at 1 per cent (refer to the report 'Recalibrating global data center energy-use estimates', Eric Masanet et al., *Science*, vol. 367, 28 February 2020). The most pessimistic experts estimate 3 per cent ('Global Warming: data centres to consume three times as much energy in next decade, experts warn', *The Independent*, 23 January 2016). A summary of these estimates is available in the article 'Data centers and global electricity use – two camps', *Hydro66*, 2 May 2020. The truth is probably somewhere between the two. In any event, data centres are believed to account for 15 per cent of the digital sector's environmental impact. Read Frédéric Bordage, *Sobriété numérique, les clés pour agir* ['Digital sobriety, the keys to action'], Buchet-Chastel, 2019. As for the growth of cloud services, see 'To decarbonize we must decomputerize: why we need a Luddite revolution', op. cit., 18 September 2019.

28 Cécile Diguet and Fanny Lopez, 'The spatial and energy impact of data centres on the territories', op. cit.

29 Frankfurt, London, Amsterdam, and Dublin, known collectively as 'FLAD'. 'Report: Dublin replaces Paris in the top four, as European hubs accelerate', *Datacenter Dynamics*, 13 October 2020.

30 Interview with Paul van Engelen, programme manager, Alliander, 2020.

31 Ibid.

32   'Internetsector: betrouwbare stroom vergtkernenergie' ['Internet sector: reliable energy requires nuclear power'], *Het Financieele Dagblad*, 10 February 2016. Interview with Marco Hogewoning, RIPE (Réseaux IP européens) Network Coordination Centre, 2020.

33   'Meer regie op vestiging van datacenters in Amsterdam en Haarlemmermeer' ['More control over the establishment of data centres in Amsterdam and Haarlemmermeer'], *Amsterdam Dagblad*, 12 July 2019.

34   'Haarlemmermeer and Amsterdam get closer to lifting data center moratorium, with restrictions', *Datacenter Dynamics*, 11 June 2020.

35   Interview with Stijn Grove, Dutch Data Centers Association, 2020.

36   'The Amsterdam Effect', *QTS Data Centers*, 12 August 2019.

37   'Establishing a new European data centre in Ireland', *TikTok Newsroom*, 6 August 2020.

38   Talk at the Data Centre World trade show by Olivier Labbé, managing director of Cap DC at Cap Ingelec, November 2019.

39   'All-Island generation capacity statement 2019-2028', EirGrid Group, SONI, 2019.

40   'High-energy data centres not quite as clean and green as they seem', *The Irish Times*, 11 September 2019.

41   Coal accounts for 19 per cent of electricity generation in the United States according to the US Energy Information Administration, 2020.

42   '"Coal is over": the miners rooting for the Green New Deal', *The Guardian*, 12 August 2019.

43   'Coal explained. Where our coal comes from', *U.S. Energy Information Administration*, 9 October 2020.

44   The connection between Altavista Power Station and No. 2 Surface mine can be made using data from the US Energy Information Administration (EIA), which publishes information on the fossil fuel consumption of the country's power stations. 'Form EIA-923', sub-section 'Fuel Receipts and Cost' states that Altavista Power Station was, until 2008, receiving a portion of its coal from No. 2 Surface Mine, which in turn was operated by Twin Star Mining. In 2013, Altavista Power Station switched to biomass energy.

45   Interview with Erin Savage, Central Appalachian senior programme manager, Appalachian Voices, 2021.

46   Using mixtures containing ammonium nitrate and diesel fuel oil.

47   Interview with Junior Walk, awareness activities coordinator at the non-profit Coal River Mountain Watch, 2021. Read 'Blasting above coal river mountain communities', Coal River Mountain Watch, 2 May 2017.

48   'Mountaintop Removal 101', *Appalachian Voices*, undated.

49   Ibid.

50 'Central Appalachia flatter due to mountaintop mining', *Duke Today*, 5 February 2016.

51 For example, see Kristofor A. Voss, Emily S. Bernhardt, 'Effects of mountaintop removal coal mining on the diversity and secondary productivity of Appalachian rivers', *Limnology and Oceanography*, vol. 62, no. 4, March 2017.

52 'Basic information about surface coal mining in Appalachia', *United States Environmental Protection Agency (EPA)*, 6 October 2016.

53 'Central Appalachia flatter due to mountaintop mining', op. cit.

54 Ibid.

55 Interview with Erin Savage, 2021.

56 In 2019, the utility's energy mix was equal parts natural gas and nuclear power (42 per cent respectively), followed by coal (12 per cent), renewable energy sources (5 per cent), and oil (less than 1 per cent). Read 'Dominion Energy power generation mix portfolio 2019', in the report 'Building a cleaner future for our customers and the world', on the website of Dominion Energy.

57 Brent Walls posted screen shots on the Facebook page of Upper Potomac Riverkeeper, 20 May 2021.

58 The Dominion group did not respond to my request aimed at formally establishing a direct connection between the Mount Storm power station and region of Washington, DC, where Ashburn's county is located.

59 Interview with Josh Stanfield, Activate Virginia, 2020.

60 '"Gob"-smacked: Dominion Energy plays both sides, double crosses everyone on Wise County coal-fired power plant closure date?', *Blue Virginia*, 28 February 2020.

61 'What a battle over Virginia's most powerful monopoly can teach Democrats everywhere', *HuffPost*, 2 December 2018.

62 'Dominion Energy nearly quadruples Virginia political contributions from 2018 to 2020', *Energy and Policy Institute*, 28 January 2021.

63 'Democratic sweep sets up confrontation with corporate giant that has loomed over Virginia politics for a century', *The Intercept*, 6 November 2019.

64 Interview with Josh Stanfield, 2020.

65 'In Virginia, a push to save country's 'cleanest' coal plant', *AP News*, 28 February 2020.

66 'Terry Kilgore', *The Virginia Public Access Project*, consulted 7 July 2021.

67 'Methane Management: the challenge', *United Nations Economic Commission for Europe (UNECE)*, undated. 'Methane, explained', *National Geographic*, undated.

68   Interview with Ivy Main, lawyer and advocate with the Sierra Club, 2021.

69   'Clicking Clean: Who is winning the race to build a green internet?', Greenpeace report, 2017.

70   House Bill (H. B) 1526 Electric utility regulation; environmental goals, also known as the Virginia Clean Economy Act, passed in 2020.

71   'Netflix streaming – More energy efficient than breathing', *The Netflix Tech Blog*, 27 May 2015.

72   Interview with Philippe Luce, 2020.

73   'Ensuring renewable electricity market instruments contribute to the global low-carbon transition and sustainable development goals', *Gold Standard*, March 2017.

74   *'Le numérique est-il source d'économies ou de dépenses d'énergie?'* ['Is digital a source of energy savings or spending?'], Institut Sapiens, Paris, 6 July 2020. 'Lean ICT: Towards Digital Sobriety', *The Shift Project*, October 2018.

75   'Un mail est aussi énergivore qu'une ampoule allumée pendant une heure' ['An email uses as much energy as a light bulb on for one hour'], *Le Figaro*, 16 May 2019.

76   'Email statistics report, 2020-2024', *The Radicati Group*, February 2020.

77   More on this topic: 'Climate crisis: The unsustainable use of online video – The practical case study of online video', Executive summary, *The Shift Project*, 2019.

78   Talk by Emmanuel Assié, founder and chairman of Webaxys, at the summer university of the E5T Foundation in August 2019.

Chapter Six: Battle of the far north

1   Interview with Anwar Osseyran, professor of business analytics and computer science at the University of Amsterdam, 2020.

2   'Greenpeace Cloud protest: do Amazon, Microsoft deserve the doghouse?', *Wired*, 2012. 'Greenpeace flies over Silicon Valley, praises Internet companies that have gone green', Greenpeace USA, 3 April 2014.

3   Facebook, Amazon, Apple, Netflix, Google.

4   'Amazon employees step up pressure on climate issues, plan walkout Sept. 20', *The Seattle Times*, 9 September 2019.

5   Keynote by Linda Lescuyer, director for energy at Interxion France, at the Data Centre World tradeshow, 2019.

6   This point is addressed in my previous book (2020) *The Rare Metals War: the dark side of clean energy and digital technologies.* Translated by Bianca Jacobsohn. Melbourne: Scribe.

7   'Apple Campus 2: the greenest building on the planet?', *The Guardian*, 7 December 2014.

8   'Amazon announces five new renewable energy projects', Amazon, 21 May 2020. For more insight into the initiatives led by the FAANG, and more specifically the GAFAM, read the article 'The greening of GAFAM: reality or smokescreen?', *Bio Ressources* blog, 19 October 2020. Greenpeace also hails the efforts of companies like Facebook, Google, Microsoft, Yahoo, and Instagram. Further reading: 'Clicking Clean, who is winning the race to build a green Internet?', *Greenpeace*, 2017.

9   Interview with Christian Déjean, then chief of business development and new markets at Hydro-Québec, 2019.

10 Interview with Yves Grandmontagne, editor-in-chief of Datacenter Magazine, 2020.

11 Ibid.

12 Interview with Philippe Luce, director of Institut Datacenter, founder of the consultancy Plus Conseil, and co-founder of the think tank 'Datacenter en transition', 2020.

13 Interview with Stijn Grove, Dutch Data Center Association, 2020. See the research report 'Les data centers, ou l'impossible frugalité numérique?' ['Data centres, or impossible digital frugality?'], *Caisse des dépôts*, 2020.

14 Interview with Philippe Luce, 2020.

15 Interview with Mariëtte Sedee, in charge of space development at the council Haarlemmermeer 2020. Another solution: computing heaters and boilers to heat buildings, and diversify heat sources. See qarnot.com and 'With Qarnot computing, ENGIE Rassembleurs d'Energies turns data into a free heat source for social housing', *ENGIE*, 31 March 2020.

16 Power usage effectiveness, or PUE, is defined as 'the relation between the total facility energy used to run a data centre and the energy used to run the IT equipment'. Read data centre cooling specialist Benjamin Petschke's article 'Power Usage Effectiveness—PUE and pPUE', *Stulz.de*, undated.

17 Interview with Erik Ferrand, chief sales officer at Qarnot Computing.

18 This is one of the solutions proposed by the Dutch company Asperitas: asperitas.com.

19 Known as Project Natick: natick.research.microsoft.com.

20 'Synthetic DNA holds great promise for data storage', *CNRS News*, 21 October 2020.

21 These speculations were laid out by Karl Andersson and Michael Nilsson, researchers at the Luleå University of Technology, Sweden, during an interview conducted in 2020.

22   Interview with Abdelali Laabi, CEO of the Moroccan IT services consultancy Axeli, 2020.

23   'Facebook to build its own data centers', *Data Center Knowledge*, 21 January 2010.

24   The article, published in January 2020 on the information website SearchDataCenter.com, is no longer available.

25   Interview with Matz Engman, head of the professional association Luleå Business Region (2011–2017), 2020.

26   Read researcher Asta Vonderau's excellent paper 'Scaling the cloud: making state and infrastructure in Sweden', *Ethnos, Journal of Anthropology*, vol. 84, no. 4, 2019.

27   Interview with Matz Engman, 2020.

28   Interview with Niklas Österberg, Arctic Business Incubator, 2020.

29   The data centre did, however, find itself next to a Natura 2000 bird protection area, and the municipality of Luleå had to negotiate with an ornithological society to stop it from obstructing the data centre's construction. See 'Han kan stoppa Facebooks bygge', *Computer Sweden*, 15 September 2011. Local resident, Lennart Hedlund, is believed to have also filed a complaint on environmental grounds; it apparently held up building operations somewhat, but was ultimately thrown out of court.

30   'Luleå gives Facebook "thumbs up"'in record bid', *The Local*, 17 March 2013.

31   Many experts agree that only the most recent data is stored in Luleå. 'Cold' data, which is older and therefore less consulted, is apparently hosted in other data centres further away from European internet users.

32   Interview with Niklas Österberg, 2020.

33   Interview with Karl Andersson, 2020.

34   Interview with Karl Andersson, 2020.

35   Interview with Niklas Österberg, 2020.

36   Asta Vonderau, 'Scaling the cloud: making state and infrastructure in Sweden', *op. cit.*

37   Jeffrey A. Winters, *Power in Motion: capital mobility and the Indonesian State*, Cornell University Press, 1996.

38   Hannah Appel, 'Offshore work: oil, modularity, and the how of capitalism in Equatorial Guinea', *American Ethnologist, vol. 39, no. 4*, November 2012.

39   'Google reaped millions in tax breaks as it secretly expanded its real estate footprint across the U.S.', *The Washington Post*, 15 February 2019.

40   'Documents for Google in Lenoir, North Carolina', *The Washington Post*, 25 January 2019.

41   Vinnie Mirchandani, *The New Technology Elite: how great companies optimize both technology consumption and production*, John Wiley & Sons Inc, 2012.

42   'Secret Amazon data center gives nod to Seinfeld', *Infosecurity*, 12 October 2018.

43   Tung-Hui Hu, *A Prehistory of the Cloud*, The MIT Press, 2015.

44   Interview with Asta Vonderau, executive director of the Centre for interdisciplinary Regional Studies (ZIRS) at Martin Luther University of Halle-Wittenberg (Germany), and author of the article 'Scaling the cloud: making state and infrastructure in Sweden', *op. cit.*, 2020.

45   As well as Randi, Parki, Seitevare, and Akkats.

46   The fight against CO_2 emissions is too often the only measure of our ecological actions. Yet although the carbon emissions of hydroelectricity are low, it is not without impacts on the environment. These are listed extensively in the literature, including the report 'Hydropower pressure on European rivers: The story in numbers' of the World Wide Fund for Nature (WWF), published in 2019: 'The number of hydropower plants in Europe is already exceptionally high and their overlap with protected areas reveal a tremendous pressure on Europe's biodiversity ...'. Quebec is also a choice destination for data centres, since 97 per cent of electricity generated by hydroelectric power stations. 'It's a gamble', says Christian Déjean, the chief of business development and new markets at Hydro-Québec at the time of our interview. 'We have electricity that is available, inexpensive, renewable, and not intermittent!' However, reckons Philippe Luce, director of Institut Datacenter, this Québécois electricity 'is not green because by submerging the valleys, we have wiped out the biotope over thousands of hectares, created reservoirs, wrecked water ways to supply the dams, and caused entire local populations to migrate. You need to look at the entire chain of electricity generation and examine its origin.' We should also consider the impact of infrastructure on the living conditions of the Sámi people, who represent the last nomads of Europe occupying northern Scandinavia and the Kola Peninsula, in Russia. 'Infrastructure like hydroelectric dams can obstruct the migration routes of the Sámi and reindeer', exposed Runar Myrnes Balto, political adviser to the executive council of the Sámi Parliament of Norway, during an interview in the Norwegian city of Tromsø in 2020. For more extensive research on the impact of hydroelectric dams on the Sámi of Norway, read Åsa Össbo and Patrik Lantto, 'Colonial tutelage and industrial colonialism: reindeer husbandry and early 20th-century hydroelectric development in Sweden', *Scandinavian Journal of History*, vol. 36, no. 3, July 2011.

47   The page is called *Vuollerim/Jokkmokk Lilla Lule Älv ska leva igen*.

48   Interview with Christer Borg, association Älvräddarna, 2020.

49   On Rennesøy island in the south of Norway, a data centre of the company Green Mountain was even built at the bottom of a fjord in a

former NATO submarine base. The data centre is cooled by pumping seawater into pipes in the server rooms. 'Except that the grids on the pipe were the wrong size, and an entire population of crustaceans, fish, and prawns were sucked in, and spawned in the pipes. It was like a slow-roast seafood barbecue in there,' says Yves Grandmontagne, editor-in-chief of *Datacenter Magazine*, who visited the facility in 2015. Interview conducted in 2020.

50 'Kolos to build world's largest data center in northern Norway', press conference in Ballangen, Norway, 18 August 2017.

51 Inspired by the name given to a train cutting through icy landscapes that was imagined in the 1980s by Benjamin Legrand, Jacques Lob, and Jean-Marc Rochette in a science-fiction comic book, later adapted for screen in 2013 by the South Korean director Bong Joon-ho.

52 For creating digital currencies. Read 'Kolos data centre park in Norway is being acquired by cryptocurrency miners', *Datacenter Dynamics*, 28 March 2018.

53 'Bitcoin mining consumes 0.5% of all electricity used globally and 7 times Google's total usage, new report says', *Business Insider India*, 7 September 2021. 'Bitcoin uses more electricity than many countries. How is that possible?', *The New York Times*, 3 September 2021.

54 Interview with Christian Andersen, editor-in-chief of *Fremover*, 2020.

55 Interview with Isabelle Kemlin, Nordics business unit director at CBRE Data Centre Solutions, 2020.

56 'Russian personal data localisation requirements', *Microsoft*, 30 November 2020.

57 Talk by Olivier Labbé, CEO of Cap Ingelec, at the Data Centre World trade show, 2019.

58 Interview with Ahmed Ahram, director of CAP DC, the French subsidiary of Cap Ingelec, 2020.

59 'No one can precisely measure the ecological gains generated by moving data centres closer to end users, but it is substantial', said Philippe Luce during an interview in 2020.

60 Interview with Christian Déjean, 2019.

61 This number was reported to me by Ian Bitterlin, consulting engineer and formerly visiting professor at the University of Leeds, United Kingdom, in an interview given in 2020.

62 Interview with Michiel Steltman, managing director of the digital infrastructure association of the Netherlands (DINL), 2020. The future will certainly be based on a combination of centralised and decentralised (edge) storage and data-processing solutions.

63 digitalcleanupday.org/

64   Interview with Anneli Ohvril, executive director of Let's Do It World, 2020.

65   Ibid.

66   Kris de Decker, 'Why We Need a Speed Limit for the Internet', *Low-Tech Magazine*, 2015.

67   Renee Obringer et al., 'The overlooked environmental footprint of increasing Internet use', *Resources, Conservation and Recycling*, vol. 167, April 2021.

68   signal.org, olvid.io/en, protonmail.com, e foundation. Users can also opt for operating systems like GrapheneOS (grapheneos.org) and LineageOS (lineageos.org). Some experts, like Agnès Crepet, head of software longevity & IT at Fairphone, reckon that Facebook has gone too far in its data collection policy, and that users are steadily moving away from the American tech titan's services.

69   duckduckgo.com

70   This is precisely what is offered by French telecommunications service provider TeleCoop, 'the first cooperative teleco operator committed to the ecological and social transition'. See telecoop.fr

71   This seems to be the opinion of US engineer and digital pioneer Vint Cerf, born in 1943, who said 'internet access will become a privilege, not a right'.

72   'En 2050, Internet sera-t-il toujours debout?' ['In 2050, will the internet still be standing?'], *CNET France*, 1 October 2019.

73   Interview with Jelle Slenters, head of business development for EMEA (Europe, Middle East, Africa) at Sims Lifecycle Services, 2020.

74   Interview with Philippe Luce, 2020.

Chapter Seven: Expansion of the digital universe

1   Steve Case, *The Third Wave: an entrepreneur's vision of the future*, Simon & Schuster, 2017.

2   For a more educational definition of the Internet of Everything and its economic potential, watch the YouTube video 'The Internet of Everything is the New Economy' (August 2014) by US firm Cisco.

3   Kevin Kelly, *The Inevitable: understanding the 12 technological forces that will shape our future*, Viking, 2016.

4   Ibid.

5   RFID stands for radio-frequency identification. With this technology a sensor is able to identify an object using radio-frequency signals, allowing two objects to communicate and share information with one another.

6   Byung-Chul Han, *In the Swarm: digital prospects*, The MIT Press, 2017. Original title: *Im Schwarm. Ansichten des Digitalen*. Translated by Erik Butler. MSB Matthes & Seitz Berlin, 2013.

7   Interview with Fredrik Kallioniemi, commercial director of Cloud company Hydro66, 2020.

8   'Nataliya Kosmyna, à la recherche d'une intelligence artificielle éthique', ['Nataliya Kosmyna, in the search for ethical artificial intelligence'], *Le Monde*, 29 September 2020. Others, including scientist Joël de Rosnay, refer to 'the symbiotic web'. Read 'Vers la fusion homme-machine. Un Web en symbiose avec notre cerveau et notre corps', *Sociétés*, no. 129, 2015/3, as well as *The Symbiotic Man: a new understanding of the organisation of life and a vision of the future*. Translated by Phyllis Aronoff, Rémy Charest, Howard Scott, and Wanda Romer Taylor. McGraw-Hill, 2000.

9   'Cisco Edge-to-Enterprise IoT Analytics for Electric Utilities Solution Overview', *Cisco*, 1 February 2018.

10   'What is 5G? Your questions answered', *CNN*, 6 March 2020.

11   Interview with Martin Péronnet, managing director of Monaco Telecom, 2020.

12   'South Korea reaches almost 13 million 5G subscribers in January', *RCR Wireless News*, 1 March 2021.

13   Interview with Cho Mu-hyun, journalist, 2020.

14   Keynote by Stéphen Kerckhove, managing director of Agir pour l'Environnement, at the conference 'La 5G: avancée technologique, recul écologique?' ['5G: technological advance or ecological decline?'), La Recyclerie, Paris, 9 March 2020.]

15   '5G: an ambitious roadmap for France', *ARCEP*, 16 July 2018.

16   Interview with Jean-Pierre Raskin, researcher and lecturer at Louvain School of Engineering (Belgium), Institute of Information and Communication Technologies, Electronics and Applied Mathematics (ICTEAM), 2020.

17   'China's telecoms carriers push to complete "political task" of 5G network roll-out amid coronavirus crisis', *South China Morning Post*, 5 March 2020.

18   'Merkel fordert mehr Tempo beim digitalen Wandel' ['Merkel urges calls for more speed in the digital transition'], *Süddeutsche Zeitung*, 1 December 2020.

19   'Le retard numérique allemand affole Angela Merkel' ['Germany is behind on digital and it's terrifying Angela Merkel'], *L'Obs*, 31 January 2017.

20   Interview with John Booth, consultant at Green IT Amsterdam, 2020.

21   'Gallium: China tightens grip on wonder metal as Huawei works on promising applications beyond 5G', *South China Morning Post*, 20 July

2019. This information on scandium was given to me by Christopher Ecclestone, a mining strategist at Hallgarten & Company, London, during an interview in 2020. Interview with Pierre-Marie Théveniaud, president of the French non-profit Robin des Toits, 2020.

22 See 'White Paper: The Road to 5G is Paved with Fiber', *The Fiber Broadband Association*, 12 December 2017, and 'Fiber Broadband Association: 1.4M Fiber Miles Needed for 5G in Top 25 U.S. Metros', IEEE Communications Society, 19 December 2017.

23 '5G's rollout speeds along faster than expected, even with the coronavirus pandemic raging', *CNET*, 30 November 2020.

24 'Canalys: 278 million 5G smartphones to be sold in 2020', *GSM Arena*, 10 September 2020.

25 Keynote by Michèle Rivasi, Member of European Parliament with Europe Écologie les Verts, at the conference La 5G: avancée technologique, recul écologique? ['5G: technological advance or ecological decline?'], *La Recyclerie*, Paris, 9 March 2020.

26 Such fears fall under what doctors call the 'the nocebo effect', which is characteristic of our modern, risk-averse societies. Unlike the placebo effect, the nocebo effect occurs when a patient believes they are suffering the effect of what is in fact an inert substance that has been presented as an active medication.

27 'It is wholly a confusion of ideas to suppose that the economical use of fuel is equivalent to a diminished consumption. The very contrary is the truth.' William Stanley Jevons, *The Coal Question: an inquiry concerning the progress of the nation, and the probable exhaustion of our coal-mines*, Nabu Press, 2010 (first edition Macmillan and Co, 1865).

28 'Fuel Consumption of Cars and Vans', *International Energy Agency (IEA)*, June 2020.

29 See the sale statistics on the website of the International Organization of Motor Vehicle Manufacturers: oica.net/category/sales-statistics/. Furthermore, 'reducing the consumption of cars did not mean a decrease in petrol consumption; it just meant motorists could do more kilometres', adds a specialist in 'Numérique: le grand gâchis énergétique' [Digital: the great energy waster'], *CNRS Le journal*, 16 May 2018.

30 'CO2 emissions from commercial aviation: 2013, 2018, and 2019', International Council on Clean Transportation (ICCT), 8 October 2020. 'CO2 emissions from aviation', Briefing EU Legislation in Progress, 23 January 2018.

31 Christopher C. M. Kyba et al., 'Artificially lit surface of Earth at night increasing in radiance and extent', *Science Advances*, 22 November 2017.

32 'It's not your imagination: phone battery life is getting worse', *The Washington Post*, 1 November 2018.

33 '5G consumer potential – Busting the myths around the value of 5G for consumers', An Ericsson Consumer & IndustryLab Insight Report, *Ericsson*, May 2019.

34 'Pourquoi la 5G est une mauvaise nouvelle pour l'environnement' ['Why 5G is bad news for the environment'], o1net, 26 January 2020.

35 Watch Orange's promotional video on YouTube boasting the merits of 5G: '5G: un réseau pour TOUS et PARTOUT' ['5G: a network for ALL EVERYWHERE'].

36 Interview with Jean-Pierre Raskin, 2020.

37 Interview with Frédéric Bordage, founder of GreenIT.fr, 2018.

38 Interview with Sébastien Crozier, chairman of CFE-CGC Orange, 2020.

39 Ibid.

40 Interviews with Françoise Berthoud, IT research engineer at the French National Centre for Scientific Research (CNRS), 2019 and 2020.

41 Christopher L. Magee et al., 'A simple extension of dematerialization theory: Incorporation of technical progress and the rebound effect', *Technological Forecasting and Social Change*, vol. 117, April 2017. The same conclusions were reached in a study on the supposed dematerialisation of 99 world economies: 'Results show that no countries exhibit a dematerialization of economic activity'. From Federico M. Pulselli et al., 'The world economy in a cube: A more rational structural representation of sustainability', *Global Environmental Change*, vol. 35, November 2015.

42 Read Isabelle Autissier's preface of Frédéric Bordage's book *Sobriété numérique, les clés pour agir* ['Digital sobriety, the keys for action'], Buchet-Chastel, 2019.

43 Over 12 billion views in 2020, earning 29.5 million dollars.

44 'Driving transformation in the automotive and road transport ecosystem with 5G', *Ericsson Technology Review*, no. 13, 13 September 2019.

45 Zia Wadud et al., 'Help or hindrance? The travel, energy and carbon impacts of highly automated vehicles', *Transportation Research Part A: Policy and Practice*, vol. 86, April 2016. There are also claims that the resulting decrease in the number of road accidents could lead to the manufacture of vehicles that are lighter—therefore releasing fewer emissions—because of the reduced risk of collisions. Read 'Connected cars could be big energy savers, or not', *Politico*, 20 October 2016.

46 Electronic control units (ECUs) control the functioning of the engine and other vehicle components (gearbox, braking system, etc.). See 'Number of automotive ECUs continues to rise', *ee News Automotive*, 15 May 2019.

47 'The race for cybersecurity: protecting the connected car in the era of new regulation', *McKinsey & Company*, 10 October 2019.

48 Ibid.

49 Interview with Mathieu Saujot, research director, 'ways of life in transition', IDDRI, Paris 2020. Even Carlos Tavares, head of Stellantis (PSA-Fiat-Chrysler), has announced that the company will discontinue research in this domain, arguing that 'given the additional cost of the technology, the price of the car will be such that whoever can afford it will in any case not be the one behind the wheel, but the one at the backseat'. Read 'Premiers coups de frein sur la voiture autonome' ['The brakes are being put on the autonomous car'], *Les Échos*, 26 March 2019.

50 Lidar (light detection and ranging) is a digital tool that uses lasers to give a 360-degree, three-dimensional scan of the driverless car's surrounding environment. It can contain up to 64 lasers, and collect millions of data points every second. Read 'Autonomous cars could drive a deluge of data center demand', Rich Miller for *Data Center Frontier*, 24 May 2017.

51 Namely, Stéphane Nègre, CEO of Intel Corporation. See 'La donnée: nouvel or noir de la voiture de demain' ['Data: the new black gold of tomorrow's car'], *La Tribune*, 22 March 2018. Also refer to Laurent Castaignède's book, '*Airvore* ou la face obscure des transports' ['*Airvore* or the dark side of transport'], *Écosociété*, 2018.

52 Interview with Mathieu Saujot, 2020.

53 'Do driverless cars really need edge computing?', *Data Center Knowledge*, 12 July 2019.

54 Nikolas Thomopoulos and Moshe Givoni, 'The autonomous car—a blessing or a curse for the future of low carbon mobility? An exploration of likely vs. desirable outcomes', *European Journal of Futures Research*, vol. 3, no. 1, December 2015. According to Thomopoulos and Givoni, there is 'the risk of autonomous cars leading to the renaissance of the private car [...] at the expense of public and NMT (non-motorised transport)'.

55 'Not all of our self-driving cars will be electrically powered – here's why', *The Verge*, 12 December 2017.

56 'Another big challenge for autonomous car engineers: Energy efficiency', *Automotive News*, 11 October 2017.

57 Mathieu Saujot, Laura Brimont, Oliver Sartor, 'Putting autonomous mobility on the path to sustainable development' (full report in French), IDDRI, June 2018. The researchers assert the additional release of 26 grams of CO_2 per kilometre versus current vehicle emissions in Europe, produces on average an additional 122.4 grams of CO_2 per kilometre.

58 Interview with Laurent Castaignède, author of the book '*Airvore* ou la face obscure des transports' ['*Airvore* or the dark side of transport'], op. cit.

59   Interview with Mathieu Saujot, 2020.

60   Nir Eyal, *Hooked: How to Build Habit-Forming Products*, CreateSpace Independent Publishing Platform, December 2013. Products, Portfolio Penguin, 2014.

61   Blue is the darkest colour after black, and offers good screen readability.

62   Watch the talk given by Paul Ray on 8 December 2009 entitled *Designing Bing: Heart and Science*.

63   Ibid.

64   'Why Google has 200m reasons to put engineers over designers', *The Guardian*, 5 February 2014. Google and Bing did not respond to my requests for interview.

65   Patrick Süskind, *Perfume*, Hamish Hamilton, 1985.

66   Interview with Karl Pineau, co-director of Designers Ethiques, 2020.

67   'Why Apple's notification bubbles are so stressful', *OneZero*, 27 February 2019.

68   Martin G. Helander, Thomas K. Landauer, Prasad V. Prabhu, *Handbook of Human-Computer Interaction*, Elsevier Science, 1997.

69   'The button color A/B test: red beats green', *Hubspot*, 2 August 2011.

70   'Introducing your new navigation', *Facebook*, 5 February 2010.

71   'Dopamine, smartphones & you: A battle for your time', *Science in the News*, Harvard Graduate School of the Arts and Sciences, 1 May 2018.

72   Interview with Sören Enholm, CEO of the Swedish firm TCO (Total Cost of Ownership), 2020.

73   Mireille Campana et al., 'Réduire la consommation énergétique du numérique' ['Reducing the energy consumption of digital technologies'], Ministry of the Economy and Finance, France, report for the General Council for the Economy, December 2019.

74   'The worrying trajectory of energy consumption by digital technology', *Institut Mines-Télécom*, 28 May 2020. Republished from the original French article 'L'inquiétante trajectoire de la consommation énergétique du numérique', *The Conversation*, 2 March 2020.

75   Talk by Inès Leonarduzzi, CEO of Digital For The Planet, at the online conference 'Croissance numérique et protection de la planète, un oxymore?' ['Digital growth and protecting the planet, an oxymoron?'] at the Institut français de Munich, 20 November 2020.

76   See the 'Take Control' section on the Center for Humane Technology website: humanetech.com/take-control.

77   'Troubles de l'attention, du sommeil, du langage ... La multiplication des écrans engendre une décérébration à grande échelle" ['Attention deficit, sleep and language problems ... The multiplication of screens is leading to large-scale decerebration"], *Le Monde*, 21 October 2019.

78   designersethiques.org

79   See *Le Guide d'éco-conception de services numériques* [French only] by the Ethical Designers: eco-conception.designersethiques.org/guide/.

80   'Is the answer to phone addiction a worse phone?', *The New York Times*, 12 January 2018.

81   Open 'Settings', then 'Accessibility', then 'Color Filters'. Push the main button of the device three times to activate Grayscale mode. This feature is also available for the current versions of Android under 'Digital Wellbeing'.

82   Interview with Karl Pineau, 2020.

83   Refer to the keynote presentation by Dr. Mike Hazas of the University of Lancaster (UK) at the conference 'Drowning in data – digital pollution, green IT, and sustainable access', EuroDIG, Tallinn (Estonia), 7 June 2017.

84   Interview with Jean-Pierre Raskin, 2020.

Chapter Eight: When robots out-pollute humans

1   Keynote presentation by Dr Mike Hazas of the University of Lancaster (UK) at the conference 'Drowning in data – digital pollution, green IT, and sustainable access', EuroDIG, Tallinn (Estonia), 7 June 2017.

2   The term 'robot' designates 'a mechanical device capable of performing tasks, with autonomy of decision-making over the basic actions comprising said tasks'. This is the definition of the French Inter-ministerial Department for Forward Planning and Prediction of Economic Change (PIPAME) and the French General Directorate for Competitiveness, Industry and Services in the report 'Le développement industriel futur de la robotique personnelle et de service en France' ['The future industrial development of personal and service robotics in France'], 12 April 2012. The scope of my analysis also includes the machines, interfaces, and connected objects that make up the digital universe.

3   Bruno Patino, *The Goldfish Civilization*. Grasset, 2019.

4   'The flourishing business of fake YouTube views', *The New York Times*, 11 August 2018.

5   'Cisco Annual Internet Report (2018–2023) White Paper', updated on 9 March 2020.

6   Read the paper 'Vivre avec les objets connectés' ['Living with connected objects'] in the journal *Third*, no. 3, November 2019. Also refer to the interview with Laurence Allard, lecturer in communication science, researcher at IRCAV (cinema and audiovisual research institute) of

Université Sorbonne Nouvelle, co-founder of the group Mobile et Création, and co-founder of Labo Citoyen.

7   Interview with Liam Newcombe, senior vice-president of engineering at Energy Internet Corporation, 2020.

8   'Send scam emails to this chatbot and it'll waste their time for you', *The Verge*, 10 November 2017.

9   Keynote presentation by Dr Mike Hazas of the University of Lancaster (UK) at the conference 'Drowning in data – digital pollution, green IT, and sustainable access', EuroDIG, Tallinn (Estonia), 7 June 2017.

10   'Training a single AI model can emit as much carbon as five cars in their lifetimes', *MIT Technology Review*, 6 June 2019.

11   A change that was already sanctioned by other global stock exchanges, such as the stock exchange in Paris, which went fully electronic in 1987.

12   Friedrich Moser and Daniel Wunderer, *Money Bots*, 90 minutes, Blue+Green communication, Arte France, RBB, 2020.

13   Interview with Stéphane Barbier de la Serre, macro-economic strategist, Makor Capital Markets, 2020. It is interesting to note that one of the mottos of this company, which uses algorithm-enhanced investment strategies, is 'We don't speculate, we calculate'.

14   Interview with Juan Pablo Pardo-Guerra, associate professor at the University of California, San Diego, 2020.

15   Interview with Stéphane Barbier de la Serre, 2020.

16   Interview with Jérémy Désir, former quantitative analyst at HSBC Bank, 2020.

17   Ibid.

18   'Intelligence Artificielle (IA) et gestion d'actifs: améliorer la stratégie d'investissement et la connaissance des Investisseurs', ['Artificial intelligence (AI) and asset management: improving the investment strategy and knowledge of investors'], *IRevue Banque*, 25 January 2019.

19   'Quants have a fundamental issue with indiscretion', *Bloomberg*, 6 April 2020.

20   Aladdin stands for asset, liability, debt and derivative investment network. See www.blackrock.com/uk/professionals/solutions/aladdin.

21   For an explainer on how Aladdin works, read 'BlackRock's Edge: why technology is creating the Amazon of Wall Street', *Forbes*, 19 December 2017.

22   Interview with Juan Pablo Pardo-Guerra, 2020.

23   Michael Lewis, *Flash Boys. A Wall Street Revolt*, W. W. Norton & Company, 2014.

24   Juan Pablo Pardo-Guerra, *Automating Finance: Infrastructures, Engineers, and the Making of Electronic Markets*, Cambridge University Press, 2019.

See also 'Book Review: automating finance', *CFA Institute*, 13 March 2020.

25   'BlackRock's black box: the technology hub of modern finance', *Financial Times*, 24 February 2020.

26   Interview with Jérémy Désir, 2020.

27   Interview with Michael Kearns, professor of computer and information science at the University of Pennsylvania, 2020.

28   'The passives problem and Paris goals: how index investing trends threaten climate action', report by the Sunrise Project, 2020. This trend is not specific to the United States: passive management has long been at the origin of half of investments on the Asian markets, and a third of investments on the European markets. Read 'Environment program request for proposal: aligning passive investment with Paris climate goals', *William and Flora Hewlett Foundation*, 28 January 2020.

29   The list can be consulted upon request on the Fossil Free Fonds website. In 2021, Encana was ranked number 30 on the list (35 in 2014).

30   'Encana needed to tap into passive investing, CEO Suttles says', *Bloomberg Markets and Finance*, 31 October 2019.

31   'Encana receives securityholder approval for reorganization', *Encana Corporation*, 14 January 2020.

32   Encana did not reply to my request for interview.

33   'Who owns the world of fossil fuels. A forensic look at the operators and shareholders of the listed fossil fuel reserves', *Finance Map*, 2018 and 2019.

34   Thermal coal intensity (TCI) is expressed in tons of carbon dioxide per million dollars of assets under management (AuM). '[Inside Story] COP24 highlights limits to financial engagement on coal-related emissions', *Novethic*, 17 December 2018.

35   'The passives problem and Paris goals: how index investing trends threaten climate action', op. cit.

36   Ibid.

37   Interview with Diana Best, senior finance strategist, Sunrise Project, 2020.

38   In fact, some financial services companies offer this kind of investment—MSCI, Stoxx, Solactive, etc. Read 'Une piste pour investir durable en Bourse à moindres frais' ['One way of investing sustainably and affordably on the stock market'], *Le Monde*, 2 November 2020.

39   Interview with Diana Best, 2020.

40   'The passives problem and Paris goals: how index investing trends threaten climate action', op. cit.

41   'Artificial intelligence gets a seat in the boardroom', *Nikkei Asia*, 10 May 2017. Vital stands for Validating Investment Tool for Advancing Life

sciences. The motto of DKV is 'Knowledge is Power; Deep Knowledge is Transcendent Power' (see company website).

42 'A.I. has arrived in investing. Humans are still dominating', *The New York Times*, 12 January 2018.

43 Interview with Juan Pablo Pardo-Guerra, 2020.

44 Two Sigma Investments LLC, 31 March 2011.

45 'Green Horizon. Driving sustainable development', *IBM*, undated.

46 'IBM expands Green Horizons initiative globally to address pressing environmental and pollution challenges', *IBM*, 9 December 2015.

47 'How artificial intelligence can fight air pollution in China', *MIT Technology Review*, 31 August 2015.

48 Ibid.

49 Interview with Lex Coors, chief data center technology and engineering officer, Interxion, 2020.

50 Michio Kaku, *The Future of the Mind: the scientific quest to understand, enhance, and empower the mind*, Doubleday, 2014.

51 David Rolnick et al., *Tackling climate change with machine learning*, Future of Life Institute, Boston, 22 October 2019.

52 'A physicist on why AI safety is "the most important conversation of our time"', *The Verge*, 29 August 2017.

53 'The Doomsday invention: Will artificial intelligence bring us utopia or destruction?', *The New Yorker*, 23 November 2015.

54 'Fourth industrial revolution for the earth. Harnessing artificial intelligence for the earth', World Economic Forum – Stanford Woods Institute for the Environment, *Pricewaterhouse Coopers (PwC)*, January 2018.

55 Interview with Stuart Russell, professor of computer science, University of California, Berkeley, 2020.

56 Interview with Tristram Walsh, Alice Evatt and Christian Schröder, researchers in physics, philosophy, and engineering science, respectively. They are also the instigators of the 2020 AI impact weekend *AI + Climate Change: building AI solutions to help solve the world's climate crisis* held in February 2020 at the Oxford Foundry, a business accelerator of the University of Oxford.

57 Interview with Lex Coors, 2020.

58 'Fourth industrial revolution for the earth. Harnessing artificial intelligence for the earth', World Economic Forum – Stanford Woods Institute for the Environment, *Pricewaterhouse Coopers (PwC)*, January 2018.

59 Keynote by Emmanuel Assié, founder and CEO of Webaxys, Data Centre World, 2019.

60   Interview with Tristram Walsh, research associate at University of Oxford, Smith School of Enterprise and the Environment, 2020.

61   Encyclopedia Britannica, *Deep Ecology*.

62   Nick Bostrom, 'Existential risks. Analyzing human extinction scenarios and related hazards', *Journal of Evolution and Technology*, vol. 9, no. 1, 2002.

63   Stuart Russell, *Human Compatible: artificial intelligence and the problem of control*, Penguin Books, 2020.

64   Interview with Stuart Russell, 2020.

65   'How the enlightenment ends', *The Atlantic*, June 2018.

Chapter Nine: Twenty thousand tentacles under the sea

1   Remarks by US vice president Al Gore at the National Press Club in Washington, DC, 21 December 1993.

2   Named after the founder of the Red Cross, Henry Dunant (1828–1910), who was also the first to receive the Nobel Peace Prize. The first cable, 'Curie', made landfall in 2019 and connects Valparaiso (Chile) and Los Angeles.

3   Orange owns two of the Dunant cable's 12 fibre-pairs. Despite my contacting the group communiations team on numerous occasions, they were unwilling to tell me the day of the cable landing. With the help of many experts, I followed the movements of the cable layers likely to be involved in laying the Dunant, using their geopositioning system in real time on myshiptracking.com. In the end, I was given the information by the company Louis Dreyfus TravOcean, which took part in the landing of Dunant in France.

4   Interview with David Walters, independent consultant in the UK, and former engineer in the telecommunications cables industry, 2020.

5   Interview with Bertrand Clesca, founder off OpticalCloudInfra (France) and consultant with Pioneer Consulting, 2020.

6   The metals are copper, steel, or aluminium. With fibre optics, light travels at approximately 66 per cent of the speed at which it travels in the air.

7   Quoted by Patrice Flichy in his book *Dynamics of Modern Communication: the shaping and impact of new communication technologies*, SAGE Publications, 1995.

8   Interview with Jean-David Fabre, sales director at Ciena, 2020. For further reading on the notion of speed through the harnessing of light, read Paul Virilio's *The Administration of Fear*. Semiotext(e), 2006.

9   'How Google is cramming more data into its new Atlantic cable', *Wired*, 5 April 2004.

10   Patrice Flichy, op. cit. The author describes optical fibres as such on account of their finesse and the pulses of light they conduct.

11   'Tonga almost entirely offline after fault develops in undersea fibre-optic cable', *New Zealand Herald*, 24 January 2019.

12   Not taking into account unofficial cables, deployed for military or intelligence purposes. In 2015, the American geographer and artist Trevor Paglen created a superb exhibition by photographing the optical cables around the world used by the National Security Agency (NSA). The images are available in the articles 'Photos of the submarine internet cables the NSA probably tapped', *Wired*, 20 September 2016, and 'Trevor Paglen plumbs the internet', *The New Yorker*, 22 September 2015.

13   Google is currently deploying a new cable, Grace Hopper, named after the American computer science researcher (1906–1992), between New York, the UK, and Spain ('Google is laying a giant new undersea internet cable stretching from New York to the UK and Spain', *Business Insider India*, 28 July 2020), while Facebook is laying another (2Africa) around the African continent ('Cabling Africa: the great data race to serve the 'last billion'', *Financial Times*, 31 January 2021). Telecom Egypt owns a fibre-pair that is about to link South Africa to Saint Helena in the South Atlantic Ocean (Equiano, see 'Telecom Egypt signs agreement with St Helena Government to provide it with its first subsea solution', *Capacity Media*, 2 November 2020), which the Viettel group is connecting Vietnam, China, Japan, and Thailand (Asia Direct Cable, see 'Asia Direct Cable Consortium to build new Asia Pacific submarine cable', nec.com, 11 June 2020).

14   The cable went into service in February 2021. Read 'The Dunant subsea cable, connecting the US and mainland Europe, is ready for service', Google Cloud, 3 February 2021.

15   The 2020 Submarine Networks EMEA (EMEA) conference.

16   Interview with Linsey Thomas, British independent consultant in telecommunications, 2020.

17   Interview with Keith Schofield, strategic adviser at Pioneer Consulting (United States), 2020.

18   'Internet: la lutte pour la suprématie se joue sous les océans' ['Internet: the fight for supremacy is taking place under the ocean'], *Les Échos*, 6 April 2019.

19   David Fayon, 'Géopolitique d'Internet. Qui gouverne le monde? ['The geopolitics of the internet. Who governs the world?'], *Economica*, 2013. 'Submarine Cables and the Oceans: connecting the world', International Cable Protection Committee, United Nations Environment Programme, World Conservation Monitoring Centre (UNEP-WCMC), December 2009.

20   See 'Undersea cables: indispensable, insecure', *Policy Exchange*, 2017.

21   'Internet, un monde bien réel' ['The internet, a physical reality'], *La Croix*, 24 April 2018.

22   'A broken submarine cable knocked a country off the internet for two days', *The Verge*, 8 April 2018.

23   'Submarine cables and the oceans: connecting the world', op. cit.

24   'Sécurité, pêche ... Une enquête publique lancée sur le plus grand câble sous-marin du monde qui passe par la Côte d'Opale' ['Security, fishing ... A public equity is opened on the world's biggest undersea cable that crosses the Opal Coast'], *France Info*, 18 November 2019.

25   Interview with Antony Viera, general secretary of the Regional Committee of Marine Fisheries and Marine Farming (CRPMEM), Hauts-de-France, 2020.

26   'Submarine cables and the oceans: connecting the world', op. cit.

27   Ibid.

28   'Vandals blamed for phone and Internet outage', *CNET*, 10 April 2009.

29   'Vietnam's submarine cable "lost" and "found"', *LIRNEasia*, 2 June 2007. This is not an isolated event: in the article, the Vietnamese coastguard explains that it has already seized hundreds of tonnes of cables lifted by fishing boats.

30   'Internet, un monde bien réel' ['The internet, a physical reality'], *La Croix*, 24 April 2018.

31   'Câbles transcontinentaux: des milliards de gigaoctets sous les mers' ['Transcontinental cables: billions of gigabytes under the sea'], *Le Monde*, 24 June 2018.

32   Of which fourteen are for New Zealand, and three for Australia.

33   'Undersea cables: indispensable, insecure', *Policy Exchange*, 1 December 2017.

34   Kim Nguyen, *The Hummingbird Project*, 111 min, Belga Production/Item 7, 2018.

35   Before the Hibernia Express was laid, the history of cables is marked by situations where speed determines the execution of trades on the stock market. 'In 1836 an affair of telegraphic fraud sparked off debate again on the use of this means of communication. Two bankers from Bordeaux had bribed a telegraph employee to add signals to official dispatches. This system permitted them to be informed of the development of the rate of government stocks', wrote Patrice Flichy in his book *Dynamics of Modern Communication: the shaping and impact of new communication technologies*, op. cit. He continues: 'The two Bordeaux bankers were not the first to discover the value of information in the establishment of stock market rates. Under the

Restauration, the Rothschilds had already set up a system of private mail which permitted them to know, before anyone else, the main political events and rates on other markets. Thus the "assassination of the Duke of Berry, in February 1829, was known in Frankfurt by the House of Rothschild well before everyone else. It then made necessary arrangements and only announced the news after having sent its mail and its orders" (Gille 1959: 262)."

36 Interview with Alasdair Wilkie, chief technical officer, marine projects, Digicel Group, 2020.

37 Shallow waters being defined as less than 1,000 metres deep.

38 'Route clearance for Hibernia Express', *atlantic-cable.com*, 28 January 2018.

39 Interview with Alasdair Wilkie, 2020.

40 Nova Scotia, New Brunswick, and Prince Edward Island.

41 'One of them was a sailor and helped us avoid traversing any of the ancestral fishing areas', explained Wilkie.

42 'Including a section of the first transatlantic cable, laid by the French [in 1869] between Brest [Brittany] and Saint-Pierre-et-Miquelon [a French archipelago south of Newfoundland, Canada]', Wilkie explained.

43 Belonging to Encana and ExxonMobil.

44 Fastnet Rock is located a few kilometres south of Ireland.

45 Interview with Laurent Campagne, senior consultant, AQEST, 2020.

46 'Hibernia Express transatlantic cable route connects New York to London in under 58.95 milliseconds', Submarine Telecoms Forum press release, 24 September 2015.

47 'Starlink, new competitor in HFT space?', *Shortwaves Solutions*, 16 September 2020.

48 'Hibernia Networks completes acquisition transaction by GTT', *Business Wire*, 9 January 2017. In 2017, Hibernia Atlantic sold its cable to GTT Communications for 590 million US dollars—almost precisely 10 million US dollars per millisecond.

49 Electronic equipment resembling torpedoes used to relay digital signals every 80 kilometres.

50 Interview with Bertrand Clesca, founder of OpticalCloudInfra and consultant with Pioneer Consulting, 2020.

51 'L'Ifremer mesure l'impact des câbles sous-marins' ['Ifremer measures the impact of undersea cables'], *Mer et Marine*, 25 June 2019.

52 'Submarine cables and the oceans: Connecting the world', op. cit.

53 Ibid.

54 Interview with Alwyn du Plessis, CEO of Mertech Marine, 2020.

55 The list of cables the company has recovered is available on its website mertechmarine.co.za.

56   The first cable recovered by Mertech Marine was a section of the 350-kilometre TAT-1 cable. The company chartered a ship in August 2008 with a view to selling the copper. By the time it came back to port, the collapse of Lehman Brothers and the ensuing financial recession sent copper prices into a tailspin, severely jeopardising the company.

57   Interview with Bertrand Clesca, 2020.

58   Interview with Laurent Campagne, 2020.

59   'YouTube and Netflix are cutting streaming quality in Europe due to coronavirus lockdowns', *CNBC*, 20 March 2020.

60   Interview with Laurent Campagne, 2020.

61   'Is the internet on the brink of collapse? The web could reach its limit in just eight years and use all of Britain's power supply by 2035, warn scientists', *The Daily Mail*, 2 May 2015.

62   The Shannon Limit was demonstrated in 1948 by the American engineer Claude Shannon. See 'Shannon's limit, or opportunity?', *Ciena*, 25 September 2017, for further reading.

63   Read the fascinating paper by Nicole Starosielski, associate professor of media, culture, and communication at New York University, 'Strangling the Internet', *Limn*, no. 10, 'Chokepoints', April 2018.

64   Namely, FLAG (Fiber-optic Link Around the Globe), SEA-ME-WE 1, SEA-ME-WE 2, SEA-ME-WE 3, and AFRICA-1. See 'Undersea cables: Indispensable, insecure', op. cit.

65   James Cowie, 'Syrian web outage no surprise', *Renesys Blog*, 9 May 2013.

66   'Strangling the Internet', op. cit.

67   Ibid.

68   According to quantum mechanics, a particle can be in two different places at once.

69   Interview with Andrew Ellis, professor of engineering and applied sciences at the University of Aston in Birmingham, UK, 2020.

70   'IARC classifies radiofrequency electromagnetic fields as possibly carcinogenic to humans', Press release no. 208, *WHO/International Agency for Research on Cancer (IARC)*, 31 May 2011.

Chapter Ten: The geopolitics of digital infrastructure

1   The cable takes its name from the Indian physicist Chandrasekhara Venkata Raman (1888–1970), who is known for his work on the molecular diffraction of light.

2   'Israel to play key role in giant Google fibre optic cable project', *Haaretz*, 14 April 2020.

3   Sunil Tagare, 'Facebook's apartheid of Israel in 2Africa', 21 May 2020. Article available on Tagare's LinkedIn profile.

4   In France, the city of Marseille in particular has become a global hub for landing fibre-optic cables. As for Brazil, read 'EllaLink's transatlantic submarine cable has already anchored in Portugal', *BNamericas*, 6 January 2021.

5   Félix Blanc, *Géopolitique des câbles: une vision sous-marine de l'Internet ['The geopolitics of cables: an underwater vision of the internet']*, Centre for technology and society, law department, Fundaçao Getulio Vargas (FGV Direito Rio Bresil), June 2018.

6   Interview with Bertrand Clesca, founder of OpticalCloudInfra and consultant with Pioneer Consulting, 2020.

7   Aborted cable projects also shed light on the territories at war, and on confrontations between nations. For example, it is impossible to link the United Arab Emirates and Oman to Turkey via dangerous Syria. And in 2018, Australia, fearing espionage, denied the Chinese company Huawei the possibility of landing a cable on its territory. Read 'Australia supplants China to build undersea cable for Solomon Islands', *The Guardian*, 13 June 2018.

8   Russian Optical Trans-Arctic Cable System.

9   'The Arctic: a new internet highway?', *Arctic Yearbook*, 2014.

10   'Geography of the global submarine fibre-optic cable network: the case for Arctic ocean solutions', *Geographical Review*, June 2020.

11   'Arctic subsea communication cables and the regional development of northern peripheries', *Arctic and North*, no. 32, September 2018.

12   'Quintillion activates Arctic subsea cable', *Submarine Cable Networks*, 13 December 2017.

13   'Charges: Ex-Quintillion CEO duped investors in Arctic broadband project', *Alaska Public Media*, 12 April 2018. Elizabeth Pierce was arrested in April 2018, then sentenced in 2019 to five years in prison. Among the cheated investors were the French companies Natixis and Alcatel Submarine Networks.

14   'Melting Arctic means new, and faster, subsea cables for high-speed traders', *Bloomberg*, 12 September 2019.

15   Including the Japanese company Sojitz Corporation and the Norwegian company Bredbåndsfylket Arctic Link AS.

16   Interview with Juha Saunavaara, assistant professor at the Arctic Research Center, Hokkaido University (Japan), 2020.

17   Ibid.

18   'Major step towards a Europe-Asia Arctic cable link', *The Barents Observer*, 6 June 2019.

19   'Data cables are the new trading routes', *The Barents Observer*, 15 June 2017.

20   Interview with Keith Schofield, strategic adviser, Pioneer Consulting, 2020.

21   'Arctic Telecom cable initiative takes major step forward', *Cinia*, 6 June 2019.

22   'Vision and actions on jointly building Silk Road Economic Belt and 21st-Century Maritime Silk Road', National Development and Reform Commission (NDRC), *Ministry of Foreign Affairs, and Ministry of Commerce of the People's Republic of China*, 28 March 2015.

23   'Full text of President Xi's speech at opening of belt and road forum', *Xinhuanet*, 14 May 2017.

24   A section of PEACE will also pass along the eastern side of the African continent up to the Seychelles. See peacecable.net; see also https://www.datacenterdynamics.com/en/news/peace-cable-completes-connection-of-pakistan-egypt-segment-to-connect-to-marsielle-france/

25   'China's 'One Belt, One Road' takes to space', *The Wall Street Journal*, China Real Time Blog, 28 December 2016.

26   Tencent's most popular app is WeChat.

27   'Interview with Laurent Campagne, senior consultant, AQEST, 2020.

28   'Huawei technicians helped African governments spy on political opponents', *The Wall Street Journal*, 15 August 2019.

29   'Made-in-China censorship for sale', *The Wall Street Journal*, 6 March 2020.

30   'La route de la soie numérique, le nouveau péril chinois?' ['The digital silk road: the new Chinese peril?'), *Le Temps*, 25 April 2019.

31   'The space and cyberspace components of the Belt and Road Initiative', in the report by the National Bureau of Asian Research, *Securing the Belt and Road Initiative. China's evolving military engagement along the Silk Road*', 3 September 2019, quoting Joe McReynolds, 'China's Evolving Perspectives on Network Warfare],'*China Brief, vol.* 15, issue: 8, 16 April 2015.

32   Ibid.

33   Ibid.

34   Interview with Jean Devos, former director of Alcatel Submarcom/ASN and former marketing director of Tyco SubCom, 2020.

35   Read 'Digital Silk Road on path to sustainable development: expert', *Xinhuanet*, 5 September 2017.

36   Repeaters are electronic components that relay the cable's digital signals every 80 kilometres on average.

37   'Huawei Marine joint venture launched', *Lightwave*, 19 December 2008.

38   Interview with Jean Devos, 2020.

39   'Global Marine Group sells its stake in Huawei Marine Networks', *Offshore Energy*, 30 October 2019.

40   Interview with Jean Devos, 2020.

41   Interview with Laurent Campagne, 2020.

42   Interview with Jean Devos, 2020.

43   Ibid.

44   Interview with Laurent Campagne, 2020.

45   'Undersea cables: Indispensable, insecure', *Policy Exchange*, 1 December 2017.

46   Ibid.

47   'Comment la France écoute (aussi) le monde' ['How France (also) listens to the world'], *L'Obs*, 25 June 2015.

48   At the time these lines were written, the construction of the CPEC was running behind schedule, as stakeholders looked for foreign investment, namely from Turkey and Russia, to boost the project. Read 'Russia Wants To Participate In The China-Pakistan Economic Corridor', oilprice.com, 14 November, 2022.

49   'Pakistani separatist groups unite to target China's Belt and Road', *Nikkei Asia*, 1 August 2020; 'Pakistani militants opposing Belt and Road kill 14 security men', *Nikkei Asia*, 16 October 2020; 'Rising attacks by Baloch separatists increase risks, costs of BRI projects in Pakistan: Report', *The Economic Times*, 20 July 2020.

50   White paper on China's National Defense, published by Beijing in 1998: china.org.cn/e-white/5/index.htm

51   'Securing the Belt and Road Initiative. China's evolving military engagement along the Silk Roads', *National Bureau of Asian Research*, op. cit.

52   'The dawn of a PLA expeditionary force?', *National Bureau of Asian Research*, 'Securing the Belt and Road Initiative. China's evolving military engagement along the Silk Roads', op. cit.

53   Blackwater Security was very active in Iraq during the Iraq War.

54   Interview with Jonathan Hillman, researcher at the Center for Strategic and International Studies (CSIS), 2020, and author of the book *The Emperor's New Road. China and the Project of the Century*, Yale University Press, 2020.

55   Guifang (Julia) Xue, 'The potential dual use of support facilities in the Belt and Road Initiative', in the report *Securing the Belt and Road initiative. China's evolving military engagement along the Silk Roads*, op. cit.

56   Interview with Jonathan Hillman, 2020.

57   Pacific Light Cable Network.

58   'Facebook and Google drop plans for underwater cable to Hong Kong after security warnings', *ZDNet*, 1 September 2020. Instead, the cable will only operate between the US, Taiwan, and the Philippines.

59   Interview with Bertrand Clesca, 2020.
60   The difference being that the 'ships laying telecommunication cables are very specific', explains Bertrand Clesca. 'The Brazilian company Padtec was bought out in 2019 by IPG Photonics, a US manufacturer of fibre lasers and laser systems, which is not doing anything with it, meaning it will gradually die. The US company Xtera is dead on its feet.'
61   Interview with Bertrand Clesca, 2020.
62   Ibid.
63   'Un océan de câbles. Puissance(s) au bout du câble' ['An ocean of cables. Power(s) at the end of the cable'), *RFI*, 28 March 2019.
64   Interview with Laurent Campagne, 2020.

Conclusion

1   Interview with Inès Leonarduzzi, director of Digital For The Planet, 2019.
2   Known as the FAIR principles (findable, accessible, interoperable, reusable).
3   Known as corporate social responsibility (CSR).
4   'Coining less expensive currency', *NIST*, 20 June 2018.
5   Interview with Victoire de Margerie, founder and vice-president of the World Materials Forum, 2018.
6   'Apple adds Earth Day donations to trade-in and recycling program', Apple, 19 April 2018. 'Volvo mines blockchain to keep ethical sourcing promise', *Forbes*, 27 January 2020.
7   waag.org
8   libreplanet.org, framasoft.org, linux.org.
9   With these networks, users, through their mobile phones, provide the wireless link of a community internet network: guifi.net.
10   'Climate Crisis: the unsustainable use of online video. The practical case for digital sobriety'. Report led by Maxime Efoui-Hess for the think tank The Shift Project, July 2019.
11   Byung-Chul Han, *In the Swarm: digital prospects,* op. cit.